P9-CJV-177

THE ASSESSMENT OF BILINGUAL APHASIA

THE ASSESSMENT OF BILINGUAL APHASIA

MICHEL PARADIS
McGill University

with the collaboration of
Gary Libben

LEA LAWRENCE ERLBAUM ASSOCIATES, PUBLISHERS
1987   Hillsdale, New Jersey   London

Lawrence Erlbaum Associates, Inc., Publishers
365 Broadway
Hillsdale, New Jersey 07642

Library of Congress Cataloging-in-Publication Data

Paradis, Michel.
The assessment of bilingual aphasia.

Bibliography: p.
Includes index.
1. Aphasia—Diagnosis. 2. Bilingualism. I. Libben, Gary. II. Title. [DNLM: 1. Aphasia—diagnosis. WL 340.5 P222a]
RC425.P366 1987   616.85'52   86-29229
ISBN 0-89859-650-5

Printed in the United States of America
10 9 8 7 6 5 4 3 2 1

Contents

Foreword

With the publication of this remarkable test instrument, both the clinician and the researcher can properly and thoroughly assess the aphasic impairments of patients who speak more than one language. The Bilingual Aphasia Test, the product of over eight years of serious scholarship and experimental investigation, covers all levels of linguistic structure in all four modalities of language use in over forty languages. For the convenience of clinicians who are more familiar with aphasia batteries from which syndromes are derived, there is a section at the end of this book outlining how subsections of the Bilingual Aphasia Test can be grouped under common aphasic syndromes. And, there is more. The test is comparable in each language. For example, the people pictured in the naming sections are dressed appropriately for their culture and climate, there is snow on the trees in the Finnish version, the dome of a mosque is pictured in the Farsi version. Contrasting linguistic elements such as case markers and pronouns are balanced across languages which make more use of one or the other feature. The great care that went into the construction of this test to make it linguistically and culturally balanced is evident in every subsection. The result, as might be expected, is an aphasia battery which is linguistically coherent in each language. This is a singular accomplishment.

Harry A. Whitaker

Preface

The object of this volume is to provide a detailed analysis of the *Bilingual Aphasia Test*, its theoretical foundations and rationale. Thus, after placing the assessment of bilingual aphasia in the context of experimental and clinical studies in the neurolinguistic aspects of bilingualism of the past decade and in the historical perspective of research on aphasia in polyglots of the last 100 years, a thorough description of the test and of the criteria of equivalence between various languages in which it has been transposed, as well as explicit instructions for implementation and scoring are provided. A framework for the interpretation of findings toward clinical diagnosis and research objectives is then suggested.

The book is therefore of interest to linguists who seek empirical verification for their theoretical constructs; to neuropsychologists who investigate brain organization associated with differences in experience; to speech therapists who will find in it a user's manual for the *Bilingual Aphasia Test;* to aphasiologists who require a diagnosis in more than one of a patient's languages; and to neurolinguists who explore the factors involved in the various recovery patterns of bilingual aphasics.

The population highest at risk with respect to aphasia—individuals aged over 65—is steadily increasing. The number of bilingual speakers has always been large (and is also increasing) but only recently has some attention been paid to the bilingual phenomenon in clinical settings. Most patients have been, and to a large extent continue to be, examined only in the majority language of the hospital community. In the past, the fact that a patient spoke other languages was at most recorded in his or her file, but nothing was done about it. In fact, very little could be done about it for lack of a standardized instrument to assess the patient's other languages. With the *Bilingual Aphasia Test,* anyone who speaks the patient's language (relative, friend, nurse on a different ward, hospital clerk), given a minimum set of instructions, can assess the patient's performance in that language. This assessment can then be compared with that of the language of the environment or whatever other language the patient may speak. Because the score in any language corresponds item per item to the score in every other language, anyone can perform the analysis by visual inspection, with the aid of a pencil (or in seconds with a microcomputer). The only parts of the analysis that require a speaker of the language are spontaneous speech, descriptive speech and spontaneous writing, even though the first two do get some (subjective) rating from the examiner (items 18-22 and 344) and some objective data (items 345–346) toward an assessment.

Fortunately, most aphasiologists today have become aware that it is not sufficient to assess polyglot patients' language deficits in only one of their languages. The language least impaired may be other than the language of the hospital staff in which the patient is being tested. Hence for a true evaluation of the patients' linguistic communicative capacities, all of their languages should be tested, and should be tested with an equivalent instrument.

Though the handful of cases reported since 1843 have seldom been assessed with comparable instruments (within as well as between patients), various patterns of recovery have nevertheless been described which establish reliably that some languages are definitely better recovered or are less impaired than others within the same patient. So far, however, no factor has been identified that might predict which language, post insult, is more likely to be the patient's best. The eventual detection of such factors is one of the reasons for the large-scale systematic use of the *Bilingual Aphasia Test*. Also, adequate batteries are not available in many of the languages covered by the *Bilingual Aphasia Test*. The material will allow screening for aphasia in languages in which standardized tests are not presently available, as well as assessing a single patient in more than one language with a comparable instrument.

This instrument is designed for the analysis of pathological language in bilingual aphasics at all levels of linguistic structure (phonological, morphological, syntactic, lexical, semantic) in all 4 modalities of language use (aural and reading comprehension, oral and written production). Further, it assesses the aphasic patients' judgments and repetition, at the level of the word, the sentence and the paragraph, from spontaneous speech to metalinguistic tasks, and it evaluates patients' translation capacities in both directions as well as their grammaticality judgments for sentences incorporating surface syntactic structures of the other language.

The research was initiated during a collaborative project with the late Professor Henry Hécaen, then Director of the Neurolinguistic Unit 111 of the Institut National de la Santé et de la Recherche Médicale, Paris, France, with the active collaboration of Marie-Claire Goldblum of the same research unit. This project was funded by the Quebec Ministry of Intergovernmental Affairs 01-07-23 from

1978 to 1980. It was pursued during a subsequent collaborative project with Professor Yvan Lebrun, Director of the Neurolinguistic Service of the Academic Hospital of the Vrije Universiteit in Brussels, Belgium from 1981 to 1983, funded by grant 01-07-K81, and with Dr. Jordi Peña, Director of the Neuropsychology and Logopedics Unit of the Municipal Neurological Institute, Barcelona, Spain (MAIQ 4-10-83). Research in Barcelona was further funded by a grant from the Generalitat de Catalunya's Interdepartmental Commission on Research and Technological Development (C.I.R.T. 4.820) to Dr. Peña, and in Donostia by a grant from the Basque Government's Department of Health and Welfare (Decreto 222/85) to Dr. Iñaki Bidegain (ASPACE). The test was then put in its final format with the collaboration of Gary Libben who designed it so that it would be computer-compatible. He is also responsible for the statistical analysis of the norms. The series of tests in over 40 languages is the result of research funded by the Quebec Ministry of Education FCAC grant EQ1660 from 1980 to 1985. The collection of norms in each of the relevant countries was funded by the Social Sciences and Humanities Research Council of Canada grant 410-83-1028 for 1984 and 1985.

Michel Paradis

Acknowledgments

Thanks are due to the numerous persons who collaborated in the adaptation of the test in their various languages and in the obtention of norm data: R. Abidi (Arabic translation, Arabic/French, Arabic norms), I. Ahlsén (Swedish translation), S. Alibhai (Gujarati translation, English/Gujarati), M. Akbarzadeh (Azari norms), J. S. Alvarez Emparanza (Basque translation), B. Bacz (English/Polish, French/Polish), J. F. Bahâr (Azari translation, Azari/Farsi), A. Baruzzi (Italian translation, Italian norms), J. C. Beaumont (French norms), J. Brunner (Norwegian norms), M. A. Canzanella (Italian translation, English/Italian, French/Italian, Italian norms), N. L. Cheng (Cantonese translation, Cantonese/English), E. Cichoń (Polish translation), P. Coppens (Dutch/English, Dutch/French, Dutch/German, Dutch norms), Y. Dehghan (Azari/Farsi, Azari norms), T. Devanathan (Tamil translation), M. Dillinger (English/Portuguese), J. Droge (American English norms), J. Elias i Bescós (Catalan and Spanish translations, Catalan/Spanish, Catalan and Spanish norms), H. Essegulian (Western Armenian translation), A. Fell (Hebrew norms), M. Folkö (Swedish norms), K. Freibergs (Latvian translation, English/Latvian), M. C. Goldblum (French version), M. M. Gonzalez Gil (Galician translation, Galician/Spanish, Galician and Spanish norms), H. Hagiwara (Japanese translation), M. Halle (Norwegian translation, English/Norwegian, Norwegian norms), C. Hedqvist-Dravins (Swedish translation, English/Swedish, Swedish norms), L. Herriondo (Basque translation, Basque/Spanish, Basque and Spanish norms), S. Hervouet-Zeiber (English/Russian), T. Hervouet-Zeiber (Russian translation), N. Hildebrandt (English/Japanese, Japanese norms), K. Hummel (English version), N. Janjua (Urdu translation, English/Urdu), L. Jensen (Danish), Å. Johansson (Swedish norms), O. Juncos Rabadán (Galician translation, Galician/Spanish, Galician and Spanish norms), L. Kamperidis (Greek/Turkish), A. Karlsson (Icelandic Translation, English/Icelandic), E. Kehayia (Greek translation, English/Greek, French/Greek, Greek norms), H. Keshish (Armenian/Farsi), H. Kremin (German translation), K. Křivinkova (Czech translation, Czech/English), P. Kukkonen (Finnish translation, Finnish/Swedish), M. Labas-Weber (Hungarian translation, English/Hungarian, French/Hungarian), Gary Libben (English version, computer programs for test administration and analysis of results), O. Lindner-Libben (German translation), A. Mazzucchi (Italian norms), C. Moes (German/Swedish, Russian Swedish), P. Nercessian (Bulgarian translation, Bulgarian/English, Bulgarian norms), R. Nilipour (Azari/Farsi, Azari and Farsi norms), A. Norgerg (Swedish norms), F. Nurmohammadi (Azari translation), R. Ong (Chinese/English), H. Osterreich (Estonian translation), I. Özkut (Turkish translation, English/Turkish, Turkish norms), H. Palanjian (Armenian/English, Armenian/French, Armenian norms, D. Parcehian (Bulgarian norms), T. Paribakht (Farsi translation, English/Farsi, Farsi norms), S. Patnaik (Oriya translation, Oriya norms), L. Pellitro Ramilo (Galician translation, Galician/Spanish, Galician and Spanish norms). H. Puente Carracedo (Galician translation, Galician/Spanish, Galician and Spanish norms), E. Purcell (Canadian English (norms), R. Qasemzadeh (Azari norms), G. Ralaisoa (Malagasy translation, French/Malagasy), G. N. Rangamani (Kannada translation, English/Kannada), X. M. Rodriguez Gonzalez (Galacian translation, Galician/Spanish, Galician and Spanish norms), T. Rossman-Benjamin (Hebrew translation, Hebrew norms), P. Saarinen (Finnish and Swedish norms), S. Saunders (English/German), M. N. San Jose Benito (Galician translation, Galician/Spanish, Galician and Spanish norms), I. Sepehrniya (Azari norms), Z. Shen (Standard Modern Chinese translation), A. M. Simões Dillinger (Brazilian Portuguese translation), M. Singh (Hindi norms), C. Stieblich (German norms), J. Struijk (Norwegian norms), L. Travis (French/Malagasy), D. Truong (Vietnamese translation, French/Vietnamese), D. Vadáz (Hungarian norms), J. Vaid (Hindi translation, English/Hindi, Hindi norms), J. Valladares Vaquero (Galician translation, Galician/Spanish, Galician and Spanish norms), D. Visintini (Italian norms), T. Vizkelety (Hungarian norms), J. Yamanaka (Japanese norms), G. Zaar (Swedish norms).

We are grateful to the following institutions for their kind cooperation in allowing us to obtain norms from non-brain-damaged patients: Mustapha Hospital, Algiers (Algeria: Arabic); Akademisch Ziekenhuis-Universiteit Brussel, Brussels (Gelgium: Dutch); General Hospital in Boyana, Dragalevtzi and Sofia (Bulgaria: Bulgarian); The Civic Hospital, Ottawa, Ontario, The Meder Nursing Home, Ottawa, Ontario, The Queensway-Carlton Hospital, Nepean, Ontario, (Canada: English); Hôpital Notre-Dame, Montréal, Québec (Canada: French); Kustaankartanon Vanhainkoti; Appartments for the aged of the city of Helsinki, The Organization of Swedish speaking pensioners of Helsinki, Svenska Folkparteit: Helsingfors Distrikt (Finland: Finnish and Swedish); Klinikum Aachen,

Aachen (Germany: German); Agios Loukas General Clinic, Thessaloniki, Evangelismos General Hospital, Athens (Greece: Greek); National Institute for Arthrytis and Physiotherapeutic care; Budapest, Istvàr Hospital, Budapest; Jànos Hospital, Budapest (Hungary: Hungarian); All India Institute of Medical Science, New Delhi, Meerut University, Meerut (India: Hindi); Bhubaneswar General Hospital, Orissa (India: Oriya); Department of Speech Therapy, College of Rehabilitation Sciences, Teheran (Iran: Azari, Farsi); Convalescent Home, Jerusalem (Israel: Hebrew); Cantù Municipal Hospital, Como; Ospedale Don Gnocchi, Parma; Parma Municipal Hospital, Parma (Italy: Italian); Kosei-in Nursing Home, Nagoya; Sakashita Hospital, Sakashita City (Japan: Japanese); The Ministry of Health and Hôpital des Spécialités, Rabat (Morocco); Ullevål Sykenhus, Oslo; Vår Frue Sykenhus, Oslo; Radiumshospitalet, Oslo; Sunnas Sykenhus, Nesoddtangen (Norway: Norwegian); Hospital Residencia Ntra.Sra.de Aranzazu, Donostia (Spain: Basque and Spanish); Hospital General Ntra.Sra.del Mar, Barcelona; Hospital de la Santa Creu i San Pau, Barcelona (Spain: Catalan and Spanish); Hospital Xeneral de Vigo (Spain: Galician and Spanish); Lazarettet i Lund (Sweden: Swedish); Center for Neurology (Tunisia: Arabic); Gülhave Askerî Tıp Akademisi, Ankara; Hacettepe Hastanesi, Ankara; Polis Emeklileri Derneği Huzurevi, Istanbul (Turkey: Turkish); Culpepper Gardens Retirement Home, Arlington, Virginia (U.S.A.: English).

We also wish to thank the 1,640 patients who volunteered to take the Bilingual Aphasia Test so that we could obtain norms.

The equivalent of 36 student-years were subsidized by the Quebec Ministry of Education's *Formation de Chercheurs et d'Action concertée* Fund and the Social Sciences and Humanities Research Council of Canada from 1980 to 1985. The following students (some of whom have since obtained their doctoral degree) have worked as research assistants for the McGill University Department of Linguistics FCAC/SSHRCC Bilingual Aphasia Project and have thus contributed in sundry capacities to the development of the Bilingual Aphasia Test: D. Allen, A. Baruzzi, J. C. Beaumont, D. Biedlingmaier, A. Bergey, M. A. Canzanella, L. DeFreitas, M. Dillinger, J. Droge, G. Farrell, J.-A. Gendron, H. Hagiwara, N. Hildebrandt, K. Hummel, K. Johnson, E. Kehayia, G. Libben, P. Nercessian, D. Patrick, E. Purcell, C. Stieblich, J. Vaid. The artists responsible for the illustrations of the various tests are Michel Côté, Max Steiner, and Wim van Eyck of the Graphics Department of McGill University's Instructional Communications Center and Per Gyllenör of Oskarshamns folkhögskola, Sweden. Dr. Molly Mack deserves special thanks for her valuable comments and for her thorough editing of the manuscript.

1 Neurolinguistic Perspectives on Bilingualism

Our understanding of bilingualism would be greatly improved if data were systematically collected about the course of aphasia in bilingual patients.

—Lambert and Fillenbaum (1959 p. 29)

The basic questions in the neuropsychology of bilingualism are whether the two languages of the same subject have different cerebral representations and whether the fact of having acquired two languages influences the cerebral organization of higher cortical functions. Several hypotheses have been proposed, each based on some isolated observational data and much speculation. Most theoretical claims still await empirical verification.

First, there is the long standing neurological claim that all languages of a polyglot are subserved by the same cortical locus or loci. A more recent theoretical linguistic position assumes that all languages share the same linguistic principles and that, therefore, the underlying cerebral representation must be the same for all the languages of a speaker-hearer. It predicts that if some aspect of competence is impaired by neurological trauma, then all languages known by the speaker must be disordered in just the same way, consistent with the impaired competence. Thus, according to this hypothesis, there is no specific cerebral representation for each language (as *langue*) but only a single undifferentiated capacity for language in general (*langage*). Consequently all languages are subserved by a common cortical area or jointly distributed over the classical language areas (e.g., Broca's, Wernicke's).

1

Questions specific to bilingual aphasia are added to those stemming from aphasia in general, such as whether aphasia is a general cognitive deficit or a language-specific impairment; whether it is a unitary phenomenon or admits of multiple syndromes; whether it is a deficit of competence or performance; and whether modality-specific deficits are aphasic symptoms. Theoretical positions on these issues will have consequences for hypotheses about bilingual aphasia and/or the representation of two languages in one brain.

Some authors, for example, argue that patients are not aphasic unless their competence is impaired. Competence is considered not to be impaired when a deficit is not equally manifested in all modalities or when a patient undergoes spontaneous recovery. Moreover, because it is assumed that competence is common to both languages, if a bilingual is agrammatic for some aspect of the grammar in one of his languages, it is predicted that she or he will be agrammatic for those same components of the grammar in the other language (Scholes, 1984). Thus, what recovers spontaneously in unilinguals and bilinguals as well as what is differentially deficient in bilinguals is not considered a result of impaired competence but of loss of access through some defective performance mechanism. Such a position therefore holds that any bilingual patient exhibiting nonparallel recovery is not aphasic.

Whether or not we call patients aphasic who have lost the use of one of their languages or who have differential postmorbid proficiency in each language, it is of interest to the neuropsychology of language in general and of bilingualism in particular to examine whether nonparallel deficits do indeed occur, and if so, to investigate the mechanisms responsible for differential, successive, selective, antagonistic, and mixed recoveries. In fact, there is no a priori reason to reject the possibility that each language might be subserved by its own competence, namely, that each grammar might be separately stored and/or processed. There is indeed no clinical evidence that there is only one underlying neurolinguistic competence for both languages, that is to say, one common neural substrate for language, undifferentiated as to specific language. If it can be shown that specific alterations in competence occur in one language and not in the other, then it is not unreasonable to assume that each language is subserved by different neurofunctional substrates. Further systematic investigations, based on large numbers of successive unselected cases and using identical testing procedures, should help us solve the puzzle of differential recoveries and eventually provide us with clues as to whether the various languages of a polyglot are stored and processed by the brain separately, each as an independent linguistic system, or together, as one single linguistic competence.

While authors from Pitres (1895) to Penfield (1953, 1959, 1965) through Pötzl (1925), Minkowski (1927, 1963), Veyrac (1931), Ombredane (1951), and Gloning and Gloning (1965) have argued against separate centers specifically assigned to each of the languages of polyglot subjects, a growing number of contemporary researchers are prepared to consider various kinds of differential representation, including distinct anatomical localization. In fact, some have come to believe that "it would be surprising if bilingualism had no effect on brain organization" (Segalowitz, 1983, p. 121). According to these authors, there are numerous reasons to believe that cerebral representation of language is not entirely the same in polyglots as in unilinguals (Lecours, Branchereau, & Joanette, 1984, p. 20). The two languages of a bilingual may not be subserved by exactly the same neuronal circuits; it may even be that they are differently lateralized (Lebrun, 1981, p. 68).

Bilinguals have two languages at their command. They can speak one or the other and understand either at any time. They can switch between them, and they can mix them at any level of linguistic structure (phonetic, phonological, morphological, syntactic, lexical, semantic). Bilingual aphasics have been reported to lose some of their linguistic abilities selectively, as well as the ability to translate in either direction or in both (Paradis, Goldblum, & Abidi, 1982). Segalowitz (1983, p. 156) considers the fact that two languages in a bilingual patient can be differentially affected by brain damage as a strong argument for some separate representation in the brain. But, as he rightly notes, the nature of their separation is still unexplained. It has given rise to a number of suppositions.

According to one of these, the various languages of the polyglot are represented in different anatomical loci within the same general language zones (the classical language areas). Though, as mentioned earlier, it has had many detractors, some of them quite vehement, this hypothesis has never had any serious proponents. Scoresby-Jackson (1867) is generally credited with having come closest to such a suggestion. Another view is that the two languages of a bilingual are represented in partly different anatomical areas in the dominant hemisphere, with some overlap (Ojemann & Whitaker, 1978; Rapport, Tan, & Whitaker, 1983).

But assuredly the most debated issue has been the successive reformulations of the basic differential lateralization hypothesis which assumes a greater participation of the nondominant hemisphere in the representation and/or processing of language in bilinguals.

First of all, the nature of the alleged participation of the right hemisphere is far from clear. The classical view is that the right hemisphere of right-handers has no linguistic capacity. It may acquire some, but only when the left hemisphere is damaged early in life, and then only to some extent. Another assumption is that the language capacity of the right hemisphere is virtually the same as that of the left, but is inhibited by the functional left hemisphere and released only when the left hemisphere is incapacitated. But assuming that the right hemisphere does participate in the processing of language, then it is legitimate to ask what the nature of this participation which supposedly increases with bilingualism could be. At least four possibilities come to mind.

Let us call the first *the redundant participation hypothesis*. According to this hypothesis, both hemispheres process information in identical ways, though the participation of the left hemisphere may be quantitatively greater. The processing by the right hemisphere is redundant and hence the removal of the right hemisphere is of little consequence for language.

Another possibility would be *the quantitatively complementary participation hypothesis* according to which, as above, each hemisphere processes the same stimuli in the same way, with greater participation of the left hemisphere. However, there is a mass effect and the whole is necessary for normal language processing. A lesion to homologous parts of either the right or the left hemisphere will cause qualitatively identical deficits proportional to the extent of the damage.

One can also conceive of *a qualitatively parallel participation hypothesis.* According to this hypothesis, the same stimulus is processed in a qualitatively different way by each hemisphere. Each hemisphere processes all aspects of a stimulus in accordance with its own inherent mode of functioning. The participation of the right hemisphere is thus qualitatively complementary to that of the left hemisphere in processing utterances.

Still another plausible candidate is *the qualitatively selective participation hypothesis.* Each hemisphere, in accordance with its intrinsic functional capacities, specializes in the processing of a different aspect of a complex stimulus. In this case, as in the previous one, the participation of the right hemisphere is qualitatively complementary to that of the left hemisphere. However, while in the qualitatively parallel participation hypothesis complementarity is with respect to each aspect of an utterance, in the qualitatively selective participation hypothesis it is with respect to the utterance as a whole.

The qualitatively parallel participation hypothesis predicts that a lesion in the right hemisphere will affect all aspects of the utterance (albeit in a specific way, distinguishable from the effects of a homologous left-hemisphere lesion; e.g., global vs. analytic-sequential decoding of the meaning of a word or phrase), whereas the qualitatively selective participation hypothesis predicts that a right-hemisphere lesion will affect certain aspects of the utterance (a homologous left-hemisphere lesion will affect the other aspects of the utterance; e.g., prosody related to emotional states vs. grammatical stress pattern or lexical tone).

The redundant and the quantitatively complementary participation hypotheses assume an identical processing of the same aspects of an utterance; the qualitatively parallel participation hypothesis assumes a different processing of the same aspects; while the qualitatively selective participation hypothesis assumes a different processing of different aspects. Among the most often mentioned intrinsic processing modes attributed to each hemisphere, one finds the analytic/global, sequential/concomitant, logical/analogical, context-independent/context dependent, and deductive/inductive. Aspects of an utterance that have been invoked as likely to be processed separately by each hemisphere are, among others, grammatical/paralinguistic, phonemic/prosodic, and syntactic/pragmatic.

The situation gets even more complex in the case of language cerebral lateralization in bilinguals. In the first place, researchers do not even agree on the facts. Then, they further disagree on the interpretation of these controversial facts. That is, while some authors decide in favor of an increased participation of the right hemisphere in the processing of a second language (Gloning & Gloning, 1965; Minkowski, 1963; Ovcharova, Raichev, & Geleva, 1968; Vildomec, 1963), others conclude that bilingualism actually intensifies the development of cerebral dominance for language (Stark, Genesee, Lambert, & Seitz, 1977). Still others see no difference between unilinguals and bilinguals with respect to lateralization of language (Gordon, 1980; Piazza Gordon, & Zatorre, 1981; Soares & Grosjean, 1981; Walters & Zatorre 1978). In fact, several hypotheses have been proposed concerning the extent of right hemisphere participation in the processing of language in bilinguals, as follows: The second language is represented (or processed) in the right hemisphere; the second language is represented bilaterally; the second language, while mostly lateralized to the left, is less so than the first; both languages are less lateralized; both languages are equally represented in the left hemisphere; both languages are more lateralized (Obler, Zatorre, Galloway, & Vaid, 1982; and Galloway, 1983; for a critique of the experimental literature, see Zatorre, 1983; for details, see Vaid & Genesee, 1980).

An additional question is whether the manner of representation (i.e., one of the above possibilities) is the same in all bilinguals, irrespective of the kind of bilingualism, or whether it is a function of one or several of the acquisitional, utilizational, or structural dimensions of bilingualism (see Table 1.1). In fact, among 15 bilinguals observed by Hamers & Lambert (1977), 3 subjects appeared to have right hemisphere dominance for both languages, 2 subjects seemed to possess one language in the left hemisphere and the other in the right, while 3 more showed a substantial left processing of one language and no left-right difference in the other. Yet, in spite of the lack of clear evidence in favor of one or the other of the above hypotheses, a number of further hypotheses have been formulated to account for the alleged greater participation of the right hemisphere found by some in the processing of language in bilinguals. Some authors have even gone so far as to suggest that the right hemisphere is specialized for the acquisition of a second language (Ovcharova et al., 1968; Vildomec, 1963). But as clinical observations and/or experimental results have invalidated this initial hypothesis, a series of tentative explanations have been formulated. In effect, each new attempt has further restricted the bilingual population to which the greater participation of the right hemisphere hypothesis was supposed to apply: *The age hypothesis,* according to which a language learned after puberty is less lateralized because of the difference in maturational states during acquisition; *the stage hypothesis,* according to which the second language is gradually lateralized to the left hemisphere as that language is better mastered; *the revised stage hypothesis,* according to which the increased participation of the right hemi-

TABLE 1.1
Variables Associated With Differences Among Bilinguals

- Degree of proficiency: ability to use two languages   "ambilingualism"   "equilingualism"
  - each like a native speaker ("true" bilingualism)
  - neither like a native speaker ("semilingualism")
  - each in a specific context (diglossia)

- Types of organization of the grammar: no interference ("coordinate")
                                            unidirectional interference ("subordinate")
                                            bidirectional interference ("compound")

- Context of acquisition: Both acquired at the same time — by speaking 1 language to 1 person or group of persons
                                                               by speaking both languages alternately & indiscriminately
                                                               to both parents and/or other speakers of the bilingual
                                                               community

  As a second language outside the home and/or at school — as language of instruction & interaction with peers

                                                            only as language of instruction, all peers being of the
                                                            same mother tongue as learner & speech community

  (In school) through formal language instruction — grammar-translation (deductive)
                                                     structuro-global audiovisual (inductive)
                                                     audiolingual pattern drill (inductive)
                                                     conversational (interactive, inductive)
                                                     communicative (interactive, inductive)

  Age of acquisition

  Motivation

- Context of use: home/community and/or work
                    frequency of use
                    one used only for specific purposes (restricted lexicon, sociolinguistic registers, etc.)
                    modality of use (for listening only, e.g., TV, or for interaction)
                    different sociolinguistic status associated with use of each language

- Structural distance between the languages: from two closely related dialects to two unrelated languages

sphere is limited to adults at the beginning of the acquisition of a language in a natural environment, but not through formal learning; *the type of bilingualism hypothesis,* according to which coordinate bilinguals (in whom the languages are supposed to be more separate) have their languages represented separately, with a greater participation of the right hemisphere than for compound bilinguals; *the context hypothesis,* according to which right hemisphere participation is greater in a second language context than in a foreign language context; *the modality hypothesis,* according to which the learning of a second language through reading and writing promotes greater left hemisphere participation while acquisition by ear promotes greater right hemisphere participation; *the language-specific hypothesis,* according to which some characteristics of a given language may foster right hemisphere participation, these characteristics ranging from differences in the organization of thought patterns, to vowel characteristics, to tone, to directionality of writing; and *the structural distance hypothesis,* according to which two languages that are structurally very different (e.g., English and Japanese) are represented more separately, with greater participation of the right hemisphere than with two closely related languages (e.g., Catalan and Spanish).

It is not the case, as has often been claimed, that studies of dominance in aphasics have demonstrated that more aphasia is found following right hemisphere lesions in bilinguals (10 per cent) than has been reported for unilinguals (2 per cent) (Hughes, 1981, p. 27). Such statistics are very misleading at best, and are probably false. The reason is very simple (and has often been quoted, including by those authors who then nevertheless go on to use those figures in support of their argument): Since most cases of aphasia subsequent to left hemisphere damage are not reported, and since most cases of crossed aphasia—unilingual or bilingual—do get reported because of their exceptional character, one cannot conclude from the few *selected* cases of aphasia in bilinguals reported (contrasted with the large populations of unselected consecutive cases of unilingual aphasics from whom incidence of crossed aphasia has been derived), that the right hemisphere plays a greater role (let alone ''a major role'') in bilinguals (yet, see Albert & Obler, 1978; Galloway, 1980; Hughes, 1981; Lebrun, 1981). In addition, the study by Nair & Virmani (1973), which represents the main source of clinical evidence adduced to bolster the hypothesis that bilinguals are less strongly lateralized for language than unilinguals, has been radically and repeatedly misinterpreted: No comparison between the incidence of crossed aphasia among bilingual and unilingual subjects can possibly be derived from their report (Solin, forthcoming).

It may be useful, at this point, to make a clear distinction between *language representation* (i.e., linguistic competence) and *language use* (i.e., performance). Clinical evidence overwhelmingly points in the direction of quasi-exclusive representation of language in the left hemisphere in at least 95% of right-handers (but see Lecours, 1980), while the right hemisphere undoubtedly participates in the normal use of language. It seems most likely that, should there be any difference between the role of the right hemisphere in bilinguals and in unilinguals, it would be in the use of processing strategies relying on right hemisphere capacities, and not in language representation (Gordon & Weide, 1983). This difference could be due to the habitual cognitive style of certain individuals who, in their use of a second language, rely less on syntactic, morphological, and phonological (algorythmic) processes than unilinguals (or than in the use of their own dominant language), and rely more on paralinguistic and situational (heuristic) elements.

This distinction between representation and use of languages may explain some of the contradictions found between clinical and experimental results, the former reflecting deficits in linguistic competence (representation), the latter reflecting defects in the processing of utterances (performance) involving cognitive processes other than grammatical coding, such as access to knowledge of the world, capacity for analogical reasoning, extraction of information from paralinguistic and situational contexts, and from emotional suprasegmental features.

Whatever the participation of the right hemisphere, the more specific question of how the representation of two languages is organized in the same brain remains. Are both languages subserved by the same neurophysiological substrate or is each language stored and processed in distinct neuroanatomical structures? The ways in which two languages could be organized in their neuroanatomical and neurophysiological representation are indeed multiple. At least four hypotheses may be considered, as presented below.

1. The Extended System Hypothesis. The languages are undifferentiated in their representation. Two languages are not substantively different from one; the bilingual language system simply contains more phonemes, more morphemes, more syntactic rules. These are treated as additional elements of the same kind within the system and are integrated into it. They are processed as allo-elements, namely used in different environments—i.e., elements of L_1 are used in the context of L_1 and elements of L_2 in the context of L_2. The two languages are no more than two different ways of encoding a message within the same system, just as two different registers within the same language (or even two different constructions within the same register) select among different elements. The two languages behave with respect to each other in the same way as two stylistic variations within the same language. Thus there is no reason to believe that they are represented in any manner different from a single language.

2. The Dual System Hypothesis. Elements of each language are stored separately, in a system of connections independent of each other. For each level of linguistic structure, each language is subserved by different networks of neural connections. The two linguistic systems are thus separately stored in the brain, with two independently represented sets of phonemes, morphemes, syntactic rules, etc.

3. The Tripartite System Hypothesis. Those items that are identical in both languages are represented by one single underlying neural substrate common to

both languages, and those that are different each have their own separate neural representation. Thus whatever two languages have in common is represented only once, and that which is specific to each language is represented separately.
4. The Subset Hypothesis. Hypotheses (1) and (2) need not be mutually exclusive but may represent two aspects of the same phenomenon. Both languages are stored in identical ways, in a single cognitive system (*langage*), though elements of each language (*qua langue*), because they normally appear only in different contexts (elements of L_1 in the environment of other elements of L_1, and elements of L_2 in the environment of L_2), form a *de facto* separate network of connections, and thus a subsystem within a larger system (that comprises both). Bilinguals have two subsets of neural connections, one for each language (and each can be activated or inhibited independently because of the strong associations between the elements) while at the same time they possess one larger set from which they are able to draw elements of either language at any time.

The ease with which a bilingual can assume a foreign accent in speaking one language with the phonemes of the other, or intentionally use syntactic and morphological rules of one language when speaking the other, or insert words and phrases of one language when speaking the other (with or without a corresponding switch in phonology) seems to support the extended system hypothesis. So does evidence that bilinguals cannot block understanding of one of their languages even when reading or speaking the other. Parallel recovery of their two languages in bilingual aphasic patients is also compatible with this hypothesis.

On the other hand, selective recovery (and to some extent any type of non-parallel recovery) tends to support a dual system hypothesis. Some patients have been reported to have lost comprehension as well as expression in one or more of the languages that they spoke fluently before insult. In cases of successive recovery, they do not regain access to one or more of their languages until another has been maximally recovered. In cases of reciprocal antagonism, one of the patient's languages regresses to the proportion that the other improves, thus demonstrating a dissociation between the two languages. Such a dissociation between the availability of one of the patient's languages over the other can be interpreted as showing that a language can be selectively inhibited and that, therefore, it must be represented neurofunctionally as a system separate from the other system to which the patient has access. Moreover, the fact that a bilingual speaker is able to produce sentences in one language quite automatically (i.e., unreflectively, without consciously constructing sentences by the deliberate application of rules and selection of words) and without interference from the other language seems to indicate that each language can be activated independently and hence that it constitutes an autonomous system. This perspective is further reinforced by certain phenomena observed in psychiatry. Bilingual psychotic patients have been reported to lose their linguistic competence (Hughes, 1981) or have hallucinations (Hemphill, 1971; Laski & Taleporos, 1977) in only one of their languages (though it can be argued that hysterical manifestations do not always have a neurophysiological counterpart). Likewise, electroshock psychotherapy has been reported to cause a transient selective aphasia in one of the patient's languages (Kalinowsky, 1975; Lipsius, 1975) and differential recovery (Chernigovskaya, Balonov, & Deglin, 1983).

The evidence from electrical cortical stimulation in bilinguals reported by Ojemann & Whitaker (1978) and Rapport et al. (1983) is compatible with a tripartite system since at some stimulation sites both languages were affected and at other sites only one was. The authors concluded that there are cortical sites common to both languages and sites with differential organization of the two languages. A detailed systematic examination of differential recovery patterns in bilingual aphasic patients should allow us to ascertain whether structural elements shared by a patient's two languages are (or are not) affected in identical ways in each language. In particular, results from studies conducted in Northern Spain and in Scandinavia where large populations of bilinguals speak either two very similar languages (Catalan/Spanish, Galician/Spanish, Danish/Swedish, Norwegian/Swedish) or two very dissimilar languages (Basque/Spanish, Finnish/Swedish) should provide enough data within the next 2 or 3 years to verify this assumption.

At this time, the subset hypothesis seems capable of accounting for, or at least is compatible with, all the observed facts. Parallel impairments can be interpreted as the result of damage to, or interference with, the linguistic system as a whole, and differential impairments as the result of damage to, or interference with, one of the subsystems. Each language, as a subsystem, is susceptible to selective pathological inhibition. Yet, subjects with intact brains have the choice of alternately using elements of one or the other linguistic system, or of simultaneously using elements of both. They have equal access to both languages and, depending on whether they are in a unilingual or bilingual context, they will choose words from one language only or indifferently from both.

One might expect that bilingual aphasics would lose the two languages they spoke before insult to an extent proportional to their relative premorbid degree of mastery. It is indeed often the case that they do, but not always. Sometimes polyglots become aphasic for only one or two of the languages that they knew (selective aphasia: Paradis & Goldblum, in press; Pitres, 1895). Sometimes they recover one language better than the other (differential recovery: April & Han, 1980; Galloway, 1978; Rapport et al., 1983, cases 1 and 4; T'sou, 1978), or one after the other has been maximally recovered (successive recovery: Ovcharova et al., 1968, case 2; Rapport et al., cases 2 and 3). Sometimes one of the languages is not recovered and remains forever unavailable (selective recovery: Nair & Virmani, 1973; Peuser & Fittschen, 1977) or a better recovered language deteriorates as the other improves (antagonistic recovery: Chlenov, 1948; Wald, 1961, cases 1 and 5). In two reported cases, the first recovered language deteriorates several times in succession, so that each language is only alternately available (alternate antagonistic recovery: Paradis et al., 1982). In some cases, the patient systematically mixes the two languages inextricably (mixed recovery: Gloning & Gloning, 1965, cases 2 and 5; L'Hermitte, Hécaen, Dubois, Culioli, & Tabouret-Keller, 1966, case 4; Perecman, 1984). Two cases of different symptoms in each language have been reported (Albert & Obler, 1978, p. 98; Silverberg & Gordon, 1979). These patterns of recovery are not mutually exclusive: Different relations may hold concurrently between different pairs of languages and pattern of recovery may change over time. Two languages may be recovered in a successive manner while another remains selectively unavailable (Minkowski, 1927, 2 cases; Schulze, 1968); reciprocal antagonism may occur after a period of successive recovery (Minkowski, 1928); or a selective aphasia may become antagonistic over time with respect to one of the two initially unaffected languages (Paradis & Goldblum, in press).

It is not possible, at this time, to determine the frequency of occurrence of nonparallel recoveries since information relating to parallel recoveries is not generally published. Furthermore, it is difficult to compare the various published cases with each other because of the lack of standardization of assessments, sometimes even between the two languages of the same patient. Too many important details are missing from most descriptions, and those that are actually given invariably differ from one study to another. These are two of the reasons why the *Bilingual Aphasia Test* was developed and transposed into 40 languages selected among those spoken by large bilingual populations around the world. With this test, one will now be able to measure with much more precision than ever before the residual language capacities of bilingual and polyglot aphasic patients in each of their languages. Only after the test has been systematically used on large unselected populations of consecutive entries in various collaborating hospital centers around the world will it be possible to address specific issues regarding patterns of recovery. These include ascertaining the frequency of occurrence of each pattern of recovery and establishing correlations among the various factors that have been suggested thus far as influencing the pattern of recovery. Such factors are order and mode of acquisition or learning; extent of use; degree of fluency; structural distance between the languages; type and degree of affect associated with each; and type and orientation of the writing system involved. Also to be considered are site and size of lesion and type of aphasia which results (Paradis, 1977, pp. 78–112).

So far, no factor seems preponderant. Neither the language acquired first, nor the one used the most, nor the one of the greatest utility to the patient, nor a standard language over a dialect consistently emerges as the language best recovered. While some patients have recovered the language of the hospital environment which was neither their mother tongue nor their most fluent language, just as many have not recovered the language of the environment even though it was their mother tongue and most fluent language. Others have recovered a language which was neither their mother tongue, nor their most fluent language, nor that of the environment.

Whatever the characteristics of the preferentially recovered language—whether it is the first acquired, the most often used, or the language of the hospital environment—an important question remains: Why is one language recovered and not another, or why is one recovered better than another? This question has given rise to three hypotheses:

1. Each language is represented in a different locus in the brain, and thus a circumscribed lesion may affect one and not the other, or one more than the other;

2. there is an area in the brain that acts as a switch mechanism which allows the bilingual to shift from one language to another; a lesion in this area—believed from Pötzl (1925) to Leischner (1948) to be located in the supramarginal gyrus—either blocks the switch in one position and the patient can speak only one language, or causes the switch to become loose and the patient uncontrollably keeps switching back and forth between languages;

3. the unrecovered language is not lost but inhibited: Differential recoveries are not caused by organic destruction of physiologically specialized (language-specific) centers but due to functional disturbances, and selective impairment is not caused by damage to the stored language itself but by an incapacity to retrieve what is stored.

As we have seen, the first hypothesis has, until recently, hardly had any proponents. One interpretation of it, which has not received much consideration so far, is that while it seems indeed unlikely that languages would be represented in different anatomical areas—if by that is meant gross anatomical areas such as convolutions or other macroanatomical divisions—it is not so improbable that each language would be subserved by neural circuits which are distinct, albeit inextricably interwoven within a same anatomical area. This view is not incompatible with the third hypothesis. Whereas the organic destruction of a given area would cause deficits in both languages stored within its limits, a functional disturbance (a failure in inhibition or disinhibition) would result in selective recovery when only one of the circuits is affected, in differential recovery when one is affected more than the other, in successive recovery when one is affected longer than the other, in antagonistic recovery when each is alternately affected, and in parallel recovery when both circuits are equally affected. Mixed recovery would be the result of a failure of inhibition/disinhibition between the two circuits.

Soon after its proposal, the second hypothesis was confronted with two types of counter evidence—selective and mixed recoveries with no damage to the temporo-parietal area (Gloning & Gloning, 1965; L'Hermitte et al., 1966; Stengel & Zelmanowicz, 1933) and parieto-temporal lesions with no selective or mixed recovery (Gloning & Gloning, 1965; L'Hermitte et al., 1966; Schulze, 1968). In fact it may not be necessary to postulate an anatomically localized (or even a neurofunctional, physiological) switch mechanism at all. The capacity to switch is not specific to the bilingual speaker. The decision to encode a message in English or in Spanish is surely of the same order as the decision to produce an active, a passive, or a cleft sentence in either language. There is no reason to believe that language switching should not depend on the same general neuropsychological mechanism of internal choice that governs the capacity to speak or to remain silent. Language switching does not even require any psychological skill peculiar to bilingualism, but rather a skill that is equally applicable in a large number of operations in which persons are asked to switch modes of response, as Macnamara, Krauthammer, and Bolgar (1968, p. 213) rightly suggest. Delays, if any, involved in switching languages in experimental tasks are of the same order as those of orienting to any new task (Lewis, 1968, p. 54; see also Dalrymple-Alford, 1985).

Switching from one language to the other can also be accounted for by the third hypothesis—namely, by a phenomenon of inhibition and disinhibition. In accordance with the general principle that whenever a mechanism necessary for the accomplishment of a given function is activated, the antagonistic mechanism is concurrently inhibited, it is not unreasonable to suppose that when an element of the language is activated, those elements that are in direct competition with it are simultaneously inhibited. In the case of the selection of a word, this entails the inhibition of all its synonyms, of all the words within the same semantic field and, eventually, of all other words. In the bilingual speaker, not only must synonyms within one language be inhibited, but their equivalents in the other language as well. It seems plausible that optimally, one language as a whole is inhibited while the other is activated. Among other things, this phenomenon would explain why it is often difficult for non-brain-damaged perfectly fluent bilinguals to translate on demand a common word or phrase.

This inhibition may be conceived of as a result of raising the threshold of activation of a circuit, and therefore as admitting of differences in degree. It may never be total (Altenberg & Cairns, 1983; Mack, 1984). Even when a bilingual is speaking to unilinguals the other system may not be totally deactivated (Grosjean, 1985, p. 474). But then, no function of the brain is "totally deactivated" in the sense that it could not be activated by an external stimulus. One may assume that the threshold of activation of the language not being spoken is nevertheless much higher than the one of the language being spoken. It is generally sufficiently high for a speaker not to activate the other system (i.e., to avoid intrusive interference) when speaking to unilinguals. This does not mean that the speaker would be prevented from understanding what she or he concurrently heard (or saw) in the other language, any more than she or he would be prevented from interpreting what she or he smells, tastes, feels, hears, and sees while speaking.

Yet, in an odorless room, before the aroma of melting chocolate reaches a person, his or her sense of the smell of chocolate is not "activated." It becomes activated by the impinging stimulus.

Similarly, L_B may be thought to be "at the ready" (though deactivated) at any time, including when L_A is being spoken (though in this case the threshold of activation may be higher). Any language known to the speaker can be activated at any time by external stimuli or by internal stimuli (i.e., self-activated), provided the inhibition is not too strong. In cases of habitual alternate use of two languages and of habitual mixing, the language other than the one currently used may be more easily disinhibited (i.e., may have a generally lower threshold of activation).

Under normal circumstances, the strength of a neural circuit underlying a linguistic element (i.e., its propensity to be activated) is assumed to be proportional to the frequency of stimulation of that circuit. A circuit that has been well established and that is used frequently would thus easily be self-activated in the absence of external stimuli. An element would be easier to understand (recognition of the stimulus) than to produce voluntarily (recall, or self-activation in the absence of the stimulus). A higher degree of inhibition would therefore be necessary to hinder the comprehension of a word than to prevent its voluntary recall (self-activation).

A pathological process might selectively raise the threshold of some circuits, making self-activation of the element it subserves more difficult or even impossible while still allowing its comprehension, as in cases of selective loss of expression with preserved comprehension in one language. A higher level of inhibition could raise the threshold of activation to such a point that even comprehension would be impossible, as in cases of selective loss of a language without residual comprehension. If each language forms a subsystem, then a pathological process could independently inhibit each language temporarily, alternately, or permanently.

Whereas the phenomenon that allows one language to be selectively or differentially impaired could be explained by the above hypothesis, the factors that impede the disinhibition of a particular language rather than another, or that give rise to an antagonistic rather than a successive or mixed recovery, remain to be identified. These factors may derive from the patient's history of bilingualism (contexts of acquisition and use, structural distance between the languages, degree of mastery of each) or from physiological and neuropathological circumstances (site and size of lesion, symptomatology, age of patient). The relevance and extent of contribution of all these potential factors will have to be determined. This will be possible, of course, only by investigating very large numbers of patients and sharing the findings through international cooperation.

However, it should be realized that, although we are dealing with six basic patterns of recovery, three or four types of aphasia, half a dozen different contexts of acquisition, and several contexts of use, which together form a very large number of possible combinations indeed, it is not necessary to examine as many groups of patients as there are possible combinations of variables. Fortunately, in the search for the factors associated with bilingual recovery patterns, a rather small number of patients can quickly eliminate a large number of possibilities. For example, when a given pattern is observed in the absence of one of the variables, that variable could not reasonably be construed as contributing in any way to the cause of the symptom, neither alone nor in combination.

It would indeed be unreasonable to expect that a female patient should exhibit pattern X only when the second language was learned after age 15 and the lesion is anterior, while a male patient should exhibit the same pattern only with a posterior lesion, provided that both languages were acquired before the age of 5. Though these combinations are logically possible (and conceivable in the course of a Cartesian hyperbolic doubt process), no plausible theoretical model could account for such idiosyncratic synergistic combinations.

Thus, if two patients of opposite sexes (with similar lesions and acquisition contexts) experience the same recovery pattern, sex is to be ruled out as a possible contributing factor to the particular recovery pattern. If both sex and acquisition contexts are different, then both are to be ruled out. Potential factors can be eliminated in this way one by one until possibly a small number of them remain coextensive with a given pattern. Then it may become more difficult to ascertain whether one of the concomitant variables is the determining factor, whether it contributes to the pattern only in conjunction with one or more of these variables, or whether it is not contributing in any way but simply happens to be present for any number of reasons.

While one may not be prepared to exclude a potential factor on the basis of a single case, a large number of cases is nevertheless not necessary. Once it is established that a particular pattern occurs in the absence of one of the variables, that variable may be dropped from the search. If only women have been observed to undergo a particular recovery pattern, then a good case can be made for the working hypothesis that sex is a contributing factor (until such time as a male patient manifesting this pattern is found). But when it is clear that both men and women exhibit the pattern, sex cannot be a contributing factor, let alone a determining one. The same holds for any of the potential factors under scrutiny: if a pattern obtains in the absence of a variable, any role attributed to this variable must be dismissed.

So, on the basis of the two cases reported by Paradis et al. (1982) it is reasonable to suppose that neither sex (the first patient was a female, the second a male) nor context of acquisition (L_2 learned after 12 by grammar-translation, acquired before 5 from the environment) nor structural distance (Arabic/French, English/French) could be a contributing factor to an alternate antagonistic recovery pattern. Etiology in this case is problematic: The first patient suffered a concussion as a contrecoup to an impact, the second an edema subsequent to surgery in the parietal lobe; both disruptions could have been the result of an edema. On the other hand, both patients suffered severe word finding difficulties and the disturbed cerebral area was posterior temporal. Lesion site and symptom may be causally related. But either factor independently (lesion site irrespective of specific symptom(s), or word finding difficulties irrespective of lesion site) or both together (i.e., word finding difficulties subsequent to posterior temporal lesion only) could be responsible for the alternate antagonistic pattern. However, it is not possible to establish this until a large number of patients exhibiting this pattern have been observed. Then, if all patients experiencing an alternate antagonistic recovery present with word finding difficulties and none present with some other symptom (in the absence of word finding difficulties), it will be possible to suspect that word finding difficulty is a necessary condition for the development of an alternate antagonistic pattern. Thus, while positive evidence (such as the absence of a suspected factor) allows one to eliminate potential variables, negative evidence (failure to find a case without a particular concomitant variable) only allows one to adopt a working hypothesis, since patients with different symptoms and/or lesions in different loci may eventually be observed to present this pattern, or patients with the same symptoms and lesion site may be observed to exhibit a different pattern. The extent to which such a working hypothesis is plausible is proportional to the number of cases observed.

A further question that may be asked is whether similarity of structure between the two languages of a bilingual has any impact on their cerebral representation and hence on the recovery pattern of aphasic patients. It has been suggested that similarity between two languages will affect their relative rates of recovery (Bychowski, 1919; Pick, 1921; Salomon, 1914; Kauders, 1929—though Kauders' own data do not confirm this hypothesis; Galloway, 1978; Lebrun, 1976; Whitaker, 1978). According to such a view, cerebral representation of bilingualism would be on a language pair-specific continuum, ranging from a bi- or multiregister unilingualism to a bilingualism involving two unrelated languages.

Albert & Obler (1978) have proposed that the proximity of structurally similar languages may entail "effort" to avoid interference, leading to more separate neural structures. In this perspective, one might expect languages that are similar to be recovered more differentially than languages whose structural distance is sufficient not to require this "effort" and consequent greater neurofunctional separation. On the other hand, the opposite argument can be put forward: The less two languages have in common, the more they are represented separately. It could be assumed that features common to two related languages would not be redundantly represented (a situation compatible with the extended system and the tripartite system hypotheses) but would form a single representation shared by both languages, whereas unrelated languages would de facto have greater neurofunctional separation since they would hardly have any features in common. A third possibility is of course that structural distance is irrelevant and that as long as two languages are spoken, they are subserved by separate neural substrates (a situation consistent with the dual system and the subsystems hypotheses).

A systematic comparison between the recovery pattern of Basque-Spanish (as well as Finnish-Swedish, Japanese-Spanish, etc.) bilingual aphasics and that of Catalan-Spanish (and Norwegian-Swedish, Galician-Spanish) should reveal whether structural distance has an effect or not, and if so, how. This investigation too will be possible only through international collaboration.

A comprehensive investigation of aphasia in bilinguals will provide empirical (clinical) evidence for testing hypotheses on the representation of two languages in the same brain. It will thus contribute valuable elements towards a theory of bilingualism. It will also provide important indications of the organizing principles that underlie language comprehension and production and suggest directions for the design of explanatory models in linguistic theory. A more immediate practical benefit of the analysis, with the same instrument, of the speech of large numbers of bilingual aphasic patients will be the gathering of data on the effects of various types of therapy in various circumstances (e.g., type of aphasia, structural distance between the languages involved), thus revealing the conditions for prescribing which type of therapy is optimal in which language.

2

Theoretical Foundations of the Assessment of Bilingual Aphasia

Aphasia testing in only one language is not sufficient to assess language deficits in the polyglot.

—Silverberg and Gordon (1979, p. 54)

THE BILINGUAL APHASIA TEST: WHAT IT IS, WHAT IT IS NOT

The need to assess language capacities in both of a bilingual's (or all of a polyglot's) languages should be obvious for a number of reasons. Assessment is essential for purposes of diagnosis, research, and prescription for treatment.

The usefulness of the *Bilingual Aphasia Test* (BAT) for diagnostic purposes is twofold. When the language of the (hospital) environment is almost nonavailable to the patient, it is important to determine whether another language may serve as a means of communication. Only when both languages have been tested with a comparable instrument can one ascertain which language is better retained or less impaired. Conversely, subtle deficits may be observable in only one of the patient's languages. These deficits may nevertheless be suggestive of the general locus and extent of cerebral damage and would go unnoticed if the better pre-served language happened to be that of the hospital environment and if the other language were not tested.

In both cases the results may help one to decide in which language the patient should receive speech therapy. In the first case, once it has been established that one language is definitely better preserved, decisions can be made with respect to the language community in which the patient may choose to live subsequently (e.g., back in the home country or in the country of immigration), and the language of therapy may be selected on the basis of the language of social reinsertion. In the second case, the language showing deficits would be treated.

For research purposes, the results obtained on the *Bilingual Aphasia Test* allow one to correlate the patient's pattern of recovery with the various acquisitional, utilizational, neurological, and pathological factors involved, and to compare such correlations with those obtained in other patients, with a view to ultimately identifying the influencing factor or hierarchy of interactive factors. Data obtained from the *Bilingual Aphasia Test* should eventually give indications about the organization of two languages in the same brain.

For purposes of prescription of language therapy, the systematic use of the *Bilingual Aphasia Test* should first serve to determine under what conditions therapy in one language has beneficial or detrimental effects on the other, and thus, when it is advisable to prescribe therapy in one (and in which one) or in both. Subsequently, once research has established these conditions, all languages of a given patient will have to be tested to ascertain which one is most accessible postmorbidly, with a view to deciding, in the light of the above findings, in which language or languages therapy should be undertaken for that patient.

Hence, what is of interest for pure research into the neurofunctional organization of the bilingual brain is also useful to the clinician for diagnostic purposes and to the therapist for prescribing the most efficient course of treatment.

The Bilingual Aphasia Test is not designed to differentiate aphasia from syndromes of confusion, dementia, or psychosis, but to determine whether performance in one language is better than in another, and, if it is, to what extent and in what language skill(s) and/or level(s) of linguistic structure. Nor is it specifically constructed to discriminate between types of aphasia. However, because it incorporates most of the tasks generally used for that purpose, the *Bilingual Aphasia Test* can be used quite reliably as a screening instrument. Hence, in addition to being used for its primary purpose—namely the assessment of differential recovery in bilinguals and polyglots, which thereby adds to the research data base—it is expected that the *Bilingual Aphasia Test* will be used to assess the residual language of unilingual aphasics in countries where no standardized test is available for that language. In such cases, items from the *Bilingual Aphasia Test* may be supplemented with *language*-independent tasks from other standardized batteries such as the color naming test and the cookie theft description of the *BDAE*.

No test can possibly cover all aspects of language exhaustively. While a battery must try to be comprehensive enough, it must remain manageable. The *Bilingual Aphasia Test* explores a substantial number of aspects of most levels of language structure (phonemic, phonological, morphological, syntactic, lexical, semantic) and language use (comprehension, repetition, judgment, propositionizing, reading, writing) in most modalities (auditory, visual, oral, and digitomanual) with the word, the sentence, and the paragraph as units of analysis. Thus it covers most of the performances that may be disturbed. It can reasonably be assumed that it contains enough items to almost eliminate variability while at the same time being of manageable size so that it can be administered in two or more languages on consecutive days, preferably in one setting each, or at most in two.

The *Bilingual Aphasia Test* is not an assessment of functional communication, but of specifically linguistic abilities in each of the patient's languages. It measures the patient's residual linguistic competence, as reflected in his/her linguistic performance. By *linguistic performance* is meant, in this context, normal language use exclusive of nonlinguistic means of communication. Thus the *Bilingual Aphasia Test* measures the patient's ability to communicate solely on the basis of linguistic means, unaided by contextual or paralinguistic clues. In other words, it is the linguistic component of communicative competence that is measured. What the patient does with language (functions, uses) depends on what the patient knows (albeit implicitly and unconsciously) about language. The latter (linguistic competence) is a prerequisite for the former (linguistic performance). Since linguistic performance (as opposed to communicative performance) entails the use of the speaker's competence (while communicative performance may, or may not involve linguistic competence), it is the patient's implicit knowledge of the grammar of each language that is assessed, not his or her overall communicative ability.

The Bilingual Aphasia Test does not measure the patient's use of language-mixing as a communicative strategy. What it does measure is the patient's ability to use each language in a unilingual setting. Paralinguistic and other non-linguistic communicative abilities as well as code-mixing abilities can be assessed independently for different purposes. It is nevertheless important to determine the nature of the patient's premorbid proficiency as well as the nature of his or her dialect, including degree of code-mixing, so as to compare his or her aphasic performance to what could realistically have been expected from his or her premorbid competence, and not to some idealized competence that would deviate from the patient's. It goes without saying that language-mixing is to be accepted as normal if it is reasonable to assume, on the basis of the history-of-bilingualism questionnaire and local bilingual usage, that it reflects the patient's premorbid habitual practice.

It is assumed that the bilingual patient does not have two sets of short-term memories, two sets of cognitive functions, two sets of mental representations of the outside world, or two sets of attention spans, used independently in conjunction with each language. Rather, it is assumed that the bilingual's higher cognitive functions and mental capacities other than language (short-term memory, long-term memory, attention, reasoning, knowledge of the world, general intelligence), are the same for that individual whether she or he uses one language or another (Paradis, 1980, 1985). Thus if performance in one language is weaker than in the other, this is to be interpreted as indicative of a language-specific weakness. The poorer performance in one language cannot be attributed to deficient sensory input, generalized cognitive deficits, or defective attention.

No doubt, access to stored conceptual knowledge and processes of reasoning interact with the grammar to allow the normal use of language. These extra-linguistic cognitive processes inevitably participate in the patient's performance on most tasks. However, they are not necessarily impaired by the aphasia-causing lesion. But even if they were, the degree of impairment would be the same, irrespective of which language is being used. Likewise, complications of the clinical manifestations of the language deficit proper (paresis of the speech musculature, poor vision or hearing, or severe intellectual impairment) are again necessarily equal for all languages in the same patient, and differences in test scores are to be taken as a sign of the dominance of one language over the other.

It could be argued that a patient may have to rely more extensively on short-term memory when processing one language than when processing the other, and that, therefore, an impaired short-term memory would affect performance in one of the languages to a greater extent than in the other. A short-term memory deficit would thus contribute to the lower linguistic score. However, it would be precisely because that language was weaker in the first place that the patient would have to rely more on short-term memory. Hence, any differential effect of short-term memory on the processing of one of the languages would simply be a further indication of that language's weakness relative to the other.

Mental processes that require the manipulation of verbal material will be sensitive to the aphasic disorder in proportion to the severity of that disorder. Thus, if one language is more or less impaired than another, these mental processes will be accordingly more or less disturbed and their differential perfor-mance will be a further reflection of the degree of impairment of each language.

In the presence of hemianopia, visual scanning in reading may be a confound-ing variable in the case of two languages read from opposite directions (e.g., Hebrew and English) though not for combinations of any two languages read from the same direction (e.g., Hebrew and Arabic or French and Russian). If pointing apraxia interferes with comprehension testing, its effects should be equal for all languages tested. In case of left-side neglect, the effects should also be the same across languages since target pictures are in the same position in all languages and have been evenly distributed on the page between left and right. No matter how artificial or metalinguistic a task may be, as long as the task is identical in all languages, a differential score is indicative of some *linguistic* differential ability.

It is not possible to select tasks that would each examine only one aspect of linguistic structure or even one skill at the exclusion of all others. Most tasks call upon phonemic discrimination, syntactic comprehension, and lexical accessibi-lity, if only to allow the patient to understand the instructions. However, a number of tasks are designed to focus on specific aspects and endeavor to control for other variables either within the task (e.g., by balancing lexical items in reversible sentences) or by cross-referencing with other sections of the test where accessibility of the lexical items involved is demonstrated. Hence an adequate assessment of the level of integrity of the patient's phonology, morphology, syntax, lexicon, and semantics, as well as his or her performance in comprehension, repetition, judgment, lexical access, propositionizing, reading, and writing, is obtained by grouping together the scores on various sections as suggested in Tables 2.1 and 2.2. On tasks concentrating on specific aspects of performance, responses are considered errors only when they relate to the task at hand (e.g., a "-" score or a wrong choice among 1, 2, 3, 4). Thus, for example, phonemic paraphasias are not scored as errors when they occur during the correct selection of a synonym (158–162) or the identification of the word that does not belong to a given semantic class (153–162). Phonemic paraphasias are scored in sections that systematically measure that dimension (521–522, 547–548, 567–569, 572–573, 574–594).

The patient's ability to understand and remember the instructions may differ on each version of the test, but only insofar as one language is weaker than the other. Since input and output modalities and whatever intervening processes involved in any given task are the same for each language being tested, the weaker performance on one version of the test must be attributed to that language's weakness relative to the other(s). The effects of intelligence and education in the measure of differential performance are minimized inasmuch as they can be presumed to be the same in a given individual, irrespective of the language in which she or he happens to communicate, and to be equal on two successive days. More educated patients may tend to obtain higher scores, but scores should be equally high or equally low in both languages. The question is not so much how well a patient does on a given version of the test but how his or her performance compares with that in the other language.

Nevertheless, education may have a differential effect in reading and writing. In fact, the patient may not be literate in one of his or her languages while being highly literate in the other. It is also often the case that one language was weaker than another before insult. This information is revealed in the answers to the bilingual history questionnaire of Part A and the first 17 questions of Part B, and the patient's performance is to be interpreted in the light of these findings.

Because premorbid reading habits and educational achievement are likely to have a greater impact on reading and writing, tasks are restricted to 10 concrete words, 10 sentences, a short paragraph, 5 concrete words for copying, and 5 concrete words and 5 sentences for dictation. Scores on these sections are obviously not compared across languages if the patient was illiterate or quasi-illiterate in one of them prior to insult. Apart from the few sections involving reading and writing, most test items are of a level compatible with a low level of education as well as with a relatively low level of second language proficiency. No matter how demanding from an intellectual standpoint a given task may be, differential results are indicative of differences in specific linguistic abilities in the two languages.

Because patients differ from each other on a number of variables, they should not be compared to each other for the purpose of determining who recovers better. Rather, once large numbers of patients exhibiting the same pattern of impairment and/or recovery—irrespective of severity—have been identified, correlations can be established between their particular pattern and factors susceptible of influencing it, such as contexts of acquisition and use, degree of premorbid proficiency, structural distance between the languages, sociolinguistic and emotional variables, age at onset, size and site of lesion, and symptomatology and etiology.

Because two languages can be affected differentially, testing in one language only cannot assess severity of aphasia. Hence, for clinical as well as research purposes, more important than how low a patient scores on a given version of the test is whether one language is more readily available than another, and if so, which one; and whether performance is significantly lower in one language than in another. The procedure to follow is to check whether the patient scores significantly lower on some or all subtests in one language than in the other, and then to check whether there are any reasons why that weaker language (or any aspect of it, e.g., reading, writing, or skills acquired mainly through schooling in a particular language, such as mental arithmetic) should have been weaker (and especially that much weaker) before insult.

Any test of aphasia faces a double double-bind. Either the test is too long and fatiguing to the patient and the examiner (Kertesz, 1979, p. 33) or not thorough enough. Either it is too difficult and aphasics may do poorly because of lack of premorbid proficiency or degree of education, or it is too easy and a ceiling effect may prevent the detection of subtle impairments. Efforts have been made to keep the BAT short without being overly brief, and comprehensive without being impractically long. We have also attempted to keep a balance between mostly easy tasks and a few slightly more difficult ones. For the sake of comprehensiveness, the number of items per task is sometimes small (5 to 10, with an overall average of more than 10). It is not the score on any specific task that serves as a basis for determining dominance, but the overall score, which is much more significant. Each individual section of the test contributes only $\frac{1}{40}$ to the total score. Subscores are nevertheless useful in showing in what particular area of the grammar or in what particular skill a patient is primarily deficient.

Compared to Weisenburg and McBride's (1935) tests, which are reported to have taken an average of 19 hours per patients (up to 94 hours for some) to administer (Darley, 1979, p. 190), the BAT may seem quite short. Compared to the reported 10–20 minutes it takes to administer Sarno's (1969) FCP (Swisher, 1979, p. 205), the BAT may seem long. Its administration takes somewhat less than half the time required for the BDAE. But then, of course, it must be administered successively in as many languages as the patient spoke before insult. It would be difficult to obtain in less time the amount of information

TABLE 2.1
Sections Focusing on Specific Aspects of Language Structure

SUBTEST AND ITEM NOS.	LINGUISTIC LEVEL TESTED				
	Phonology	Morphology	Syntax	Lexicon	Semantics
1. Spontaneous Speech 18-22, 514-539	x	x	x	x	x
2. Pointing 23-32				x	
3. Commands 33-47			x	x	
4. Verbal Auditory Discrimination 48-65	x			x	
5. Syntactic Comprehension 66-152			x		
6. Semantic Categories 153-157				x	x
7. Synonyms 158-162				x	x
8. Antonyms 163-172				x	x
9. Grammaticality Judgment 173-182			x		
10. Semantic Acceptability 183-192					x
11. Repetition of Words 193-251	x			x	
12. Lexical Decision 194-252				x	
13. Repetition of Sentences 253-259			x		
14. Series 260-262					
15. Verbal Fluency 263-267				x	
16. Naming 269-288				x	

SUBTEST AND ITEM NOS.	Phonology	Morphology	Syntax	Lexicon	Semantics
17. Sentence Construction 289-313			x		
18. Semantic Opposites 314-323				x	x
19. Derivational Morphology 324-333		x			
20. Morphological Opposites 334-343		x			
21. Description 344-346, 540-565	x	x	x	x	x
22. Mental Arithmetic 347-361					
23. Listening Comprehension 362-366					x
24. Reading Words Aloud 367-376	x			x	
25. Reading Sentences Aloud 377-386			x		
26. Reading Comprehension (paragraph) 387-392					x
27. Copying 393-397				x	
28. Dictation of Words 398-402				x	
29. Dictation of Sentences 403-407			x	x	
30. Reading Comprehension (words) 408-417				x	
31. Reading Comprehension (sentences) 418-427			x		
32. Spontaneous Writing 813-835		x	x	x	x

TABLE 2.2
Sections Focusing on Specific Language Skills

	Comprehension	Repetition	Judgment	Lexical Access	Propositionizing	Reading	Writing
LINGUISTIC SKILL TESTED							
1. Spontaneous Speech 18-22, 514-539				X	X		
2. Pointing 23-32	X						
3. Commands 33-47	X						
4. Verbal Auditory Discrimination 48-65	X						
5. Syntactic Comprehension 66-152	X						
6. Semantic Categories 153-157				X			
7. Synonyms 158-162				X			
8. Antonyms 163-172				X			
9. Grammaticality Judgment 173-182			X				
10. Semantic Acceptability 183-192			X				
11. Repetition of Words 193-251		X					
12. Lexical Decision 194-252			X				
13. Repetition of Sentences 253-259		X					
14. Series 260-262			X				
15. Verbal Fluency 263-267				X			

	Comprehension	Repetition	Judgment	Lexical Access	Propositionizing	Reading	Writing
16. Naming 269-288				X			
17. Sentence Construction 289-313					X		
18. Semantic Opposites 314-323				X			
19. Derivational Morphology 324-333				X	X		
20. Morphological Opposites 334-343				X	X		
21. Description 344-346,540-565				X	X		
22. Mental Arithmetic 347-361				X			
23. Listening Comprehension 362-366	X						
24. Reading Words Aloud 367-376						X	
25. Reading Sentences Aloud 377-386						X	
26. Reading Comprehension (paragraph) 387-392	X					X	
27. Copying 393-397							X
28. Dictation of Words 398-402	X						X
29. Dictation of Sentences 403-407	X						X
30. Reading Comprehension (words) 408-417	X					X	
31. Reading Comprehension (sentences) 418-427	X					X	
32. Spontaneous Writing 813-835				X			X

necessary for a valid assessment of a sufficient number of components of language ability to allow a meaningful comparison between a patient's languages.

In order to be able to compare the patient's performance in both languages, it is essential that versions of the BAT in various languages not be mere translations of one another, but be linguistically equivalent transpositions. In addition to adjustments for cultural appropriateness, each section in each language must be adapted to reflect a similar level of linguistic complexity, frequency, and naturalness of use as in every other language. Of course, the nature of the equivalence between elements varies with the type of task involved.

In order to determine the richness of the lexicon at the patient's disposal, a measure whose criteria are not language-specific but applicable to all must be used. These criteria must be simple enough to be interpretable by all educated persons and not only by a handful of specialists in morphology (e.g., not every intelligent, educated person could accurately count morphemes). These criteria should have similar consequences in all languages and not yield a considerably smaller or larger number of words in a particular class of languages (e.g., highly inflected languages as opposed to relatively uninflected languages). Yet these criteria should not be totally arbitrary and should be informative with respect to the richness of the lexicon available to the patient.

A good measure of the diversity of the lexicon accessible to the patient would seem to be the type/token ratio. It consists in dividing the number of different words (types) in a corpus by the total number of words (tokens) in that corpus. The more varied the vocabulary in a corpus (i.e., the greater the number of different words used), the closer is the ratio to 1. (A ratio of 1 would reflect a corpus in which not a single word was repeated.) Conversely, the more the same words are used repeatedly, the smaller the value, reflecting a proportionately reduced vocabulary. A high type/token ratio is thus indicative of a rich diversified vocabulary, whereas a low ratio is indicative of a restricted vocabulary.

However, a problem arises when it comes to deciding what counts as a word within each language. Languages without articles or copula (e.g., Hungarian and Slavic languages) tend to yield higher type/token ratios than languages in which articles, accompanying almost every noun, represent many tokens of the same type in a corpus (e.g., English and Romance languages). A language in which noun phrases are commonly realized as compound words (e.g., Dutch) tends to have relatively fewer words in a corpus of equal length because what counts as three or four words in another language counts as only one in this type of language.

Ideally, two words in a corpus are considered as tokens of the same type if they belong to the same grammatical class (e.g., *play* (V) and *play* (N) are two different types); have the same phonology apart from a possible added inflection (*boy* and *boys* are two tokens of the type *boy*; *do* and *does* are two different types); and have the same lexical meaning. Various inflected forms of a word are counted as tokens of the same type provided their radical remains unchanged (e.g., *eats* and *eating* are tokens of the type *eat*). Derived forms, on the other hand, are considered different types (e.g., *nation/national, drive/driver, boy/boyish*). Note that they generally change grammatical categories and/or pronunciation of the radical.

Heuristically, we may distinguish between a lexical meaning and a grammatical meaning. The latter conveys case, gender, number, tense, and aspect without really affecting the intrinsic lexical meaning of the word. Generally, inflectional morphology does not alter the lexical meaning of the word. *To hit* is always "the action of hitting" whether it is occurring today, yesterday, or repeatedly, whether it is in process, and whether it is carried out by one or several persons. A *hitter*, on the other hand, is not "the action of hitting" in some context, but "a person who hits." Derivational morphology thus changes the meaning of the word (and sometimes its grammatical class). All words of the language that are idiosyncratic in some way, i.e., that are not derived by a productive rule, are considered to be stored independently and are counted as different types for the purpose of this analysis (e.g., while *girl* and *girls, walk* and *walked* are tokens of the same type, *man* and *men, bring* and *brought* are different types).

Operationally, any form, listed separately in the dictionary either as a separate entry or, in parentheses, as an irregular form of the word, is counted as a different type. Inflected forms that do not have a separate entry or indication in parentheses are counted as tokens of the same type. (Hence, in English, *am, is, are,* and *be* are counted as separate words. So are *bring,* and *brought,* but not *bring* and *bringing.* Similarly, *man* and *men* are counted as two different words, whereas *car* and *cars* are counted as two tokens of the same word.) In languages with agglutinative tendencies, each part of a word that has a separate entry in the dictionary (whereas the entire word does not) is counted as a separate word type. (Hence, in Dutch, *Gemeentereinigingsdienst* is counted as 3 words since *gemeente, reiniging,* and *dienst* each has a separate entry. Unlike *bona fide* compound words such as *blackbird* and *fireball* in English, *gemeentereinigingsdienst* does not have an entry of its own in the dictionary; only its component parts do.) In this way, patients speaking agglutinative languages will not appear to have a poorer vocabulary than those whose languages are not agglutinative.

The use of a dictionary as a criterion for deciding what counts as a different word may not be as theoretically discriminative as one might wish, but it has the overwhelming advantage of ensuring uniformity of analysis across patients and across languages. This procedure should reduce to a negligible number the cases to be resolved by individual decision. Besides, the desirable criteria are fortunately captured for the most part in single/separate dictionary entries: *play* (N) and *play* (V) have separate entries; *boy* and *boyish* have separate entries, *boy* and *boys* do not—nor is *boys* specified as the plural of *boy* because it is derived by rule; *men* either gets a special entry or is given in parentheses as the plural form of *man,* depending on the dictionary. However, it remains impractical to stipulate which specific dictionary to use as a reference for each of the 40 languages

involved at the present. (There is sufficient agreement among various diction-
aries to make this requirement unnecessary.) Any standard one-volume comprehensive unilingual dictionary containing about 40,000 vocabulary entries should
be adequate.

In an effort to further reduce interlanguage variation, closed class words
(articles, prepositions, particles, conjunctions, pronouns) are not to be counted in
the calculation of the type/token ratio. This effectively cancels out any difference
that would obtain between languages that contain prepositions and those that
contain case markers; between languages with and without articles; and between
languages that obligatorily express subject pronouns and those in which pronouns are either optional or obligatorily dropped in certain contexts. Moreover,
the type/token ratio is meant to be a measure of *lexical* diversity, not grammatical competence. It will better reflect this aspect once grammatical morphemes have been deleted from the analysis. The type/token ratio is obtained
from spontaneous speech (519), descriptive speech (545), and spontaneous writing (817).

Together with word-finding difficulty, paraphasias are among the most per-
vasive characteristics of aphasic speech. The preponderance of one type of
paraphasia over another may be of diagnostic significance. Phonemic, semantic,
and verbal paraphasias have each been associated with specific syndromes. They
are therefore tabulated separately in spontaneous (521–524) and descriptive
speech (547–550). Literal, semantic, and verbal paragraphias are likewise computed in spontaneous writing (819–822).

Because phonemic paraphasias may accidentally result in real words, the
latter have been distinguished from *bona fide* verbal paraphasias having no
phonemic resemblance to the target word. The relative occurrence of verbal
paraphasias compared to phonemic paraphasias resulting in nonwords may give
an indication as to whether paraphasias resulting in real words are in fact mostly
phonemic or verbal paraphasias.

Whether or not paraphasias—reported to be present in the speech of Broca's
and conduction as well as Wernicke's aphasics—discriminate between types of
aphasia, they may nevertheless be much more prominent in one language than in
another. A count of paraphasias is therefore included as a means of capturing
differences in degree of impairment between the two languages, not only in
spontaneous and descriptive speech, but also in repetition (567–569; 574–594)
and in reading aloud (624–626; 629–658). The same reasoning holds for the
production of neologisms (520, 546, 566, 616–622, 623, 299–708, 724–728,
754–758, 804–808, 818) and perseverations (525, 551, 570, 595–601, 628,
669–678, 729–733, 764–768, 824).

A number of measures traditionally used in the language development literature, in particular in the analysis of the complexity of adult speech addressed to
children (Snow & Ferguson, 1977), have been included in the posttest analysis to
measure the syntactic complexity of the aphasic patient's output in spontaneous

and descriptive speech and in spontaneous writing. The longer the utterance, the more syntactically complex it tends to be. Therefore the mean length of utterance (516, 542, 815) gives a general indication of complexity, and the MLU of the 5 longest utterances produced by the patient (517, 543) provides a rough estimate of the upper limits of his or her productive capacity. The number of verbs per utterance (529, 555, 828) is a further indication of sentence complexity. The number of subordinate clauses (530, 556, 829) specifies whether these sentences containing more than one verb are simply conjoined or genuinely complex.

Independently of their complexity, utterances may be grammatically deviant. Syntactic and morphological features may either be used erroneously (526, 552, 825) or may be deleted (527, 553, 826). Word order may also be affected, especially through intrusions of features of the other language (528, 554, 827). These items combined to yield a measure of accuracy.

Semantic acceptability can be measured at the level of each sentence (537, 563, 833) and at the level of discourse cohesion (538, 564, 834). Fabulation should be apparent if the patient makes declarations that are obviously implausible, unreasonable, or known to be clearly untrue (539, 565, 835).

A measure of the patient's fluency can be derived from the total number of utterances and the total number of words produced in a 5-minute sample of extemporaneous speech (514, 515) and during the description of a sequence of pictures (540, 541), as well as from the number of intraphrasal pauses (531, 557) and other indications of word-finding difficulty (534, 560).

In the BAT, language is tested at various levels of spontaneity and formality ranging from extemporaneous speech to descriptive speech, and from sentence construction on request to metalinguistic grammatical transformations in accordance with a set of instructions and examples. For instance, in extemporaneous speech (spontaneous speech, 514–539) the patient is called upon to "propositionize" (Jackson, 1878), that is, to generate sentences from scratch, using what Chomsky (1965) calls the creative aspect of language use, i.e., the production of sentences without being given a structural model or vocabulary (as could be provided by questions addressed to the patient). In descriptive speech (540–565) the patient must likewise engage in the microgenesis of a sentence (Pick, 1913), i.e., in verbal planning and selection, though here the topic is suggested by the sequence of pictures. In addition, in both extemporaneous and descriptive speech (possibly more in the latter) the patient is to produce sentences that are strung together to form connected discourse. Also, in the sentence construction section (289–313), the order in which the lexical items are provided does not correspond to the word order in the simplest possible sentence constructed with them. Hence the patient is expected to recombine the words to truly construct a sentence, not simply fill in the blanks.

While various levels of linguistic structure are involved in all tasks (and all levels in some tasks), some subtests are nevertheless intended to assess abilities at one specific level. For example, while it is necessary to make use of phonemic as well as syntactic cues to be able to judge whether a sentence makes sense or not, the section on Semantic Acceptability specifically explores the patient's awareness of the semantic incongruity of a sentence if phonemic discrimination and syntactic comprehension, systematically tested elsewhere, have been shown to be operative. Similarly, in the Syntactic Comprehension section, the use of reversible sentences allow one to untangle the basic interrelationships between syntax and the lexicon: Since the lexicon is the same throughout the series of structures for each set of pictures, only the syntactic component varies from one stimulus to the next.

A number of tasks are undoubtedly artificial with respect to the normal conversational use of language, and draw on the patient's implicit metalinguistic competence. These tasks are nevertheless within the capacity of any non brain-damaged fluent speaker. Besides, most sections involving these tasks consist of recognition tasks (i.e., multiple choice) and they are the least demanding of metalinguistic items. The few production tasks are assuredly more difficult. Failure on the part of the patient to produce a morphological derivation on demand is no indication that she or he could not use such a derivation in a different, more natural situation. Nevertheless, a marked inability to perform in one language only does point in the direction of which language is less well preserved, at least for that particular task. When a patient consistently scores significantly better in one language than in the other in this domain, it can be safely assumed that she or he has retained (or has access to) more linguistic abilities in at least some aspect of that language than in the other.

In order to minimize the likelihood that the patient will obtain low scores because of his or her premorbid level of competence, the BAT has been designed to allow anyone able to function in the language to reach criterion on most subtests. This has been done even at the risk of being unable to measure very subtle deficits. Further, some subtests are sensitive to years of education, but not necessarily to degree of bilingualism. A *fortiori*, whenever the most impaired language is the native language and/or the most fluent language at the time of insult, lack of premorbid competence can clearly not be incriminated.

Inasmuchas the BAT is to be administered to bilingual aphasic patients, it is appropriate to ask what is meant by the use of the term "bilingual." Indeed, definitions of this term are extremely diverse, ranging from reference to an individual who has a mere smattering of knowledge of a second language to an individual who has native-like control of both languages. Some authors are willing to consider as bilingual a person who possesses even to a minimal degree only one of the language skills (e.g., reading comprehension) in a second language (Macnamara, 1969, p. 82). For others, "a true bilingual is someone who is taken to be one of themselves by the members of two different linguistic communities, at roughly the same social and cultural level" (Thiery, 1978, p. 146), in other words, someone who has equal control of two mother tongues (Blocher, 1910, p. 666). Thus, persons commonly called bilingual differ from each other considerably in the skill with which they use their languages. In fact, individual bilinguals differ in the degree of proficiency between each skill (understanding, speaking, reading, and writing) as well as between each level of linguistic structure (phonology, morphology, syntax, lexicon). In addition, a bilingual's internalized grammars are organized in terms of a three-dimensional continuum (coordinate, compound, subordinate), independent at each level of linguistic structure. A bilingual subject may thus demonstrate degrees of unidirectional or bidirectional interference in varied proportions at each level (Paradis, 1977, pp. 96–97). This organization is moreover susceptible of change over time as a result of linguistic experience. Bilinguals also differ in the extent of their various types of language-related competence—not only in their linguistic competence (i.e., the grammar), as mentioned earlier, but also in their communicative competence (which in addition to the former includes sociolinguistic and paralinguistic competence), and in their metalinguistic competence in each of their languages. Hence bilingualism denotes an extremely relative phenomenon indeed.

Obviously, the BAT is not intended to be used only with "true" (Smith & Wilson, 1980, p. 199), "perfect" (Meyer, 1979, p. 828), or "ideal" (Weinreich, 1963, p. 73) bilinguals, i.e., with individuals "who possess the full range of competence in both languages that a native unilingual speaker has in one" (Lyons, 1981, p. 282), assuming that such individuals can be found. But neither is it intended to be used with persons who have only "a minimal knowledge of a second language" (Crystal, 1980, p. 44). Rather, the BAT may be advantageously used with any person who has "a practical command of two languages" (Hockett, 1958, p. 8) and uses them "with no appreciable effort" (Lehmann, 1983, p. 170). (A pilot study for the BAT in three languages—Chinese, English, and French—has shown that subjects who have had no more than 400 hours of instruction in one of these languages score within the norms obtained by unilinguals.)

Clearly, results in each case will have to be interpreted in the light of information about the patient's premorbid state of bilingualism gathered from answers to questions 1–50 in Part A and 1–17 in Part B. This information may be obtained from the patients themselves but also from relatives, friends, and colleagues. These questions do not test the patient's language capacity and do not contribute to the score. The ideal situation, of course, is to test the patient premorbidly and postmorbidly, and to compare performance in each language. This is generally possible only in cases of elective surgery and is likely to occur with a very small percentage of the patients who will be examined. In the absence of premorbid testing however, a detailed account of the history of acquisition and use of the two languages should provide, in many cases, adequate clues to the probable degree of fluency in each language before insult.

Arsenian (1937) claimed that "because of its numerous variations and the fluidity of its boundaries, a typical classification of bilingualism cannot be definite enough for an objective treatment and fruitful research" (p. 19). Nonetheless, a sufficient number of patients with a (however ill-defined) practical command of two languages do find themselves in aphasia wards to allow us to eventually ascertain whether degree of mastery of a second language is a determinant in their recovery type, and if so, what other circumstances are determinants (e.g., age of onset, type of aphasia, history of acquisition and use, or any other factor identified in Table 1.1). See p. 6.

Thus, given the total number of countries in which individuals could participate in administering the BAT, and given a conservative estimate of 2 bilingual aphasic patients hospitalized each week in each participating country, it should be possible to examine 4,000 bilingual patients in one year, 40,000 in 10 years. (In a country like the U.S.A. one may expect the rate of 2 bilingual patients per week in any single large cosmopolitan city.) With such large numbers of patients it should be possible to find sufficiently homogeneous groups and hence to isolate the relevant variables.

STANDARDIZATION AND OBJECTIVITY

Every time a patient speaks a language unknown to the hospital staff, an inexperienced person (a relative, a friend, a hospital employee on another ward) may be called upon to administer the test. Therefore maximum standardization of administration and scoring procedures is necessary to ensure that results are consistently obtained and thus comparable between the various collaborating centers around the world. Explicit and comprehensive instructions as well as strictly quantitative, objective scoring procedures maximize the likelihood that the test will be administered in the same way each time.

For each section, instructions given to the patient by the test administrator are specified *in extenso*, leaving no room for addition, subtraction, or substitution, down to the last example before the patient is asked if she or he is ready. There is to be no prompting at any time and limits for answering are clearly stipulated. Test administration and conditions under which it is administered are kept as controlled as possible: The various versions are to be administered on successive days at the same time of day. In the event that the test must be split into several sessions, the portions in which it is split are to be identical in all languages tested.

Specific directives to the test administrator pertaining to manner of presentation of stimuli and scoring procedure are also stipulated in detail before each section, prior to the instructions to be read to the patient. The patient's performance is assessed each time according to the same objective and, inasmuch as possible, according to exact criteria. Scoring is made as simple and explicit as possible with as little room as possible for interpretation. Thus, whenever there is a possibility of more than one correct response, the administrator is to score "+" only if the patient provides the expected answer, and "1" if she or he provides a different, albeit equally acceptable answer, so that "+" and "1" are eventually to count as a correct score. However, in the case of a score of "1," the examiner is requested to write the actual response produced by the patient so that it can later be ascertained that it was indeed an adequate response. (This response should also be recoverable from the tape.) Thus, whenever the examiner is called upon to make the slightest decision, it can be verified later if all instances where a score of "1" was recorded instead of "+" are checked.

To further minimize the need for interpretation, the patient is not asked to point to objects or to pictures but to *touch* them. (Whereas some interpretation may be needed to decide whether a patient actually pointed in the right direction, especially when there is hesitation on his or her part, it is clear whether she or he touches the item or not.) Moreover, the administrator reports what the patient did, not whether she or he was right or wrong. Because everything the patient says is tape-recorded, verbal responses can later be checked for accuracy of scoring as well as for further analysis.

Objective, descriptive, operational definitions are provided for terms used in the posttest analysis. Ratings making use of relative terms such as "little," "very little," "mild," "severe," "very severe," "some," "a few," "many," or "frequently," are replaced by reports of presence and number of occurrences or absence of a specific feature. In the posttest analysis, as in the test itself, the scores are strictly quantitative. Spontaneous speech is not evaluated on the basis of (necessarily subjective) judgments on a discrete point scale, but in terms of (objective) quantified data (e.g., number of paraphasias, number of missing obligatory grammatical morphemes). The scores, revealing the patient's characteristic deficits and their relative frequency of occurrence in various tasks (e.g., spontaneous speech vs. repetition) may then be interpreted by the aphasiologist as indicative of particular syndromes.

When appropriate, for each task, instructions specify test object alignment, as well as order and manner of stimulus presentation. Instructions also specify under what circumstances and how many times a stimulus may be repeated, as well as the criterion for proceeding to the next stimulus (5 seconds per item) and for abandoning a particular subset (5 consecutive incorrect answers or failures to answer).

Identical explicit instructions in all languages help ensure that the test will be implemented everywhere in the same way. The identical format in all languages further ensures strict equivalence of implementation: Linguistically equivalent items are presented in exactly the same sequence in every language and the pseudorandom pattern of correct responses is identical for all subtests in all languages (Table 2.3). This also ensures that factors of nonlinguistic difficulty do not vary across languages. In addition, the same computer program can be used to score all language versions.

Therefore, the *Bilingual Aphasia Test* can be administered by persons without a background in speech-language pathology. Likewise, the comparison of scores

TABLE 2.3
Syntactic Comprehension Answer Patterns in all Languages

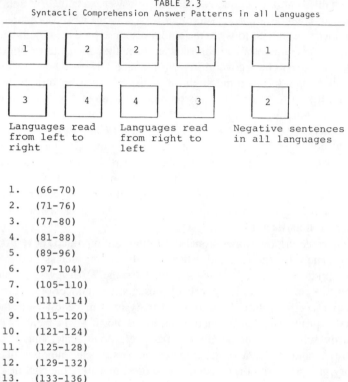

| 1 | 2 | 2 | 1 | 1 |
| 3 | 4 | 4 | 3 | 2 |

Languages read   Languages read   Negative sentences
from left to   from right to   in all languages
right   left

1.   (66-70)
2.   (71-76)
3.   (77-80)
4.   (81-88)
5.   (89-96)
6.   (97-104)
7.   (105-110)
8.   (111-114)
9.   (115-120)
10. (121-124)
11. (125-128)
12. (129-132)
13. (133-136)

between languages does not require any special training. On the other hand, the transformation of quantitative scores into qualitative profiles and their interpretation for diagnosis must be performed by an experienced aphasiologist.

While the grouping of sections is suggested in Table 4.4 by linguistic level, and in Table 4.3 by language skill, no attempt has been made to provide an interpretation of the scores in terms of the classical taxonomies of aphasia. Each clinician is free to classify patients in accordance with his or her own preferred criteria. This should be an easy task, given Tables 2.1 and 2.2 and the results of the posttest analysis. The scores on the various tasks provide a sufficient basis for a diagnosis, whatever classification is adopted, whatever each individual neurologist chooses to select as indicative of a particular syndrome as defined within a particular school of thought.

Because of the proliferation of labels for aphasic syndromes (motor, Broca's, expressive, executive, anterior, transcortical motor, dynamic, afferent motor, conduction, phonemic, efferent motor, amnestic, receptive, sensory, Wernicke's transcortical sensory, syntactic, semantic, among others), and because many authors call the same syndrome by different names, or different syndromes by the same name (see Benson, 1979, pp. 60–62; Kertesz, 1979, pp. 4–5; Lesser, 1978, p. 11), it has been judged best not to choose one of the existing taxonomies or to impose a new one, but to give the data from which any aphasiologist can derive a profile in accordance with his or her own theoretical framework.

In a deliberate attempt to avoid reliance on the skill and biases of the scorer, and thus to ensure greater consistency of the scoring method, descriptive assessments and rating scales have been replaced by plus-or-minus scoring. This method has the advantage of being quantifiable and objective. Whatever subtlety may be lost in this procedure corresponds to subjective judgments that are close to uninterpretable anyway when they come from a large number of examiners in different settings.

Even operationally defined category scales leave room for subjective interpretation. Ratings (good, fair, etc.), no matter how clearly specified, remain subjective and hence lack intertester reliability. Different judges' ratings often show discrepancies, even after common training. For example, after 40 hours of intensive instruction and practice under the supervision of a well-trained clinician, testers still score with only "good" agreement (i.e., with a 20% margin of discrepancy) on the PICA (Porch, 1967, p. 7). The definitions used for ratings are themselves often fraught with relative terms (e.g., "Comprehension is slow and uncertain," Hécaen & Angelergues, 1964. But how slow is slow? How uncertain is it?).

As indicated by Schuell, Jenkins, & Jiménez-Pablon (1964), the loss of information in scoring can be resolved by appropriate test construction. In the BAT, complex behavior such as speech comprehension and production is explored by more than one type of test. Error pattern (consistent or inconsistent errors) on syntactic comprehension, verbal auditory discrimination, reading comprehension, and all multiple-choice tasks may reveal very specific deficits (e.g., loss of the voiced/devoiced feature in auditory discrimination; interpretation of the passive construction in English as the canonical SVO—agent, action, object). In tasks not involving multiple choice, the scoring method records whether the patient did nothing or gave evidence of not understanding the instructions (i.e., by giving a response inappropriate to the task) by a score of "0"; whether the patient gave a wrong answer (i.e., a response appropriate to the task, but incorrect, such as pointing to the wrong object in a pointing task) by a score of "−"; and whether the patient gave a correct response by a score of "+." In some cases a score of "1" indicates a correct though unexpected response, and the acceptability of that response can be confirmed later by independent judges, as explained above.

By having all of the patient's linguistic output tape-recorded, it is possible to satisfy Goldstein's (1948) legitimate requirement that a record should be kept of what the patient is saying in as much detail as possible. What the patient is *doing* is actually recorded in the scores.

Moreover, and contrary to Goldstein's (1948) assumption, plus-or-minus scoring can reveal symptoms when performance on various tasks are compared. A systematic failure to respond or a consistent pattern of erroneous responses can easily be interpreted as indicative of specific syndromes. Qualitative data are derivable from cumulative and comparative scores (see Chapter 4). When some of the patient's deficits are milder in one language than in the other (as evidenced by the numerical scores), or are absent altogether while present in the other, it may safely be assumed that one language is proportionately less affected than the other (provided, of course, that it has been ascertained that the patient's premorbid proficiency was well above the level of the task).

In addition, it is preferable to compare numerical values than to convert them into a rating scale where cut-off points are necessarily arbitrary. If a patient were to score 39 on a scale ranging from 31–40, she or he would differ in labeling from a person who scored 42. Yet, a difference between 32 and 39, which is much greater, would not be revealed. Patients scoring respectively 32 and 39 would be grouped together in the same category, whereas patients scoring 39 and 42 would belong to different categories. Since the purpose of the BAT is to compare performance between languages, it is less useful to use labels such as "mild" or "severe" than to know what the discrepancy between the two languages actually is.

While every precaution should indeed be taken to ensure that test administration is constant from patient to patient and from one examiner to another, even if there were discrepancies in method of implementation between centers (and there are bound to be some), results obtained in different centers could still be compared, because what is compared across centers is not performance on individual languages, but the relative performance between pairs of languages in the same patient, each language of the same patient presumably being tested under the same conditions. Whatever intercenter variation there may be should be the same for, and similarly affect, both languages of the same patient.

Because tasks requiring the patient to provide definitions tend to penalize the uneducated, less intelligent subject (Spreen & Risser, 1983, p. 78), they have been avoided in the BAT. Instead, easier tasks, including multiple-choice tasks, have been incorporated. The latter, in turn, may place a higher demand on short-term memory. However, partly due to their higher demand on short-term memory, these tasks may be good indicators of differential language accessibility by enhancing the difference in scores between the weaker and the stronger language (assuming that the weaker language relies more on short-term memory for processing). Having words printed on cards to counteract short-term memory load was ruled out in order to avoid giving an advantage to the language in which the patient may be literate relative to the one(s) in which he may not be. (It is not uncommon to find patients literate in only one of their languages.)

The Token Test, which is generally found to be too difficult for most aphasics (Kertesz, 1982) and for many normals as well, has been adapted to the manipulation of real objects. Relative size and color relationships are not tested, only locative prepositions (or other type of locative marker in some languages).

The scoring procedures on the BAT have been designed in such a way as to allow a possibly untrained speaker of the language to administer the test with minimal difficulty. Only those features of the patient's performance that could be identified as clearly right or wrong, or could be objectively reported (e.g., which item is selected in a multiple-choice task) are scored by the test administrator. This allows the administrator to concentrate on the patient's performance without having to pay attention to more than one aspect of what the patient is saying or doing at any given time.

After the patient has been tested and all verbal production has been tape-recorded, it is possible to further analyze the patient's performance. The scores obtained during the administration of the test by the examiner (by portable computer, microcomputer, or by hand) are sufficient to derive a first clinical assessment of the patient's abilities in each language. However, for research purposes, as well as for a more detailed clinical assessment, a number of additional measures are available following the testing session. The posttest analysis can be performed either by the test administrator or by some other speaker of the language at some later time and possibly at a different place (e.g., in a center where the patient's language is spoken). In the posttest analysis (514–835), in addition to a detailed scrutiny of spontaneous and descriptive speech and spontaneous writing, such features as paraphasias, neologisms, perseverations, and deletions are examined in repetition, reading, and writing tasks. Here again, all scores are numerical.

VALIDITY

The notion of test validity determines the overall success of a test—the extent to which design goals are realized in the application of the test instrument. The validity of any test lies in its ability to measure those abilities which it explicitly purports to measure.

The BAT is a criterion-referenced test. Each subtest of the BAT has been designed to be easy enough so that any native speaker/writer of the language can perform the tasks successfully. Fundamental to this approach is the assumption that any bilingual could have scored above criterion in both languages prior to language impairment. A score below criterion in any language can therefore be interpreted as unambiguous evidence of impairment in that language.

The lowest possible ceiling approach to test design states that it is desirable that the success criterion score be as close as possible to 100% correct for each subtest of the BAT. In the ideal, therefore, any native speaker/writer of the language would obtain a perfect score on every subtest of the BAT. This approach makes the BAT an inadequate tool for the testing of normal subjects because it virtually guarantees information loss. It has not, however, been designed to be a test of normal language ability. Rather it is a tool with which language impairment can be distinguished from normal ability. In this context, it can be seen that the lowest possible ceiling approach has a number of interesting consequences: It ensures that all normal bilinguals obtain identical scores (100%) in any pair of languages. It also allows the clinician to interpret differences between a patient's test scores against the knowledge that the patient would have shown identical scores across languages prior to language impairment. In addition, this approach creates a flat distribution of scores in normals. In other words, for any language, any two individuals would have identical scores. Therefore, any observed difference between scores on the various versions of the BAT is attributable to differences in language impairment and not to differences in premorbid language abilities (as they relate to the BAT tasks). Finally, the lowest possible ceiling approach permits the comparison of a patient's scores across subtests, or subtests grouped by language function. Again, any differences observed may be interpreted against the knowledge that the patient's premorbid scores would have been identical (100%) for each subtest.

It is in this last area—the comparability of BAT subtests—that a conflict arises between the lowest possible ceiling approach and the goal of providing a test of divergent language skills. The two come into conflict because not all language functions are of equal difficulty. The Syntactic Comprehension subtest, for example, tests a broad range of syntactic constructions. Some of these constructions, however, are inherently more difficult (as measured by the BAT task) than others. The more difficult constructions cannot be tested if one adheres to the 100% correct criterion. It was decided, therefore, that a modified version of the lowest possible ceiling approach would be employed in the BAT. Thus, as far as possible, the 100% criterion has been maintained. In addition, where necessary, success criteria of 90% and 80% (for particularly difficult subtests) have been used (see Table 4.2). The success criteria are identical across languages, and thus only affect the comparison of subtests within the BAT.

The BAT is primarily intended to be a test of differential language impairment in bilinguals and polyglots. Its validity, therefore, depends on its being a test of differential *linguistic* ability. The approach taken in the design of the BAT ensures that differential linguistic ability is measured, since all other sources of variation across languages have been controlled. As has already been discussed, many of these possible sources of variation are handled by the lowest possible ceiling approach. The remaining question, then, is whether the BAT may test something other than pure linguistic ability.

In the administration of the BAT the patient himself or herself offers the theoretical control for all nonlinguistic variables. When the BAT yields positive results, i.e. differential impairment across languages, it must be the case that linguistic variables are being measured and that these variables are uncontaminated by extralinguistic subject variables.

The design of the BAT is influenced greatly by the view that the components of general language behavior are isolable. The design also reflects the view that insights into the workings of language are to be gained by an investigation of these isolated subcomponents. The test therefore contains specific tests of phonemic discrimination, syntactic comprehension, and word repetition, as well as the more integrated tasks of story telling and text reading.

The arrangement of subtests in the BAT is intended to provide a measure of the patient's ability over a broad range of language skills. These skills are selected to include those which are known to be commonly impaired in aphasia and to allow for hypothesis testing in a clinical setting. To this end, subtests are carefully balanced across modalities (visual, auditory) and response types (recognition, production). This allows the clinician to investigate, for example, a patient's ability to process a particular syntactic construction in tasks of reading, listening, writing, and repetition.

As indicated above, the sampling of the language skills in the BAT is determined by factors other than the distribution and relative importance of these skills in everyday language behavior. It therefore does not claim to be a valid test of overall language ability or communicative competence. It does claim, however, to be a valid test of the language skills which it tests.

The specific components of language behavior tested in the BAT include subtests of word repetition, naming, single-word comprehension, sentence comprehension, and text comprehension. The validity of the BAT as a whole is dependent on the subtests being true tests of the ability they claim to measure.

It is clearly the case, however, that any attempt to obtain a measure for an isolated language skill that is comparable to other language skills must take into account the fact that language skills are often hierarchically organized. This fact can present a serious problem for the construction of a valid test of a specific language skill. It is impossible, for example, to construct a test of syntactic (sentence type) comprehension in the auditory modality that does not measure phonemic discrimination ability and (at least to some extent) lexical comprehension. It may be the case then, that what appears to be a syntactic deficit is in fact a phonemic deficit. In such cases, the phonemic deficit may completely block the measurement of syntactic comprehension.

In the BAT these problems are handled by the repeated use of test stimuli across subtests. For example, the words used in the auditory comprehension subtest are also used in the repetition subtest, the lexical decision subtest, the copying subtest, and the reading subtest. The clinician can therefore test the finding that a patient shows poor lexical comprehension against the alternative hypothesis that the patient is hearing something other than the test stimuli. The explicit testing of the components of language behavior and the use of recurring test stimuli ensure the isolability of the specific language skills in subtests of the BAT.

With respect to the validity of the specific subtests of the BAT and the validity of the BAT as a whole, the following can be said: The use of recurring stimuli serves as a means of ensuring subtest validity. That validity, however, is dependent on the equivalence of subtests across languages. In Chapter 3, a description of each subtest of the BAT is given. This description includes a discussion of language equivalence for that subtest.

The overall validity of the BAT is dependent on its ability to handle the effects of subject variables and the extent to which a number of simplifying assumptions can be made about a patient's premorbid test performance. The problem of subject variables contamination is handled by the use of the patient as his or her own control. The problem of premorbid performance is handled by the lowest possible ceiling approach. The success of this approach requires that each language test of the BAT have the same low ceiling. If this condition is met, the consequences of the lowest possible ceiling approach discussed earlier follow.

Many of the problems of language test equivalence are solved at the construction stage. These are discussed fully in Chapter 3, in the section entitled "Instructions to Translators." The present discussion will be limited to the methods by which the low ceiling is ensured after each language version of the test has been constructed.

The first step in the testing of the BAT is the collection of the native-speaker responses to the test items. Part B of the BAT is administered to sixty native speakers in a country in which each language is spoken. All subjects are hospitalized, non brain-damaged, nonpsychotic patients. The sample is stratified according to age and sex. Specifically, 20 subjects aged 50–59, 20 subjects aged 60–69, and 20 subjects over 70 years of age are selected. In each of these groups half the subjects are male and half are female.

The test administrator, a native speaker of the language, brings back the data to us and reports on items that caused problems because of language or picture ambiguity, unexpected difficulty, or adverse patient reaction.

The native-speaker responses to the test are then analyzed and the performance of the group on each item of the test is reported. Those items that do not meet the success criterion are investigated. This investigation yields two possible causes: In the first case the data are inaccurate because of an error in the test answer key, a human transcription error, or a computer data transmission error. These problems can be solved easily. In the second case, the test item is found to be unsuitable (ambiguous, difficult, etc.). The procedure then is to have those items retranslated and later retested with native speakers of the language.

For item retesting, 60 native speakers of the language are again used, with the subject sample stratified according to age and sex. The data obtained from the retest are analyzed in the same manner as the data from the original test. The process of retest analysis is repeated until all items on the test meet the success criteria.

To conclude, a testing instrument for the assessment of bilingual aphasia has been developed. It is uniform across languages. It incorporates tests of language abilities which have only recently been the subject of experimental investigation in aphasia, as well as classic ones. Each version of the BAT has been administered to nonbrain-damaged hospitalized controls in order to ensure that every fluent speaker of each language represented meets criterion on each section, and to obtain norms for the rare language-specific items. While sufficiently comprehensive, it is relatively brief.

Of necessity, the test cannot present large numbers of examples of each linguistic structure in each task, nor can it present an exhaustive list of different structures. As a consequence, though it may be possible to tell that a patient is not performing within the normal range on the test as a whole or on a large subtest within the entire battery, the recognition of aphasic performances on individual structures may not be reliable for individual patients. It is nevertheless possible to compare performance in one language to that in another.

The BAT may thus not provide a sufficient data base for detailed error analyses regarding individual patients' performance on certain specific linguistic structures. Because a version of the BAT is to be given to a patient in each of his or her languages (minimally, two), the BAT must be kept relatively short. When an interesting performance pattern seems to emerge from the limited sample provided by the test, more examples of the same task may be given. The results of such supplementary tests may be revealing to the extent that they disclose a certain specific deficit in a specific language (or in both, or all) but they are not essential for the purpose of comparing the patient's performance in each language with a view to determining which one is more accessible.

While there is indeed no limit to how detailed an investigation of a patient's linguistic abilities can be, the BAT will nevertheless provide sufficiently detailed profiles of the linguistic ability of individual patients (certainly more detailed than hitherto possible) to determine whether one language is more impaired or better recovered than the other(s), not only with respect to language in general, but for specific skills and for specific levels of structure. What the BAT may not do is determine whether, for example, the negative passive construction is statistically better preserved in one language than in the other. But due to the nature of the test—and to the nature of the various languages involved—that is not even a possible task. (Various languages have different canonical word order and do or do not use the passive construction with equal frequency, etc. Furthermore, in itself, the passive construction varies in linguistic complexity from one language to another.)

Though it may eventually help to shed some light on such issues, the purpose of the BAT is not to explain the mechanisms of aphasia or the nature of the compensatory strategies used by the patient, but to determine whether one language is better recovered than another, to what extent, and in what area of functioning. These results, collected from large numbers of patients, can then be correlated with the different neurobiological, neuropathological, and environmental variables in search of a pattern.

3

Description of the Bilingual Aphasia Test

Aphasia refers to the disturbance of any or all of the skills, associations, and habits of spoken or written language produced by injury to certain brain areas that are specialized for these functions.
—Goodglass and Kaplan (1983, p. 5)

The *Bilingual Aphasia Test* uses a quadrimodal, linguistically multidimensional approach. It is quadrimodal in that it examines language performance in all four modalities—hearing, speaking, reading, and writing. It is linguistically multidimensional in that, for each modality, language performance is investigated along three dimensions—linguistic level (phonological, morphological, syntactic, lexical, semantic), linguistic task (comprehension, repetition, judgment, lexical access, propositionizing), and linguistic unit (word, sentence, paragraph). This approach allows one to detect task-specific or task-independent, modality-specific or modality-independent deficits in syntax (or any other aspect of linguistic structure), as well as task- or modality-specific (or -independent) deficits at the level of the paragraph, the sentence, or the word in each of the patient's languages (Table 3.1).

The *Bilingual Aphasia Test* is comprised of 32 subtests (each with its individual score) which can be grouped to obtain a number of measures of specific abilities, in the oral and visual modalities. Measures in the oral and visual modalities may be obtained separately or in combination (separately if one of the modalities is obviously selectively impaired, in combination if there is no significant difference in performance in each modality).

Because the purpose of the test is not to measure communicative skills but specifically *linguistic* ability, the possible influence of extralinguistic context has been minimized (even though nonlinguistic factors are assumed to be equal for

44

TABLE 3.1
Linguistic Units of Analysis by Modality

TASK	WORD	SENTENCE	PARAGRAPH
Comprehension	A – V	A – V	A – V
Repetition	A – V (copying)	A	
Judgment	A	grammaticality A semantic acceptability A	
Production	A – V (naming) (reading aloud) (writing under dictation)	A – V (construction) (reading aloud)	A – V (spontaneous speech; story description) (spontaneous writing)

Modality: A = auditory & speech
V = visual: reading & writing

each language in the same patient). The test is constructed in such a way that each modality can be examined with minimal interference from other modalities. Performance on a given task can be compared with performance on the same task in each modality. It is thus possible to establish whether the deficit is modality-specific or central.

To some extent, almost every task involves all levels of linguistic structure. However, each task may require greater involvement of a particular level, and when other factors are controlled, each task may measure one specific ability (e.g., syntactic comprehension). Though the many components of comprehension may not be entirely separated, phonemic, syntactic, and semantic aspects of comprehension are assessed separately. Though many items (in particular writing sentences to dictation) presuppose comprehension, it is not comprehension *per se* that is tested in these items.

Each of the 32 subtests has a separate score, and scores are combined into sections (comprehension, syntax, writing, etc.). Because more than one ability may be involved in any given subtest, the score obtained on a subtest may be included in the computation for more than one skill. For a given patient, the score obtained in each language for the whole test, for each of the 32 subtests, or for each skill may be compared.

Performance in any two of the patient's languages may be compared along a number of dimensions in which scores may overlap. Each dimension may be of interest for diagnostic or research purposes. In spontaneous speech and cartoon-strip description, different aspects of performance may enter into the assessment of a particular ability.

In this chapter, the *Bilingual Aphasia Test* is examined section by section under six rubrics: the description of each task, the description of the stimuli involved in each task, design considerations in the construction of each subtest, the contribution of each section to the overall assessment, cross-references with other sections for comparative assessment, and cross-language equivalence criteria that ensure comparability between versions of the test in all languages.

PART A

HISTORY OF BILINGUALISM
50 items (1–50)

In this section, the patient's language history is established. It is not part of the aphasia test itself, but is only intended to obtain information about the patient's premorbid state of bilingualism and contexts of acquisition. The information is obtained from the patient whenever possible. However, if the patient is unable to respond, answers to the questions may be supplied by friends, relatives, colleagues, etc.

The history of bilingualism section is concerned with all the languages acquired by the patient. Therefore it is administered only once, regardless of the number of languages in which the patient is tested. The information is obtained in the language of the hospital or in the language most accessible to the patient.

The questionnaire is designed to accommodate a patient with a fairly complicated history of bilingualism (i.e., one in which multiple languages were spoken at home and at school). Most patients' linguistic histories will be much less complicated than that anticipated by the questionnaire. In order, therefore, to avoid irrelevant questions in the less complicated cases, a branching format was adopted in the questionnaire. In this format, a block of questions is introduced by a yes/no question (e.g., 31, "Did you change to a school with another language of instruction after that?"). If the answer to the question is "yes" then the set of following questions about that part of the patient's linguistic history is asked. If the answer is "no" then the test administrator is instructed to jump to the next block of questions (in this case question 49). The branching format allows the questionnaire to conform to the patient. In the most complicated case, the maximum of 50 questions is asked. In the simplest case, the minimum of 17 questions is asked.

There are two parts of the history of bilingualism section. The first part is concerned with the patient's linguistic environment at home as a child. The second part is concerned with language(s) of education.

The questions about the home ask first about the language(s) spoken by the child. The next questions ask about the languages spoken to the child by each of his or her parents and/or caretakers and about the languages spoken by these people to each other. Finally, for each parent and/or guardian, there are questions about his or her native language and other languages, if any.

The questions about school concentrate on the language of instruction and the language of play. The branching structure of the questionnaire accommodates the possiblity that there were multiple languages of instruction at some time in the patient's educational history and the possiblity that the language of instruction may have changed during the course of the patient's education.

The final questions of this section ask about the patient's occupation and about the number of languages she or he was able to speak premorbidly. This determines which language tests of the BAT will be used. Questions about the patterns of use for each language tested are administered at the beginning of Part B.

HISTORY OF BILINGUALISM

1. What was your date of birth? _____ (1)

2. Where were you born? _____ (2)

3. As a child, what language did you speak most at home? _____ (3)

4. As a child, did you speak any other languages at home? + - 0 (4)

*** If the answer to (4) is "no" then go to question (6).

5. What other languages did you speak at home as a child? _____ _____ _____ (5)

6. What was your father's native language? _____ (6)

7. Did he speak any other languages? + - 0 (7)

*** If the answer to (7) is "no" then go to question (12).

8. What was your father's other language(s)? _____ _____ (8)

9. What language did your father speak most to you at home? _____ (9)

10. Did your father speak any other languages at home? + - 0 (10)

*** If the answer to (10) is "no" then go to question (12).

11. What other languages did your father speak at home? _____ _____ _____ (11)

12. What was your mother's native language? _____ (12)

13. Did she speak any other languages? + - 0 (13)

*** If the answer to (13) is "no" then go to question (18).

14. What was your mother's other language(s)? _____ _____ (14)

15. What language did your mother speak most to you at home? _____ (15)

16. Did your mother speak any other languages at home? + - 0 (16)

*** If the answer to (16) is "no" then go to question (18).

17. What other languages did your mother speak at home? _____ _____ _____ (17)

18. Did anyone else take care of you as a child? + - 0 (18)

*** If the answer to (18) is "no" then go to question (25).

19. What was his/her native language? _____ (19)

20. Did he/she speak any other languages? + - 0 (20)

*** If the answer to (20) is "no" then go to question (25).

21. What was his/her other language(s)? _____ _____ (21)

22. What language did he/she speak most to you at home? _____ (22)

23. Did he/she speak any other languages at home? + - 0 (23)

*** If the answer to (23) is "no" then go to question (25).

24. What other languages did he/she speak at home? _____ _____ _____ (24)

25. What language did you speak most with friends as a child? _____ (25)

26. How many years of education have you had? _____ (26)

27. When you started school what was the language of instruction? _____ (27)

28. At that time, did you take any subjects in another language? + - 0 (28)

*** If the answer to (28) is "no" then go to question (30).

29. What were the other languages of instruction? _____ _____ _____ (29)

48

30. What language did most of the other students speak at this school? _____ (30)

31. Did you change to a school with another language of instruction

after that? + - 0 (31)

*** If the answer to (31) is "no" then go to question (49).

32. What was this language? _____ (32)

33. After how many years did you switch to this new language of instruction? _____ (33)

34. At that time, did you take any subjects in another language? + - 0 (34)

*** If the answer to (34) is "no" then go to question (36).

35. What were the other languages of instruction? _____ _____ _____ (35)

36. What language did most of the other students speak at this school? _____ (36)

37. Did you change to a school with another language of instruction

after that? + - 0 (37)

*** If the answer to (37) is "no" then go to question (49).

38. What was this language? _____ (38)

39. After how many years did you switch to this new language of instruction? _____ (39)

40. At that time, did you take any subjects in another language? + - 0 (40)

*** If the answer to (40) is "no" then go to question (49).

41. What were the other languages of instruction? _____ _____ _____ (41)

42. What language did most of the other students speak at this school? _____ (42)

43. Did you change to a school with a different language of instruction

after that? + - 0 (43)

*** If the answer to (43) is "no" then go to question (49).

44. What was this language? _____ (44)

45. After how many years did you switch to this new language of instruction? _____ (45)

46. At that time, did you take any subjects in another language? + - 0 (46)

*** If the answer to (46) is "no" then go to question (48).

47. What were the other languages of instruction? _____ _____ _____ (47)

48. What language did most of the other students speak at this school? _____ (48)

49. And after your education was completed, what was your

occupation? _____ _____ _____ (49)

60. Before your accident/illness what languages were you able

to speak? _____ _____ _____ (50)

PART B

LANGUAGE BACKGROUND
17 items (1–17)

This first section of Part B provides information relating to the patient's experience with each of the languages tested.

The questionnaire is designed to give an overview of the patterns of language use and acquisition. The questionnaire is presented to the patient in the language being tested. If the patient is unable to respond to the questions, the information may be obtained from a relative, friend, or colleague in whatever language possible.

As in the History of Bilingualism questionnaire (Part A, 1–50), a branching questionnaire structure is employed. This minimizes test length and ensures that the patient is asked only relevant questions.

The questionnaire asks about the environment in which the patient used the language, his age of acquisition, and his self-rated premorbid proficiency. In addition, the questionnaire investigates the frequency with which the language was used. Each modality is treated separately, so that questions are repeated for the patient's speaking, reading, and writing abilities.

Because it provides a measure of the probable level of competence for each modality, the Language Background section of the BAT may play an important role in the interpretation of the patient's actual test scores.

SPONTANEOUS SPEECH
5 items (18–22)

In this section, 5 minutes of the patient's spontaneous speech are recorded. The patient is asked a lead question about some aspect of his or her life. The test administrator's goal is essentially to ensure that 5 minutes of speech are obtained from the patient. She or he may therefore prompt the patient or change topics as is necessary.

Items 18–22 represent a multiple-choice assessment of the patient's performance. The scores are provided by the test administrator, who rates the patient's total production, fluency, pronunciation, syntax, and vocabulary. This provides a preliminary, quick, clinical assessment of the patient's spontaneous speech.

The complete analysis of the spontaneous speech section takes place after the BAT has been administered to the patient. The recording of his or her spontaneous speech is subjected to the posttest analysis (514–539). This analysis provides quantitative measures for the various components of the patient's verbal production.

ENGLISH BACKGROUND

Now, I will ask you some questions about your English. Ready?

1. Have you ever lived in a/another country where English was spoken? + - (1)

*** If the answer is "no" then skip to question (4).

2. What was the name of the country?   ____ (2)

3. How long did you live there?   (years) ____ (3)

4. Before your illness, was your English speaking...

    1) not good, 2) good, 3) very fluent   (4)

5. How old were you when you learned to speak English?   (years) ____ (5)

6. Before your illness, did you speak English at home?   + - (6)

7.   Did you speak English at work?   + - (7)

8.   Did you speak English with friends?   + - (8)

9. In your daily life before your illness, did you speak...

    1) every day, 2) every week, 3) every month, 4) every year,

    5) less than once a year   (9)

10. Did you ever learn to read English?   + - (10)

*** If the answer is "no" then skip to "SPONTANEOUS SPEECH" (question 18).

11. How old were you when you learned to read English?   (years) ____ (11)

12. Before your illness, was your English reading...

    1) not good, 2) good, 3) very good   (12)

13. In your daily life before your illness, did you read English...

    1) every day, 2) every week, 3) every month, 4) every year,

    5) less than once a year   (13)

14. Did you ever learn to write English?   + - (14)

*** If the answer is "no" then skip to "SPONTANEOUS SPEECH" (question 18).

15. How old were you when you learned to write English?   (years) ____ (15)

16. Before your illness, was your English writing...

    1) not good, 2) good, 3) very good   (16)

17. In your daily life before your illness, did you write English...

    1) every day, 2) every week, 3) every month, 4) every year,

    5) less than once a year   (17)

Cross-reference. The posttest analysis of spontaneous speech should be compared to the posttest analysis of the Description subtest (540–565) and the Writing subtest (813–835).

In the Description subtest, the patient is presented with a nonhumorous cartoon strip and is required to tell the story depicted in the pictures. This task is more constrained than spontaneous speech. An additional difference is that in the Description task, the patient has the pictures which represent the story plot in front of him or her while she or he is telling the story.

The writing task is essentially the same as the spontaneous speech task in that the patient's production is unconstrained. Comparison of these sections allows for an investigation of detailed quantitative measures across modalities. Such comparisons, however, must take into account normal differences that exist between speaking and writing, particularly in the areas of sentence length, grammaticality, and register.

POINTING
10 items (23–32)

Task. The patient is presented with an array of objects set on a table before him or her. The patient hears the name of an object and must touch the appropriate object on the table.

```
POINTING


23.  Please touch the RING           +   -   0   (23)

24.           the BUTTON             +   -   0   (24)

25.           the MATCHES            +   -   0   (25)

26.           the GLOVE              +   -   0   (26)

27.           the KEY                +   -   0   (27)

28.           the SCISSORS           +   -   0   (28)

29.           the WATCH              +   -   0   (29)

30.           the ENVELOPE           +   -   0   (30)

31.           the GLASS              +   -   0   (31)

32.           the BRUSH              +   -   0   (32)
```

Stimuli.   The stimuli are common names for everyday objects. This reduces the demands on the patient's ability to abstract and reduces the artificiality of the task in general.

In each language, the same objects are used. The linguistic characteristics of the names (lexicalization, length, etc.) is a random factor within each language and between language tests. The subtest therefore measures the patient's ability to recognize the names for common familiar objects without regard to their linguistic peculiarities.

Test contribution.   The pointing test is essentially a test of auditory comprehension with a very low ceiling on message length and vocabulary difficulty. The task is intended to be transparent to the patient, and thus requires no special instructions.

The pointing test is the easiest and the purest of the tests of auditory comprehension given in the BAT. A patient who does not obtain a satisfactory score on this test displays a very low level of auditory comprehension ability. In this case the scores on the subsequent more complicated tests involving auditory comprehension may be difficult to interpret.

Design considerations.   The selection of the stimuli was constrained by considerations of availability, portability, and cross-cultural familiarity.

The objects must be readily available to the test administrator at the testing site, and must be small and light enough to be easily transported.

The section tests the patient's ability to understand the names for common objects. The same objects are used for all languages tested. Therefore, the objects must be common in all cultures in which the test is administered. Generally, this cultural neutrality has been achieved. However, when cultural neutrality is not possible, appropriate changes have been made.

Cross-reference.   The score on the pointing task is compared to the patient's performance on the naming test (questions 269–288) which also uses small common objects as stimuli. In the naming task, the patient is presented with the objects, one at a time, and is required to name them. The examination of both the pointing and naming scores gives a measure of the retention of these common vocabulary items. Patients with word finding difficulty may have a high score on pointing (recognition) but a very low score on naming (recall).

Cross-language equivalence.   Most of the 10 items are the same in all languages. Only a very small number of objects had to be changed in a small number of languages because of cultural or climatic conditions. For instance, for languages spoken in tropical countries, where gloves are seldom worn, the item "glove" has been replaced by "bangle."

SIMPLE COMMANDS
5 items (33–37)

Task. The patient must carry out verbal commands given to him or her by the test administrator.

Stimuli. The stimuli are 5 verbal commands. All commands require only that the patient perform some body movement.

The stimuli used in this subtest differ from most other BAT stimuli in that they are not unique linguistic events. Any patient would have heard these exact commands many times in his or her life. In addition, the correct response for each item is a natural well-practiced motor movement. These factors contribute to the ease of the task.

Contribution. This subtest tests the patient's basic ability to understand a message. Because of the simplicity of the task and the predictability of the correct response, it may be the case that a full parse of the command is not necessary to perform the task correctly. For this reason the subtest is best seen as a test of message comprehension.

Design considerations. In this subtest the design objective was to use only body movements that are both well-practiced and easy to perform on command.

```
SIMPLE AND SEMI-COMPLEX COMMANDS


I am going to ask you to do a few things for me.  Are you ready?

33.  Please close your eyes.              +   -   0   (33)

34.  Open your mouth.                      +   -   0   (34)

35.  Raise your hand.                      +   -   0   (35)

36.  Stick out your tongue.                +   -   0   (36)

37.  Clap your hands.                      +   -   0   (37)

38.  Put the ring on the matches.         +   -   0   (38)

39.  Put the glass next to the pencil.    +   -   0   (39)

40.  Put the matches under the fork.      +   -   0   (40)

41.  Put the pencil in front of the ring. +   -   0   (41)

42.  Put the fork in the glass.           +   -   0   (42)
```

Cross-reference.   The patient's performance on this subtest should be compared to his or her performance on the more difficult semicomplex commands subtest (38–42) and the complex commands subtest (43–47).

Language equivalence.   The same commands are given in all versions of the BAT.

SEMICOMPLEX COMMANDS
5 items (38–42)

Task.   The patient is presented with 5 objects on a table. She or he is instructed to move one object so that it is in a specified spatial relation to one of the other objects.

Stimuli.   The objects used as stimuli in this subtest are common, small, and easy to manipulate on a table. The 5 stimuli are taken from distinct semantic domains (i.e., there is only one piece of cutlery, one writing instrument, etc.).

All of the commands in this subtest have the general form, "Put X in some spatial relation to Y." The spatial relations are expressed in common locative expressions in all languages.

Contribution.   This subtest measures the patient's ability to understand and carry out commands that require the manipulation of common objects. It is therefore an extension of the pointing subtest (23–32) (see cross-reference below).

Design considerations.   The commands in this subtest were selected to be natural and easy to perform, but unpredictable. The subtest contains, therefore, no commands which require predictable actions (e.g., put the paper in the envelope) or strange actions (e.g., put the key in the brush).

Cross-reference.   The score on this subtest should be compared to the score on the pointing subtest (23–32). In the pointing subtest, the patient must simply touch a single object. In this subtest, she or he must be able to recognize two objects and be able to perform some action with them.

The semicomplex commands subtest is also cross-referenced to the complex commands subtest (43–47) which requires actions to be performed with three objects taken from the same semantic domain.

Language equivalence.   The stimuli in this section are translation equivalents in all of the languages.

COMPLEX COMMANDS
5 items (43–47)

Task. The patient is given 3 objects and is told to do something with each of the items. The patient begins to respond only after all 3 instructions have been given.

Stimuli. The 5 stimulus commands are patterned after Pierre Marie's Three Papers Task which in fact constitutes the first command.

COMPLEX COMMANDS

43. Here are three pieces of paper.
    Give me the small one, put the
    middle sized one on your lap,
    and throw away the large one.   + 3 2 1 0 (43)

44. Here are three pencils.
    Drop the yellow one on the
    floor, give me the blue one
    and pick up the red one.   + 3 2 1 0 (44)

45. Here are three coins.
    Push the large coin toward me,
    turn over the middle-sized one
    and cover the small one with
    your hand.   + 3 2 1 0 (45)

46. Here are three sticks.
    Put the short one in the glass,
    give me the medium one, and tap
    on the table with the large one.   + 3 2 1 0 (46)

47. Here are three books.
    Open the first one, turn over
    the second, and pick up the
    third one.   + 3 2 1 0 (47)

Contribution. This subtest is a relatively complex test of the patient's comprehension and mnemonic ability.

Design considerations. The major consideration in the design of this subtest was the manner in which the responses would be scored. In the final scoring procedure that was decided upon, a response is either perfect (i.e., all commands were performed correctly in the correct order) or imperfect. If it is imperfect, a record is kept of how many component commands were performed correctly, irrespective of order.

Cross-reference. The subtest is cross-referenced to the semicomplex commands subtest (38–42). That task places much less demand on the patient's memory.

Language equivalence. The stimuli in this section are translation equivalents in all of the languages.

VERBAL AUDITORY DISCRIMINATION
18 items (48–65)

Task. The examiner reads a word to the patient. The patient has before him or her an array of four pictures and a square containing a large 'X'.

For 15 of the 18 items in the section, one of the four pictures represents the stimulus word and the other three pictures represent very similar sounding words. The patient is required to touch the picture that best illustrates the stimulus word.

In 3 of the 18 items, the stimulus is not represented in any of the four pictures, and the patient is required to touch the X.

Stimuli. The words used in this section are all picturable words that form minimal pairs with three other picturable words.

In 15 of the 18 items, the stimulus word is represented in one of the pictures. For these items, the three alternative pictures represent words that differ from the target in their initial consonant or consonant cluster. Whenever possible, the differences are limited to a single phonetic feature (voicing, place of articulation, manner of articulation, nasalization).

Because the initial consonants and consonant clusters are manipulated in this section, a broad sampling of such segments is given for each language. Thus, in English, 16 of the initial segments are unique.

Test contribution. The Verbal Auditory Discrimination test (VAD) is a composite test of phonemic discrimination and auditory word comprehension.

```
VERBAL AUDITORY DISCRIMINATION

You are going to hear a word.  Please touch the picture that

shows the meaning of the word.  If none of the pictures show the

meaning of the word then touch the large "X".  So, for example,

if I say "rain" you would touch this picture because it

represents the rain.  If I say "bird" you touch this X because

there is no picture of a bird on that page.  Are you ready?

48.  Mat                      X   1   2   3   4   0   (48)

49.  Ball                     X   1   2   3   4   0   (49)

50.  Duck                     X   1   2   3   4   0   (50)

51.  Brew                     X   1   2   3   4   0   (51)

52.  Thick                    X   1   2   3   4   0   (52)

53.  Knees                    X   1   2   3   4   0   (53)

54.  Van                      X   1   2   3   4   0   (54)

55.  Jar                      X   1   2   3   4   0   (55)

56.  Shin                     X   1   2   3   4   0   (56)

57.  Plate                    X   1   2   3   4   0   (57)

58.  Cramp                    X   1   2   3   4   0   (58)

59.  Pear                     X   1   2   3   4   0   (59)

60.  Chip                     X   1   2   3   4   0   (60)

61.  Rose                     X   1   2   3   4   0   (61)

62.  Crane                    X   1   2   3   4   0   (62)

63.  Dead                     X   1   2   3   4   0   (63)

64.  Lice                     X   1   2   3   4   0   (64)

65.  Drip                     X   1   2   3   4   0   (65)
```

As a test of auditory word comprehension, it assumes that the patient's perception of the stimulus is (in phonological terms) correct. It is therefore a test of vocabulary for these picturable monomorphemic nouns and verbs.

As a test of phonemic discrimination, the test assumes that the patient would be able to understand the word if she or he could perceive it correctly. The test measures the patient's ability to form a correct phonological representation for the stimulus word.

  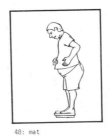 

Example: rain

48: mat

 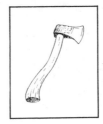 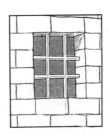 

49: ball

50: duck (X)

59

51: brew

52: thick

 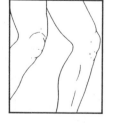  

53: knees

54: van

  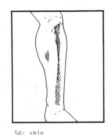 

55: jar   56: shin

  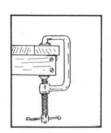 

57: plate (X)   58: cramp

59: pear

60: chip

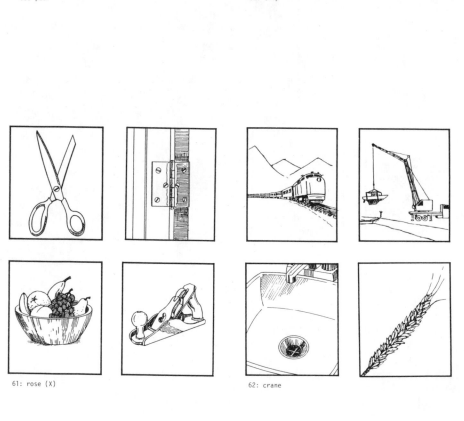

61: rose (X)

62: crane

62

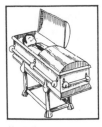   

63: dead

64: lice

 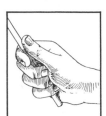

65: drip

Because of the composite nature of the test, a correct score on an item in this section indicates both phonemic discrimination and auditory comprehension ability.

Design considerations.   The stimulus words and their selected minimal pairs must be easily picturable, such as concrete nouns and action verbs. Sometimes an abstract noun or an adjective is used when its illustration is a sufficiently obvious representation of the word. It is not necessary that the picture should unambiguously evoke one single word. It suffices that, given a particular word, a speaker of the language unambiguously chooses the correct picture among the 4 presented. The picture is not to be named, only to be recognized as illustrating a given word. Thus the picture of a cobra may be used to illustrate the words "snake," "serpent," "reptile," or "cobra," for, given the picture of a teapot, a tomato and a pig as choices, whichever of the 4 words (snake, serpent, reptile, cobra) is pronounced, the patient should automatically match the stimulus with the appropriate picture.

Items 50, 57, and 61 are words not represented by any of the 4 pictures shown to the patient. The patient must consequently touch the X rather than any of the pictures. This contributes to determining the degree of confidence with which the patient points to one of the pictures. If, for these 3 items, the patient touches the X, it may be assumed that she or he touches a picture only when confident that she or he heard the word that names the picture. If, on the other hand, the patient touches one of the pictures on these 3 items and not the X, then it may be assumed that the patient touches one of the 4 pictures whether he recognizes the word or not.

Cross-reference.   Ten of the stimuli from the VAD subtest are used in the repetition subtest and the judgment subtest (193–252).

Items that serve as alternatives in the VAD subtest (i.e., represent minimal pairs of the correct answer) are used as stimuli in other sections of the BAT. Ten of these are used in the reading subtest (367–376) and in the reading comprehension subtest (408–417). Five VAD alternatives are used for copying (393–397). Finally, five VAD alternatives are used as stimuli in the dictation subtest (398–402), which integrates many of the skills tested in the other, less complex, subtests.

Cross-language equivalence.   Minimal pairs differ of course from language to language. Hence different stimuli and consequently different pictures are used for each language. However, items 50, 57, and 61 are identical across all languages, with few exceptions, as detailed below. These items are, respectively, the translation equivalent of the words for *duck* (50), *plate* (57), and *rose* (61). The pictures for these items are the same in all languages and represent objects that cannot possibly be taken to represent the stimulus word: a pitcher, a tin can,

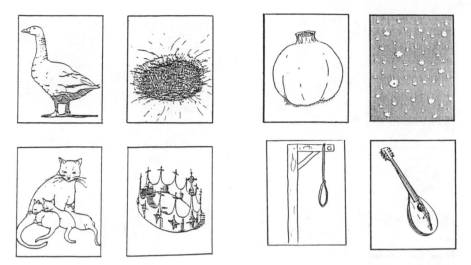

Armenian: /sak/ /dzak/ /tzak/ /ĉak/

Azari: nār qār dār tār

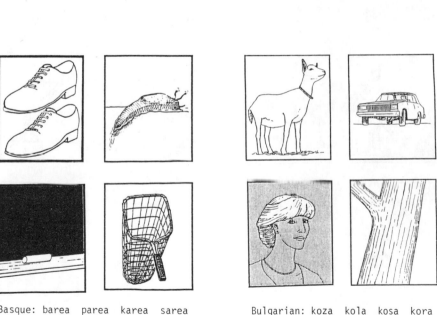

Basque: barea parea karea sarea

Bulgarian: koza kola kosa kora

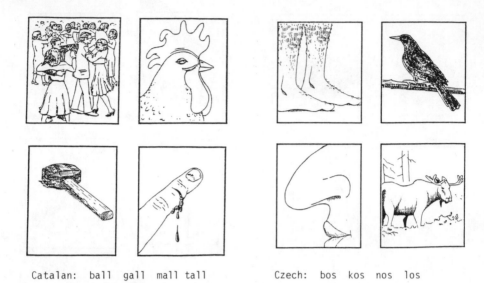

Catalan: ball gall mall tall

Czech: bos kos nos los

Dutch: dak tak bak pak

Farsi: /xɔne/ /dɔne/ /šɔne/ /čɔne/

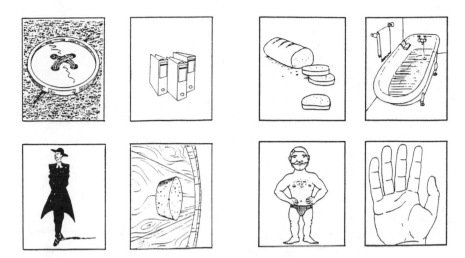

Finnish: mappi nappi pappi tappi

French: pain bain nain main

Galician: faba pava cava lava
(N.B. b=f phonemically)

German: Bach Fach Dach Schach

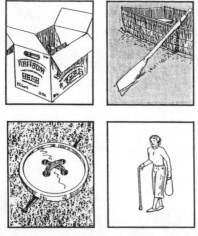

Greek: /kuti/ kupi/ /kubi/ /kutsi/

Hungarian: sör szőr csőr kör

Italian: tacco pacco Bacco sacco

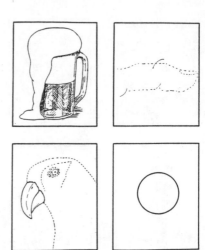

Japanese: /take/ /sake/ /Kake/ gake/

68

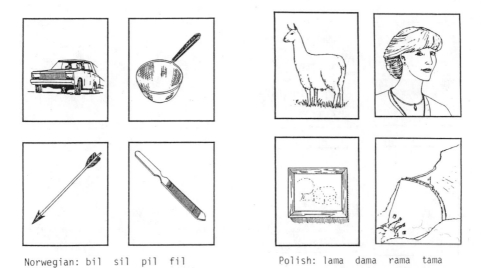

Norwegian: bil sil pil fil

Polish: lama dama rama tama

Portuguese: dália palha malha calha

Russian: /sapka/ /lapka/ /papka/
/bapka/

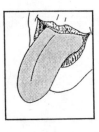

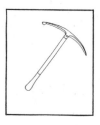
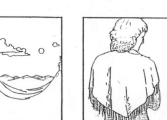

Spanish: mar bar par dar

Swedish: sal tal dal schal

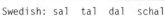

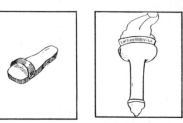

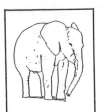

Turkish: dil zil fil pil

Vietnamese: guôć thuôć cuôć đuôć

70

bars on a prison window, and an axe for the word *duck* (or equivalent); a paper clip, a sailboat, an inkspot on a page, and a man slipping off balance for the word *plate* (or equivalent); a door hinge, a pair of scissors, a plane, and a fruit bowl for *rose* (or equivalent). These pictures were selected because they do not illustrate homophones or quasi-homophones of the stimulus word in any of the languages (e.g., a road would be too close to the English stimulus *rose,* and a picture of *rows* would be equally inappropriate). In the few cases where one of these words is used in a set of minimal pairs in a language, or when the word would differ in length from all other stimuli in this section, a different but similar word is used as the stimuli. In such cases, *goose* may be used in place of *duck, bowl* instead of *plate,* and a different, equally common flower replaces *rose.*

In a very small number of languages, particularly those in which mono-syllabic words are the exception, minimal pairs are not abundant. In these languages, for some of the items, only 3 of the words meet our criterion. A fourth word (always a foil) as close as possible in sound to the other three has been selected.

SYNTACTIC COMPREHENSION
87 items (66–152)

This section is entitled "Syntactic Comprehension" because it measures comprehension of sentences in which syntactic construction is systematically varied. For purposes of analysis, this section is subdivided into 8 parts, corresponding to the 8 constructions tested, namely, standard sentences (S), nonstandard sentences of type 1 (NS1), nonstandard sentences of type 2 (NS2), pronominal reference to animate items (P), pronominal reference to inanimate entities or self vs. third-person reference (A), negative standard sentences (Sn), negative nonstandard sentences of type 1 (NS1n), and the possessive construction (RP).

Affirmative Sentences
47 items (66-110, 117, 120)

Task. The patient has before him or her an array of 4 pictures. She or he hears a sentence and must touch the picture that best represents the meaning of that sentence.

Stimuli. The stimulus sentences in this subtest all represent picturable actions. This subtest measures comprehension of sentences in which syntactic construction is systematically varied.

SYNTACTIC COMPREHENSION - AFFIRMATIVE SENTENCES

You are going to hear a sentence. Please touch the picture that
shows the meaning of the sentence. So if I say 'the boy sits'
you should touch this picture that shows the sitting boy.

***Page 1

66.	The boy holds the girl.	1	2	3	4	0	(66)
67.	The girl holds the boy.	1	2	3	4	0	(67)
68.	She holds him.	1	2	3	4	0	(68)
69.	She holds her.	1	2	3	4	0	(69)
70.	She holds them.	1	2	3	4	0	(70)

***Page 2

71.	The father washes his son.	1	2	3	4	0	(71)
72.	The mother washes her daughter.	1	2	3	4	0	(72)
73.	He washes him.	1	2	3	4	0	(73)
74.	He washes himself.	1	2	3	4	0	(74)
75.	She washes herself.	1	2	3	4	0	(75)
76.	She washes her.	1	2	3	4	0	(76)

***Page 3

77.	The boy holds the girls.	1	2	3	4	0	(77)
78.	He holds him.	1	2	3	4	0	(78)
79.	He holds her.	1	2	3	4	0	(79)
80.	He holds them.	1	2	3	4	0	(80)

***Page 4

81.	The girl pushes the boy.	1	2	3	4	0	(81)
82.	The boy pushes the girl.	1	2	3	4	0	(82)
83.	The boy is pushed by the girl.	1	2	3	4	0	(83)
84.	The girl is pushed by the boy.	1	2	3	4	0	(84)
85.	It's the boy who pushes the girl.	1	2	3	4	0	(85)
86.	It's the girl who pushes the boy.	1	2	3	4	0	(86)
87.	It's the boy that the girl pushes.	1	2	3	4	0	(87)
88.	It's the girl that the boy pushes.	1	2	3	4	0	(88)

```
***Page 5

89.   The dog bites the cat.            1   2   3   4   0   (89)

90.   The cat bites the dog.            1   2   3   4   0   (90)

91.   The dog is bitten by the cat.     1   2   3   4   0   (91)

92.   The cat is bitten by the dog.     1   2   3   4   0   (92)

93.   It's the dog that bites the cat.  1   2   3   4   0   (93)

94.   It's the cat that bites the dog.  1   2   3   4   0   (94)

95.   It's the cat that the dog bites.  1   2   3   4   0   (95)

96.   It's the dog that the cat bites.  1   2   3   4   0   (96)

***Page 6

97.   The truck pulls the car           1   2   3   4   0   (97)

98.   The car is pulled by the truck.   1   2   3   4   0   (98)

99.   The truck is pulled by the car.   1   2   3   4   0   (99)

100.  The car pulls the truck.          1   2   3   4   0   (100)

101.  It's the truck that pulls the car. 1  2   3   4   0   (101)

102.  It's the car that the truck pulls. 1  2   3   4   0   (102)

103.  It's the car that pulls the truck. 1  2   3   4   0   (103)

104.  It's the truck that the car pulls. 1  2   3   4   0   (104)

***Page 7

105.  The mother dresses her daughter.  1   2   3   4   0   (105)

106.  The father dresses his son.       1   2   3   4   0   (106)

107.  She dresses herself.              1   2   3   4   0   (107)

108.  He dresses him.                   1   2   3   4   0   (108)

109.  She dresses her.                  1   2   3   4   0   (109)

110.  He dresses himself.               1   2   3   4   0   (110)
```

The stimulus sentences in this subtest all represent picturable actions. For each item, the patient is presented with 4 pictures. She or he then hears a stimulus sentence. For each stimulus, one picture represents the meaning of the sentence, another represents the reverse situation, and the other two represent situations that are highly related to the meaning of the sentence (i.e., they share actors and actions).

The syntactic constructions which are manipulated in this subtest can best be described in terms of sentence types. There are five types of affirmative sentences in the subtest.

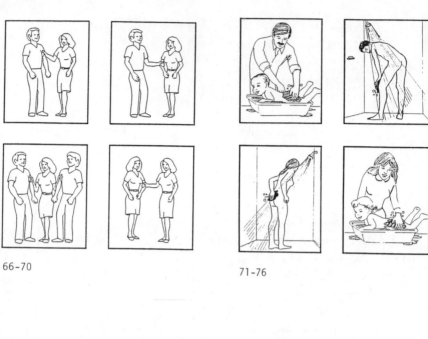

66-70

71-76

77-80

81-88

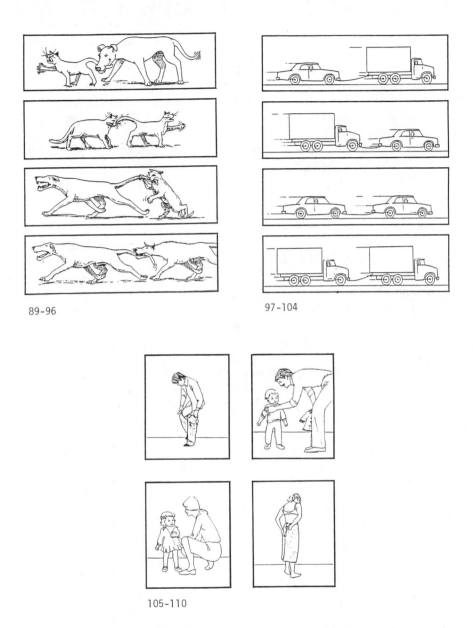

89-96

97-104

105-110

1. Standard sentences (S).   The standard sentences comprise a subject, a verb, and an object, with nouns as subject and object. These sentences are modeled on the pattern considered to be the simplest (canonical) in each language tested (SVO in English, SOV in Japanese).

Because of its relative simplicity, the standard I section of the syntactic comprehension subtest provides a baseline measure to which performance on the other sentence types can be compared. There are 13 standard sentences stimlui (66, 67, 71, 72, 77, 81, 82, 89, 90, 97, 100, 105, 106).

2. Pronominal reference (P,A).   These sentences are constructed on the same pattern as the standard sentences, but with pronouns instead of animate nouns in languages where pronouns are marked for gender (e.g., "He holds her"). See the cross-language equivalence section below for languages in which this is not the case. There are 6 stimuli for pronominal reference (68, 69, 70, 78, 79, 80).

In addition, in languages that have more than one gender for inanimate objects (e.g., in French, *elle le tire; il la tire,* referring to a truck [masculine] and a car [feminine]), these sentences include subject and object pronominal reference to gendered inanimate object (arbitrary gender). In languages for which arbitrary gender cannot be used, self-reference is contrasted with reference to a third person (e.g., "She dresses her," "She dresses herself"). There are 8 stimuli for the A sentences (73, 74, 75, 76, 107, 108, 109, 110).

3. Nonstandard 1 sentences (NS1).   The nonstandard 1 type sentences all have nouns as subjects and objects. The term nonstandard here refers to the fact that the word order is different from that of the (simpler) "standard" sentences; it is not meant to imply that these sentences are *nonstandard* in the sociolinguistic sense.

The passive construction is used as the nonstandard 1 type sentences in languages for which it is appropriate (English: e.g., "The boy is pushed by the girl.") In these languages the passive voice is possible, sufficiently common, and assumed to represent a level of complexity equivalent to the passive in English.

For languages in which the passive is nonexistent, too artificial, uncommon, or too simple (e.g., marked by the simple adjunction of an affix to the verb), some other nonstandard structure is used (see cross-language equivalence below).

There are 8 affirmative nonstandard 1 type sentences (83, 84, 91, 92, 98, 99, 117, 120).

4. Nonstandard 2 sentences (NS2).   In the second type of nonstandard sentences, topicalization is manipulated. There are 12 nonstandard 2 type sentences. Half of these are subject-topicalized and half are object-topicalized. In English and many other languages, cleft constructions of the type "It is the girl who pushes the boy" and "It is the boy that the girl pushes" are used.

The 6 subject-topicalized nonstandard 2 sentences (NS2S) are given in items 85, 86, 93, 94, 101, 103. The 6 object-topicalized sentences (NS2O) are given in items 87, 88, 95, 96, 102, 104.

Negative Sentences
24 items (111–116, 118–119, 121–136)

SYNTACTIC COMPREHENSION - NEGATIVE SENTENCES

***Page 8

111. The girl does not push the boy.   1   2   0   (111)

112. The boy does not push the girl.   1   2   0   (112)

113. The girl is not pushed by the boy.   1   2   0   (113)

114. The boy is not pushed by the girl.   1   2   0   (114)

***Page 9

115. The girl does not spray the boy.   1   2   0   (115)

116. The boy does not spray the girl.   1   2   0   (116)

117. The girl is sprayed by the boy.   1   2   0   (117)

118. The boy is not sprayed by the girl.   1   2   0   (118)

119. The girl is not sprayed by the boy.   1   2   0   (119)

120. The girl is sprayed by the boy.   1   2   0   (120)

***Page 10

121. The truck does not pull the car.   1   2   0   (121)

122. The truck is not pulled by the car.   1   2   0   (122)

123. The car does not pull the truck.   1   2   0   (123)

124. The car is not pulled by the truck.   1   2   0   (124)

***Page 11

125. The young boy does not wake up his mother. 1   2   0   (125)

126. The mother does not wake up the young boy. 1   2   0   (126)

127. The young boy is not woken up by his mother. 1   2   0   (127)

128. The mother is not woken up by the young boy. 1   2   0   (128)

***Page 12

129. The dog is not bitten by the cat.   1   2   0   (129)

130. The cat is not bitten by the dog.   1   2   0   (130)

131. The dog does not bite the cat.   1   2   0   (131)

132. The cat does not bite the dog.   1   2   0   (132)

***Page 13

133. The man does not kiss the woman.   1   2   0   (133)

134. The woman is not kissed by the man.   1   2   0   (134)

135. The woman does not kiss the man.   1   2   0   (135)

136. The man is not kissed by the woman.   1   2   0   (136)

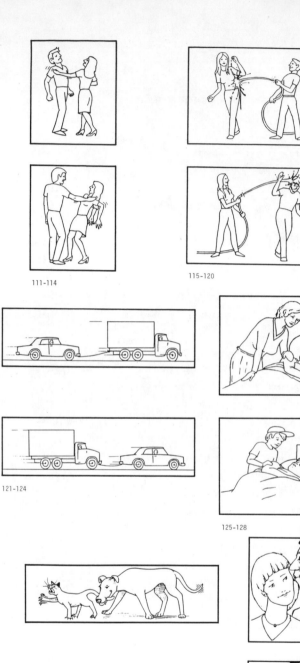

111-114

115-120

121-124

125-128

129-132

133-136

Task.   The patient has before him or her 2 pictures. She or he hears a sentence and must touch the picture that best represents the meaning of that sentence.

Stimuli.   All the sentences used in this subtest are negative and have nouns as their subjects and objects. Sixteen of the stimuli are negations of the standard 1 type sentences from the affirmative section of the syntactic comprehension subtest.

For languages such as English in which the passive is used as the first type of nonstandard sentence, the sentences are negative passives (e.g., "The boy is not pushed by the girl"). For languages in which the passive is not used as the nonstandard 1 sentence type, the 8 stimuli are negations of the alternative non-standard 1 form.

In the negative section of the syntactic comprehension subtest, the subject is presented with two pictures to choose from. In the affirmative section, she or he is presented with four pictures. A four-picture choice is desirable because it lessens the probability of a chance correct response. However, only two pictures are possible in the negative section because any situation other than the actual reverse of a negative sentence would be a correct choice. Thus in the negative section the two pictures depict, for any given sentence, an action and its reverse. For example, for the stimulus, "The girl does not push the boy," the patient is exposed to one picture depicting a boy pushing a girl and another depicting a girl pushing a boy.

The pictures used in this section are arranged one above the other in the center of the page. This avoids the effects of left or right visual-field neglect.

There are 12 standard negative (Sn) stimuli (111, 112, 115, 116, 121, 123, 125, 126, 131, 132, 133, 135) and 12 nonstandard 1 negative (NS1n) stimuli (113, 114, 118, 119, 122, 124, 127, 128, 129, 130, 134, 136).

Reversible Noun Phrase Constructions
16 items (137   152)

Task.   The patient hears an instruction that begins: "Show me . . ." followed by a noun phrase. She or he has before him or her a single picture, or in a few instances two pictures. One of the characters or objects represented in the picture corresponds to the target noun phrase. The patient responds by touching the appropriate object or character in the picture.

Stimuli.   The stimuli for this subtest are 8 pairs of reversible possessive constructions (e.g., "The baby's mother"; "The mother's baby"). These are further divided into two sets of four pairs each. The first construction type is found in items 137, 138, 142, 143, 145, 146, 150, 151. The second construction type is

SYNTACTIC COMPREHENSION - REVERSIBLE NOUN PHRASES

***Page 14

137. Show me the mother's baby.   1   2   0   (137)

***Page 15

138. Show me that niece's uncle.   1   2   0   (138)

***Page 16

139. Show me the vase of this flower.   1   2   0   (139)

***Page 17

140. Show me the manager of this restaurant.   1   2   0   (140)

***Page 18

141. Show me the book of this author.   1   2   0   (141)

***Page 19

142. Show me the dog's master.   1   2   0   (142)

***Page 20

143. Show me the doctor's patient.   1   2   0   (143)

***Page 21

144. Show me the director of the film.   1   2   0   (144)

***Page 22

145. Show me the baby's mother.   1   2   0   (145)

***Page 23

146. Show me that uncle's niece.   1   2   0   (146)

***Page 24

147. Show me the flower of this vase.   1   2   0   (147)

***Page 25

148. Show me the restaurant of this manager.   1   2   0   (148)

***Page 26

149. Show me the author of this book.   1   2   0   (149)

***Page 27

150. Show me the master's dog.   1   2   0   (150)

***Page 28

151. Show me the patient's doctor.   1   2   0   (151)

***Page 29

152. Show me the film of the director.   1   2   0   (152)

137/145

138/146

139/147

140/148

found in items 139, 140, 141, 144, 147, 148, 149, 152. For a description of construction types, see the cross-language equivalence section below.

In the affirmative section and the negative section of the syntactic comprehension subtest, stimulus sentences that require the same picture array are grouped together. This reduces the number of times that the patient must familiarize himself with a picture array, and therefore reduces the amount of time required to administer the test.

In the construction of the noun phrase section, however, this strategy was not possible. Only a single picture is presented and this picture has, in most cases, only two objects or characters. Presenting the pair members consecutively would encourage the patient to guess on the second stimulus. For this reason, the members of a stimulus pair are separated by eight items.

Cross-reference. As was indicated in the stimuli section above, this subtest has several tests within it. The patient's response patterns across these sections should be examined.

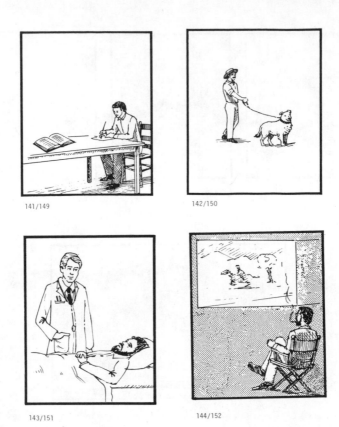

141/149

142/150

143/151

144/152

The scores for the standard 1 and nonstandard 1 type questions are to be compared to the corresponding scores for the test of syntactic comprehension of negatives (111–136).

Stimuli from both the affirmative and negative sections of the syntactic comprehension subtest are used in four other subtests of the BAT.

In the grammaticality judgment section (173–182), the patient must judge whether stimuli from the syntactic comprehension subtest and highly related ungrammatical sentences are in fact sentences of the language.

The sentence repetition section (253–259) allows for the close examination of the patient's ability to reproduce syntactic comprehension stimuli. Information from this subtest can be of value in the interpretation of the patient's performance in the syntactic comprehension subtest.

In the visual modality, there are two tests whose scores can be compared to the syntactic comprehension scores. First is the reading aloud section (377–386) which requires the patient to simply reproduce visually presented stimuli from the syntactic comprehension section. This has the same value to the interpretation of syntactic comprehension scores as does the repetition section. The use of both these tests allows the separation of reproduction difficulties attributable to a general syntactic deficit from those which are input modality specific. Second is the reading comprehension section (418–427) which offers a test very similar to the syntactic comprehension subtest. The differences between these two tests are in their length and, more significantly, in the modality in which the stimulus sentences are presented. This again allows for the separation of general and modality-specific deficits.

Cross-language equivalence.   Some languages have a very rich (i.e., complex) inflectional morphology, marking person, tense, aspect, mood, and gender. Others have a relatively simple inflectional system, with fewer distinctions within the above categories or without some of these categories altogether. Verbal inflectional morphology, like case and gender marking, is inherent to each language and cannot be controlled. Any speaker of a language has mastered its syntax and its morphology. The ability to speak a given language implies that one has mastered its various grammatical systems.

To the extent that languages differ, the complexity of a particular construction (e.g., a construction involving a nominal subject, a nominal direct object, and an action verb) will vary. In some languages, subject-object relationships are marked by word order only, in other languages by case markers as well as word order, and in still others, by case markers only.

Given that the structures of two languages necessarily differ, stimulus sentences in this test are nevertheless as close to being equivalent in complexity across languages as can be expected. An equal number of items of the same structural type (S, P, A, NS1, NS2S, NS2O, Sn, NS1n, RP) are distributed in the same way across all languages.

1. *Standard sentences.*   Inasmuch as possible, the standard sentences are translation equivalents of each other in all languages. Hence, the same sets of 4 pictures are used, with minor modifications such as dress and features of the characters, and scanning direction of the pictures, to suit specific ethnic conditions in a small number of languages. Six of the following 12 verbs are used in each language: bite, chase, dress, follow, hit, hold, lift, look at, pull, push, spray, and wash. Ten of the following 15 nouns are used in each language: ambulance, boat, boy, broom, bus, car, cat, daughter, dog, girl, man, mother, son, truck, and woman. Some of these words are used in a restricted set of languages (e.g., only languages sharing the animate/inanimate pronoun distinction use *boat* and *broom*).

2. *Pronominal reference.*   In some languages (e.g., French), subject and object personal pronouns are marked for gender whether they refer to animate or inanimate entities. In other languages (e.g., English), pronouns are marked for gender only when they refer to animate entities. In yet other languages (e.g.,

Hungarian), pronouns are not marked for gender but for animacy vs. inanimacy. Further, in some languages (e.g., Oriya), pronouns are not marked for gender or animacy. Finally, in some languages (e.g., Chinese), pronouns are not marked for gender in spoken language but are marked in written language.

For items 68–70 and 78–80, in all languages with gendered animate pronouns, masculine and feminine subject and object pronouns are systematically permuted (masc. subj./fem. obj.; masc. sub./masc. obj.; fem. subj./masc. obj.; fem. subj./fem. obj.), as well as singular subject and plural object (sing. fem. subj./plur. masc. obj.; sing. masc. sub./plur. fem. obj.). In languages marked for animacy/inanimacy, pronominal reference to animate and inanimate subject and object is systematically permuted, in the singular and in the plural.

In languages without a gender or animacy/inanimacy distinction, singular and plural subjects and objects are systematically permuted in all possible combinations (single subject/single object; single subject/plural object; plural subject/single object; plural subject/plural object).

In languages where neither gender nor number is marked, demonstrative pronouns are used instead of personal pronouns, when they can be marked at least for number (e.g., in Malagasy).

For items 73–76 and 107–110, in languages with gendered inanimate pronouns, masculine and feminine subject and object are permuted in all possible combinations. In languages without gendered inanimate nouns, self-reference vs. reference to a third person is tested. Nouns are used as subjects in languages without gender distinction among animate pronouns.

3. *Nonstandard 1 sentences.* In most languages the passive construction is used as the first type of nonstandard sentence. For languages in which the passive is too artificial, too simple, or nonexistent, some other structure that changes the basic word order is used (e.g., OSV sentences in an SOV or SVO language, or the "ba" construction in Chinese, i.e., S particle OV in an SVO language).

4. *Nonstandard 2 sentences.* In most languages a cleft construction is used as the second type of nonstandard sentence, with both topicalized subject (e.g., "It is the cat that bites the dog") and topicalized object (e.g., "It is the dog that the cat bites"). For languages in which the cleft construction is not appropriate, another construction involving a change from the standard word order different from that used in NS1 sentences is selected.

5. Reversible noun phrases. In most languages, the stimuli for this subtest are reversible possessive constructions. In languages which, like English, admit of two different constructions, the first construction is tested in the first set of items (RP1) and the second construction in the second set (RP2).

In languages with only one form but two genders, the first set contains pairs of one gender (e.g., masculine) and the second set contains pairs of another gender (e.g., feminine or neuter). In either case, the words are selected so that word order is the sole indicator of possessor and possessed (e.g., French: *Le garage du camion/le camion du garage, la classe de la maîtresse/la maîtresse de la classe;* Czech: *Zakaznika advokata/advokata zakaznika*). When the nouns are marked for case, the morphophonemic process must be the same for both words (e.g., Czech: *Ucitelku tridy/tridu ucitelky*).

Finally, in languages such as Chinese, Finnish, German, and Swedish, reversible compound nouns are very common (e.g., tap water/water tap). In these languages, pairs of reversible compounds are used as the second type of construction (RP2).

Contribution.   The syntactic comprehension section measures the patient's ability to understand sentences on the basis of their syntactic form. If the patient is unable to identify the pictures that correspond to the meaning of simple standard sentences with canonical SVO word order (or SOV, depending on the language), and with nouns as subject and direct object, nothing much can be said about failure on the other types of sentences in this section. The problem might then stem from sources other than a disruption of syntax (and should be revealed by scores on pointing, simple commands and verbal auditory discrimination), or independently from tests of visual agnosia or apraxia.

However, when the patient does demonstrate comprehension of the simple affirmative standard sentences, his or her performance on negative and/or nonstandard forms can be compared to that on the standard sentences. The score pattern indicates whether the patient does not understand the nonstandard sentences and scores randomly, or whether she or he systematically interprets the nonstandard sentences (that differ in word order and/or case markers, with the possible addition of prepositions or particles, depending on the language) in accordance with standard word order correspondence with θ roles (agent as subject, patient as direct object, in their respective canonical positions), disregarding case markers and/or prepositions, or whether they adopt some other strategy (e.g., always point to the top right picture). The reversibility of all sentences guarantees that comprehension must be syntactic (i.e., the patient uses his or her knowledge of syntax to decode the meaning of the sentence).

In the final section dealing with the possessive (137–152), the patient's ability to discriminate between possessor and possessed, strictly on the basis of word order, is determined. In languages with only one possessive construction and no gender, for half the items the ability to distinguish between the meaning of reversible compound nouns on the sole basis of word order is tested.

Together, the various types of construction tests give a general measure of the patient's ability to use syntax in decoding the meaning of sentences.

Design considerations.   The syntactic comprehension section tests the patient's ability to assign syntactic analyses to input strings in which the critical cues to relational meaning are provided by prepositions, inflections, and/or word order. A cross-linguistic study of word order (Slobin & Bever, 1982) has shown that canonical sentence schemas play a central role in processes of perception and interpretation of utterances, even in languages in which word order is relatively free. In all languages of the BAT, word order is a variable in the three types of structures tested (S, NS1, and NS2). The reversibility of the sentences allows for the verification of whether word order plays some role in comprehension and whether a word-order strategy replaces the processing of grammatical morphemes in aphasic patients, leading them to interpret NS1 and NS2 type sentences as though they were of the S type.

Possessive noun phrases (or, in some languages, compound words) were selected for the same reason. In these phrases word order is the only clue to which word represents the possessor and which word represents the possessed (or which is the head noun). The word order in these phrases is language specific: While the possessor is the first word in some languages (e.g., in the English phrase "the master's dog"), it is the second word in others (e.g., in the equivalent French phrase "*le chien du maître*").

The stimulus sentences were selected on the basis of what verbs in any given language would take a direct object. Subjects and objects were then selected so as to make the sentences as pragmatically reversible as possible. Because an action rendered in some languages by a verb requiring a direct object may be rendered in another language by a verb requiring an indirect object, the same action (and hence the same pictures) could not be used in all languages. However, one set of verbs common to all languages, with very few exceptions, has been used.

The lexical items involved vary between groups of languages so as to ensure the necessary masculine/feminine or animate/inanimate distinction in pronouns. The same pictures are used for all languages that share the same characteristics.

The major design consideration in this section was to find in each language a representative sample of sentence patterns which were not too uncommon but which, at the same time, permitted testing within reasonable time limits. Thus, in order to balance the number of different patterns against the number of tokens of each pattern, within a manageable total number of items, 8 patterns were selected. They are presented from 6 to 16 times each in the following constructions: simple standard setntences (S), pronominal reference with animate subjects and objects (P), pronominal reference to inanimate gendered nouns or self-reference vs. reference to a third person (A), passive or similar construction with subject/object word order change (NS1), cleft sentences or similar constructions with topicalized subject and topicalized object, simple standard sentences in the negative (Sn), passive negative or equivalent construction in the negative (NS1n), and the possessive (RP).

Because syntactic features associated with various constructions (e.g., the passive) differ in complexity between languages, structures of comparable linguistic complexity rather than particular constructions are examined across languages. (Constructions still happen to be the same within each group of languages sharing a particular feature.) Considerations of change of word order, adjunction or deletion of prepositions, and case markers or inflections are more important than identity of construction across languages in the choice of sentence pattern stimuli. Thus universal characteristics of everyday language use (i.e., simple statement, pronominal reference, negation, topicalization and attribution of possession) are tested in a form that makes them equivalent from the point of linguistic complexity across all languages tested.

In (P) sentences for languages without gendered personal pronouns, the singular/plural aspect of the pronouns was systematically permuted. Both the animate/inanimate and the singular/plural dimensions are tested in languages marked for animacy but not for gender.

In the (A) sentences of some languages some nouns involved had to be changed because of gender incompatibility (e.g., *car* and *truck* are of opposite genders in French and Italian but not in Catalan or Spanish; therefore, an ambulance was substituted for the car in these two languages).

The (RP) sentences are the ones with the greatest diversity in the selection of lexical items because of different constraints in different languages on gender or various morphophonemic phenomena.

The negative sentences (Sn and NS1n) are tested against only two pictures (one corresponding to a statement and the other to its opposite) since any situation other than the actual reverse of a negative statement would be a correct choice. For each sentence type, twice as many tokens of negative as of affirmative sentences are used. This somewhat compensates for the reduced significance of a correct choice caused by the fact that there are only two pictures to choose from, instead of four.

Syntactic negation is an interesting construction for at least two reasons. First, its surface form varies greatly across languages: The mark of the negative is respectively placed before the verb, after the verb, before and after the verb, inside the verb (I.e., between the verb stem and its tense and person inflection), or is used in conjunction with a specific auxiliary verb (e.g., "El niño *no* come", "der Junge ißt *nicht*"; "le garçon *ne* mange *pas*"; "erkek ye*miyor*"; "the boy *does not* eat"). Second, the negative passive construction in English (and presumably any NS1n sentence in other languages) has been demonstrated to be among the most complex constructions to understand. Yet, syntactic negation is a relatively frequently used construction in every language and is therefore part of any fluent speaker's competence. But because of its complexity, it is expected to discriminate between the stronger and the weaker language of mildly impaired patients.

Hence, even though testing the comprehension of negative sentences presents considerable practical difficulties, negative sentences (Sn and NS1n) were nevertheless included in the syntactic comprehension section.

SEMANTIC CATEGORIES
5 items (153–157)

Task. The patient hears four words. He is told that three of the four words form a group. He must repeat the word that does not belong to the group.

Stimuli. For each item four words are heard. Three of these are subordinate names within some superordinate category. The fourth name is a member of some other category. The five semantic categories and the contrasting member of each are flowers–animal, fruits–vegetable, body parts–clothing, pieces of furniture–vehicle, birds–fish. All the names used are designed to be within the vocabulary of any fluent speaker.

```
SEMANTIC CATEGORIES


You will hear four words. Please tell me which ONE word does not belong in the

group. For example, you might hear:  hat, glove, elephant, shirt. You would

choose elephant. Ready?


153.  1) tulip, 2) rose, 3) frog, 4) daisy        1   2   3   4   0   (153)

154.  1) cabbage, 2) apple, 3) banana, 4) cherry   1   2   3   4   0   (154)

155.  1) hand, 2) foot, 3) sock, 4) ear            1   2   3   4   0   (155)

156.  1) chair, 2) table, 3) bed, 4) car           1   2   3   4   0   (156)

157.  1) blackbird, 2) sardine, 3) pigeon, 4) eagle  1   2   3   4   0   (157)
```

Test contribution. This is a complex test of language use. It requires the patient to hold an array of four words simultaneously in memory. He must also understand each word. In this case, however, comprehension is not limited to the ability to match the words to a visual representation of the objects. The patient must also understand the relationship of each word to the other words with which he is presented.

The subtest is therefore a test of the patient's ability to reason logically with the words of the language.

Design considerations. The semantic categories test requires special design consideration when the stimuli are presented auditorily. The test places great demand on the patient's short-term memory. That demand increases with the number of stimuli per item.

To perform the task correctly, however, the patient must recognize that all but one of the names that he hears belong to a particular semantic category. Each stimulus can be regarded as a clue to the solution of the problem. The ease of the task therefore increases with the number of stimuli per item.

In this section the number of stimuli was chosen through consideration of these opposing constraints. Four stimuli per item represents the minimum number required for the easy recognition of these semantic categories.

Cross-reference.   The semantic categories subtest forms a unit with the following synonym subtest (158–161). In these tests the patient must demonstrate the ability to identify the relationships that exist between common nouns. The names used in the semantic categories subtest and the synonym subtest are of the same type as those used in the pointing subtest (23–32) and the naming subtest (269–288). It is to be expected that the skills tested in the semantic categories subtest are dependent on the skills tested in the pointing subtest. Interpretation of the semantic categories score should therefore be done in view of the pointing score.

Cross-language equivalence.   The five semantic categories are basically the same in all languages and each item is the closest translation equivalent across languages.

SYNONYMS
5 items (158–162)

Task.   The patient is presented with a target word and then four other words. She or he must choose which one of those four words has a meaning similar to that of the target word.

Stimuli.   The nouns used as target words are all concrete nouns that represent familiar objects. The four other words that the patient hears are also names of familiar objects. Three of these objects are unrelated to the target. The other word represents an object which is highly related to the object. In English, for instance, the pairs are seat–armchair, clock–watch, pencil–pen, sandal–shoe.

The emphasis in this section is on the relationship of similarity between the objects, and only secondarily between the words which represent them. This increases the probability of equivalence across languages.

Test contribution.   This subtest measures the patient's ability to identify precise meaning relationships between words. He must hold the target word in memory while evaluating its similarity to each alternative. The test is therefore a member of the group of BAT subtests which measure the patient's ability to reason with the words of the language (see cross-reference below).

```
SYNONYMS

Now you will hear a single word.  I will ask you to give me another word which

has a similar meaning.  I will give you four choices.  So for example I would say

"jacket" and then give you four choices:  "table," "house," "coat," "car."  You

would choose "coat" because its meaning is the most similar to "jacket."  Ready?

   158.  SEAT:

           1) vase, 2) pencil, 3) armchair, 4) watch       1   2   3   4   0   (158)

   159.  CLOCK:

           1) shoe, 2) drawer, 3) banana, 4) watch         1   2   3   4   0   (159)

   160.  PENCIL:

           1) pen, 2) hat, 3) ashtray, 4) apple            1   2   3   4   0   (160)

   161.  SANDAL:

           1) wheel, 2) shoe, 3) letter, 4) garden         1   2   3   4   0   (161)

   162.  CANOE:

           1) match, 2) boat, 3) newspaper, 4) tree        1   2   3   4   0   (162)
```

Design considerations.   Like the semantic categories test, the synonyms subtest places great demand on short-term memory. In this test, however, the patient doesn't have to hold all the stimuli in memory simultaneously to perform the task correctly. She or he can mentally compare each alternative to the target as it is presented.

It seems, however, that for tasks of this sort there is a tendency for the patient to forget the target word when a large number of alternatives are presented.

Presenting the subjects with very few alternatives increases the probability of a chance correct response. This is an important consideration for the synonyms subtest which only has five items.

Cross-reference.   The synonym subtest is complementary to the semantic categories subtest (153–157). Both of these tests require the patient to use his or her lexical knowledge. In such tests it is generally difficult to distinguish between logical, computational, and linguistic abilities. In presenting these two tests no attempt was made to distinguish these skills. Rather two tasks which require all of these skills are presented in slightly different proportions. The synonym subtest requires less computation than the semantic categories subtest, but more precise lexical knowledge.

90

A differential score between languages is to be interpreted as a linguistic difference since the nonlinguistic demands (logical, computational abilities, short-term memory) are assumed to be identical in the same patient.

Cross-language equivalence.   Translation equivalents for the same or related words are used in all languages, depending on the availability of synonyms in each language.

ANTONYMS I
5 items (163–167)

Task.   The patient hears a word and then four alternatives. She or he must choose which one of the four alternative words has a meaning opposite to that of the target word.

Stimuli.   The target words used in this subtest are all common adjectives that have obvious unambiguous opposites.

For each of the items, the four alternatives are high associates of the target word. Only one of these associates, however, has the opposite meaning.

Test contribution.   The subtest measures the ability of the patient to recognize the opposites of common adjectives. Like the semantic categories subtest and the synonym subtest, there is a nonnegligible memory load due to the fact that the test is presented auditorily.

In the two tests that precede this one, the semantic categories test and the synonym test, the patient's task is basically to determine which words in an array of words are in some way related to one another and which ones are not. In this test, however, the patient must identify the relation of opposition from among the other relationships that exist between the target word and the alternatives. The alternatives are therefore also distractors.

The adjectives used in this section are common, but as adjectives they are expected to be somewhat more difficult than the common picturable nouns used in the previous two sections.

For the reasons given earlier this section is expected to be more difficult than the previous multiple choice tests of lexical relations. It is, however, expected to be much easier than the production test of semantic opposites to which it is matched (see cross-reference below).

Design considerations.   The major design difficulty in this section is the selection of target stimuli which are frequent, which have an unambiguous opposite, and which have three common high associates. In some languages this is a simple matter, while in others there are few adjectives for which all conditions can be satisfied.

ANTONYMS II
5 items (168–172)

ANTONYNS

Now, you will hear a word and then four choices. But this time I want you to
choose the one that has the OPPOSITE meaning. So, for example, if you hear
"down" and then the choices: "house," "up," "under," "big" you would choose "up"
because its meaning is most opposite to the meaning of "down." Ready?

163. HAPPY:

    1) glad, 2) sad, 3) rich, 4) baby   1 2 3 4 0 (163)

164. DARK:

    1) shy, 2) black, 3) light, 4) silent   1 2 3 4 0 (164)

165. YOUNG:

    1) big, 2) old, 3) green, 4) small   1 2 3 4 0 (165)

166. SICK:

    1) sad, 2) quiet, 3) alive, 4) healthy   1 2 3 4 0 (166)

167: WRONG:

    1) right, 2) way, 3) funny, 4) mistake   1 2 3 4 0 (167)

***Pause here and read the following instructions to the patient.

Now for these, the choices look very similar BUT ONLY ONE is the opposite of the
word you will hear. Ready?

168: UGLY:

    1) beautiful, 2) beauty, 3) beautifully   1 2 3 0 (168)

169: SILENT:

    1) noise, 2) noisily, 3) noisy   1 2 3 0 (169)

170: SAD:

    1) happily, 2) happiness, 3) happy   1 2 3 0 (170)

171: FAST:

    1) slow, 2) slowness, 3) slowly   1 2 3 0 (171)

172: BOLD:

    1) careful, 2) carefully, 3) care   1 2 3 0 (172)

Cross-reference. This subtest is directly comparable to the semantic opposites
subtest (314–323) in which the patient hears a common adjective and is required
to produce its opposite. The antonym multiple-choice section is designed to

determine if the patient is able to simply recognize adjective opposite pairs. This section therefore aids in the interpretation of the patient's ability to produce them.

The subtest is also related to the semantic categories subtest (153–157) and the synonym subtest (158–162). It is important to note, however, that although all three of these tests require the patient to determine logical relations between words, the antonyms subtest uses adjectives which are not strictly comparable to the common nouns used in the other two tests.

Cross-language equivalence.   Inasmuch as possible, the stimulus words are translation equivalents in all languages. For each stimulus, the correct response is its natural lexical opposite in the language. The incorrect choices are high associates of the stimulus in each language. The pairs of adjectives and their opposites may vary somewhat from language to language, depending on which adjective in each language has an obvious unambiguous opposite.

Task.   The patient hears a target word and then three other words, one of which is an exact opposite of the target word. She or he must choose the alternative that is the opposite.

Stimuli.   All five of the target words are adjectives that have obvious semantic opposites. For each item, all three alternatives are morphological forms of the semantic opposite root. So, in English for example, the patient is presented with a noun form, an adverb form, and an adjective form.

Test contribution.   Although this subtest measures the patient's ability to distinguish adjectival forms from adverbial, nominal, and/or verbal forms in particular, it measures, in general, the patient's metalinguistic knowledge in this area.

The object of this subtest is generally not transparent to the patient. With this type of task, however, metalinguistic knowledge can be tested without the test administrator having to ask questions like "Which one is the adjective?" Such questions test the patient's metalinguistic vocabulary and only secondarily his or her metalinguistic knowledge.

Design considerations.   The major design problem in this section was to find a task that could serve as a multiple-choice counterpart of the test of derivational morphology (see cross-reference below). Once such a task was found, the problem remained to find stimuli in each language for which three distinct morphological forms are available. In German, for example, in which the surface forms adverb and adjective are identical, a verb was used instead of the adverb.

Cross-reference.   This subtest is to be compared to the derivational morphology subtest (324–333). In that subtest, the patient is presented with a word and must change it to a different morphological form. So in English, for example, the patient is given a noun and must produce the adjective form. The derivational morphology subtest is complex, difficult, and sensitive to the patient's educational background. The antonym II subtest, therefore, plays a large role in separating the patient's knowledge of the morphological forms from his or her productive ability in a metalinguistic task.

Cross-language equivalence.   In most languages it is possible to contrast a noun form and an adverb form with the target adjective form. In some languages adjectives and adverbs have the same form. In these languages, a verb form is used instead of an adverb. In a few languages (e.g., Cantonese, Mandarin), the noun and the adjective have the same form and hence a verb form and an adverb form are contrasted with the targer adjective.

GRAMMATICALITY JUDGMENT
10 items (173–182)

Task.   The patient hears a sentence. She or he must decide whether it is a grammatically correct sentence of the language.

Stimuli.   The stimuli are 7 ungrammatical and 3 grammatical sentences. The grammatical sentences are taken from the syntactic comprehension subtest (66–152). The ungrammatical sentences are formed by altering sentences from the syntactic comprehension subtest so as to make them ungrammatical. This is done by the deletion of a morpheme, by the addition of a morpheme, by the use of an inappropriate morpheme, or by the use of wrong word order.

Contribution.   The subtest measures the patient's ability to recognize the syntactic well-formedness of sentences. This is a test of general metalinguistic ability and may aid in the interpretation of performance on other production and comprehension tasks of the BAT (see cross-reference below).

   Paired with sentence comprehension disturbances and failure in sentence construction, grammaticality judgments may be useful because the performance of some agrammatic patients on grammaticality judgments has been reported to display a remarkable sensitivity to structural information (Linebarger, Schwartz, & Saffran, 1983a, 1983b). Results of the grammaticality judgment task may indicate greater sparing of syntactic knowledge in one language than in another, despite failure in both on other more difficult tasks.

Design considerations.   The goal in the design of this subtest was to create a set of ungrammatical sentences that are comparable to real sentences used in the BAT. The systematic altering of a variety of sentence types taken from the syntactic comprehension subtest (66–152) serves to establish this comparability.

Cross-reference. The subtest is primarily cross-referenced to the syntactic comprehension subtest (66–152) and secondarily to all other subtests of the BAT which use syntactic comprehension stimuli. These include the sentence repetition subtest (253–259), the reading sentences aloud subtest (377–386), the sentence dictation subtest (403–407), and the sentence reading comprehension subtest (418–427).

Cross-language equivalence. The nature of the alterations depends on the structure of each language. In all languages, sentences are made ungrammatical by the deletion or insertion of a grammatical morpheme, by the use of an inappropriate morpheme, or by the use of the wrong word order. The patient is asked whether the sentence is a correct sentence in the language being tested.

```
GRAMMATICALITY JUDGMENT


Now, you will hear some sentences. Please tell me if the sentence is a correct

English sentence. For example, if I say "The boy sits on a chair," it is a

correct English sentence and you say 'yes.' But if I say "The boys on a chairs

sit," it is not correct and you say 'no.'  Ready?


173.  She pushes him.                      judgment   +   -   0   (173)

174.  He dresses herself.                  judgment   +   -   0   (174)

175.  The cat is biting by the dog.        judgment   +   -   0   (175)

176.  It's the boy kiss the girl.          judgment   +   -   0   (176)

177.  The truck is pulled by the car.      judgment   +   -   0   (177)

178.  It's truck that pulls car.           judgment   +   -   0   (178)

179.  The girl is sprayed the boy.         judgment   +   -   0   (179)

180.  The boy not wake up his mother.      judgment   +   -   0   (180)

181.  It's the boy that pushes the girl.   judgment   +   -   0   (181)

182.  The dog not is bitten by the cat.    judgment   +   -   0   (182)
```

SEMANTIC ACCEPTABILITY
10 items (183–192)

Task. The patient hears a sentence and must decide whether the sentence makes sense.

```
SEMANTIC ACCEPTABILITY


The next sentences are all correct English sentences. BUT some of them do not
make sense. I will read the sentence to you. You tell me if it makes sense.
For example, if I say "she cuts her hair with pencils" you say 'no' because it
does not make sense. "She cuts her hair with scissors" makes sense and you say
'yes.' Ready?


183.  The sun shines by night.              judgment  +  -  0  (183)

184.  The cat sits on the roof.             judgment  +  -  0  (184)

185.  The flowers grow in the gravy.        judgment  +  -  0  (185)

186.  The season comes out of the chimney.  judgment  +  -  0  (186)

187.  He is wearing a new suit today.       judgment  +  -  0  (187)

188.  They dribble their cars to work.      judgment  +  -  0  (188)

189.  The sausage ate the dog.              judgment  +  -  0  (189)

190.  They had radios for breakfast.        judgment  +  -  0  (190)

191.  She combs her hair in front of the mirror.  judgment  +  -  0  (191)

192.  He drinks sand when it is hot.        judgment  +  -  0  (192)
```

Stimuli.　　The 10 sentences used in this section are all grammatically well
formed. Seven, however, are semantically or pragmatically unacceptable.

In this section, semantic unacceptability has been operationalized. That is, a
sentence is unacceptable if it is rejected by native speakers of each language
tested. Items that do not meet this criterion in individual languages have been
changed in those languages.

Test contribution.　　This subtest is firstly a test of general sentence comprehension. A high degree of comprehension is required if the patient is to decide
whether a sentence makes sense.

As a judgment task, the subtest offers a view of the interface between the
patient's real world knowledge and his linguistic knowledge in each language
tested.

Design considerations.　　In this section it proved to be surprisingly difficult to
find sentences that are semantically unacceptable in a wide variety of cultures. It
seems that cultures differ greatly in their willingness to consider a sentence that
could have a metaphorical interpretation as semantically acceptable.

Cross-reference. The stimuli used in the semantic acceptability section are unique to this section. However, a comparison should be made to the preceding grammaticality judgment section (173–182).

Cross-language equivalence. In this section, semantic unacceptability has been operationalized by rejection by native speakers of each language tested. Items that do not meet this criterion in individual languages are changed in those languages. So, for languages spoken in Scandinavian countries familiar with the midnight sun, the sentence "The sun shines by night" is replaced by "Christmas is celebrated in August." In Arabic, any reference to common concrete objects susceptible of a "poetic" interpretation is avoided.

REPETITION AND JUDGMENT

The repetition and judgment section of the BAT extends from item 193 to item 252. In this section, the patient hears a word. She or he must repeat the word and then decide whether it is an existing word in the language.

The repetition and judgment tasks are administered as a single section for the sake of convenience to both the test administrator and the patient. Within the repetition and judgment section, however, are six discrete subtests. Each of these tests is described separately below.

Repetition of Real Monosyllabic Words
10 items (193, 195, 197, 201, 207, 211, 213, 215, 217, 221)

Task. The patient hears a word. She or he must then repeat it.

Stimuli. The 10 words used here are all monosyllabic. For most languages, all the items in this section are stimuli from the VAD subtest (48–65). In some languages in which monosyllabic minimal pairs are extremely rare, ten monosyllabic words were not available. For those languages, VAD stimuli are found in both the monosyllabic and bisyllabic repetition subtests.

Contribution. The subtest measures the patient's ability to repeat simple monosyllabic words of the language. It is a composite test of listening and speaking. The score should therefore be compared to the scores of simpler tests of listening and production as well as those of the test of monosyllabic nonword repetition (see cross-reference below).

Design considerations. The design of this section is relatively uncomplicated except in those cases where fewer than ten monosyllabic stimuli were available from the VAD subtest (see stimuli above).

REPETITION OF WORDS AND NONSENSE WORDS, AND LEXICAL DECISION

I am going to ask you to repeat some words. Some of them are real
English words. Some are not really English words. They don't
make sense. Please repeat after me, and then tell me if the word
is a real English word. Ready?

193.	MAT	repetition	+	-	0	(193)
		judgment	+	-	0	(194)
195.	BALL	repetition	+	-	0	(195)
		judgment	+	-	0	(196)
197.	BREW	repetition	+	-	0	(197)
		judgment	+	-	0	(198)
199.	CHAY	repetition	+	-	0	(199)
		judgment	+	-	0	(200)
201.	THICK	repetition	+	-	0	(201)
		judgment	+	-	0	(202)
203.	GOOM	repetition	+	-	0	(203)
		judgment	+	-	0	(204)
205.	FLUP	repetition	+	-	0	(205)
		judgment	+	-	0	(206)
207.	VAN	repetition	+	-	0	(207)
		judgment	+	-	0	(208)
209.	ROP	repetition	+	-	0	(209)
		judgment	+	-	0	(210)
211.	PEAR	repetition	+	-	0	(211)
		judgment	+	-	0	(212)
213.	CHIP	repetition	+	-	0	(213)
		judgment	+	-	0	(214)
215.	CRANE	repetition	+	-	0	(215)
		judgment	+	-	0	(216)
217.	LICE	repetition	+	-	0	(217)
		judgment	+	-	0	(218)
219.	BIM	repetition	+	-	0	(219)
		judgment	+	-	0	(220)
221.	JAR	repetition	+	-	0	(221)
		judgment	+	-	0	(222)

98

Cross-reference.   This subsection is cross-referenced to three other parts of the test.

First, the score on this subtest is to be compared to the test of multisyllabic real-word repetition (223, 225, 229, 235, 237, 241, 243, 245, 249, 251). These tests differ only in difficulty. Together they form a stratified test of repetition ability.

Second, the monosyllabic real-word repetition score should be compared to the monosyllabic nonword score (199, 203, 205, 209, 219). Interpretation of the difference between these scores can be aided by examination of the monosyllabic lexical decision subtest (194–222). The lexical decision subtest is made up of the stimuli from the monosyllabic real-word and nonword subtests. Conclusions based on the patient's differential word-nonword repetition ability must be evaluated in view of the patient's own judgments about the "wordness" of the stimuli.

Third, the monosyllabic real-word repetition score can be compared to the score on the VAD section (48–65). These sections share the same stimuli (see stimuli section above). If the patient obtains a high score on the VAD subtest and a low score on the repetition subtest there is evidence that the low repetition score is attributable to difficulties in production only.

If, on the other hand, the patient's VAD score is low and the repetition score is high, the evidence suggests that the low VAD score is a result of a deficit in verbal comprehension rather than phonemic discrimination.

Repetition of Multisyllabic Real Words
10 items (223, 225, 229, 235, 237, 241, 243, 245, 249, 251)

Task.   The patient hears a word. She or he must then repeat it.

Stimuli.   The 10 stimuli in this section can be subdivided into five bisyllabic (223, 225, 229, 235, 237) and five trisyllabic (241, 243, 245, 249, 251) real words All the multisyllabic words used in this section are monomorphemic.

Contribution.   This subtest is an extension of the monosyllabic real-word repetition subtest. Repetition performance plays an important role in the categorization of aphasic patients' behavior. For that reason, the comparatively difficult multisyllabic real-word repetition subtest was included to offer a more sensitive measure of the patient's repetition ability.

Design considerations.   It is important that the words in this section be monomorphemic in all languages tested. This increases comparability between languages. It must be considered, however, that for each language, the subjective "length" of a trisyllabic word is dependent on the number of syllables in an average word.

223.	SIGNAL	repetition	+	-	0	(223)
		judgment	+	-	0	(224)
225.	PAPER	repetition	+	-	0	(225)
		judgment	+	-	0	(226)
227.	CHETTY	repetition	+	-	0	(227)
		judgment	+	-	0	(228)
229.	LIQUID	repetition	+	-	0	(229)
		judgment	+	-	0	(230)
231.	BARSEN	repetition	+	-	0	(231)
		judgment	+	-	0	(232)
233.	SUMMIP	repetition	+	-	0	(233)
		judgment	+	-	0	(234)
235.	DOLPHIN	repetition	+	-	0	(235)
		judgment	+	-	0	(236)
237.	PROMISE	repetition	+	-	0	(237)
		judgment	+	-	0	(238)
239.	KIMMID	repetition	+	-	0	(239)
		judgment	+	-	0	(240)
241.	MELODY	repetition	+	-	0	(241)
		judgment	+	-	0	(242)
243.	ELEPHANT	repetition	+	-	0	(243)
		judgment	+	-	0	(244)
245.	POTATO	repetition	+	-	0	(245)
		judgment	+	-	0	(246)
247.	SOLLICK	repetition	+	-	0	(247)
		judgment	+	-	0	(248)
249.	DISASTER	repetition	+	-	0	(249)
		judgment	+	-	0	(250)
251.	SEMINAR	repetition	+	-	0	(251)
		judgment	+	-	0	(252)

Cross-reference.   The score on this subtest is to be compared to the score on the simpler monosyllabic subtest (193, 195, 197, 201, 207, 211, 213, 215, 217, 221) with which it forms a unit.

The subtest score should also be compared to the score on the multisyllabic nonword repetition score (227, 231, 233, 239, 247). The difference between the word and nonword scores can be evaluated in comparison to the patient's lexical decisions for these stimuli (224–252).

Repetition of Monosyllabic Nonwords
5 items (199, 203, 205, 209, 219)

Task.   The patient hears a word. She or he must then repeat it.

Stimuli.   The stimuli are monosyllabic phonotactically well-formed nonwords in each language. The nonwords were formed by taking a real-word of the language and changing one consonant or consonant cluster.

Contribution.   This subtest provides a measure of the patient's ability to re-produce a single syllable of the language with some degree of exactitude. Performance on this test is independent of comprehension (unless the patient thinks she or he heard a similar real-word). This characteristic of nonword repetition makes it a good measure of the patient's ability to hear and produce phonemic distinctions.

Design considerations.   The nonword stimuli in this test must be read to the patient by the test administrator. Care must be taken therefore to ensure that within each language, the stimuli are spelled so that they will be pronounced in the same way by all test administrators.

Cross-reference.   This subtest is matched to the test of real monosyllabic word repetition (193, 195, 197, 201, 207, 211, 213, 215, 217, 221) The stimuli used in both the real-word and nonword subtests are used in the lexical decision subtest (194–222).

Repetition of Multisyllabic Nonwords
5 items (227, 231, 233, 239, 247)

Task.   The patient hears a word. She or he must then repeat it.

Stimuli.   The five stimuli in this section are bisyllabic nonwords. All the non-words are phonotactically well-formed. They were formed by changing one consonant or consonant cluster of a bisyllabic, monomorphemic real-word of the language.

Contribution.   The bisyllabic section of the nonword subtest offers a more difficult test of receptive and productive phonemic discrimination.

Design considerations.   In this section, the nonwords must be represented orthographically so that pronunciation (including stress or tone when appropriate) will be consistent across test administrators.

Cross-reference.   The patient's score on this section can be compared to his repetition performance for real multisyllabic words (223, 225, 229, 235, 237, 241, 243, 245, 249, 251). It should be noted that in the real-word section both bisyllabic and trisyllabic words are used. The nonword repetition score is therefore only strictly comparable to the score for bisyllabic real words (223, 225, 229, 235, 237). As has already been stated, any interpretation of the differences between the patient's repetition performance for words vs. nonwords requires consideration of the patient's lexical judgments for those stimuli. Lexical decision for multisyllabic words is tested in items 224, 226, 228, 230, 232, 234, 236, 238, 240, 242, 244, 246, 248, 250, 252.

Cross-language equivalence.   The words for repetition have been selected in accordance with the same criteria in every language. There are 20 real words: 10 monosyllabic, 5 bisyllabic and 5 trisyllabic. Polysyllabic words are monomorphemic. Nonsense words are formed by taking a real word in the language and changing one consonant to form a phonologically acceptable nonword. The following distribution of items obtains in all languages:

Monosyllabic real words: 193, 195, 197, 201, 207, 211, 213, 215, 217, 221
Bisyllabic real words: 223, 225, 229, 235, 237
Trisyllabic real words: 241, 243, 245, 249, 251
Monosyllabic nonwords: 199, 203, 205, 209, 219
Bisyllabic nonwords: 227, 231, 233, 239, 247

In all languages, like Oriya, in which no monosyllabic words are found (except for 3 pronouns, the words for "no" and "mother" and the 2nd person informal imperative form—though even these would have an appended vowel in many dialects), 10 words are selected from the bisyllabic Auditory Verbal Discrimination stimuli.

In languages where less than 10 VAD stimuli are monosyllabic, the balance is made up of bisyllabic VAD stimuli. In all languages, however, the monosyllabic and bisyllabic words are distributed in accordance with the above chart, irrespective of their VAD status.

LEXICAL DECISION: MONOSYLLABIC WORDS
15 items (194, 196, 198, 200, 202, 204, 206, 208, 210, 212,
214, 216, 218, 220, 222)

Task. The patient hears a single phonotactically well-formed syllable of the language and must repeat it. She or he must then decide whether the syllable is an existing word of the language.

Stimuli. Ten of the stimuli in this subtest are real words of the language. They are taken from the stimuli used in the verbal auditory discrimination section and are the same stimuli as those used for real monosyllabic word repetition.

Five of the stimuli presented are nonwords. These are the same words used in the monosyllabic nonword repetition section. The nonwords are formed by taking a real monosyllabic word of the language and changing a single consonant or consonant cluster.

Contribution. This test is essentially a test of auditory comprehension, since the only distinction between a real word and a phonotactically well-formed nonword is that one has meaning and the other does not.

There may, however, exist alternative strategies for success in this subtest. The fact that the items in this subtest are matched to both the repetition section and the VAD section (see cross-reference) allows for the isolation of these alternative strategies or perhaps "intermediate" levels of word comprehension. It is conceivable that a patient could distinguish correctly between words and nonwords solely on the basis of the familiarity of the stimulus. Such a patient would then score high on the repetition task, high on the lexical decision task, but low on the VAD task. In this case, the score on the lexical decision task is a unique measure of the patient's word recognition ability.

The score on this subtest may also reflect the patient's confidence in his or her knowledge of the words of the language. This would be reflected in the distribution of lexical decision errors. One would expect a disproportionate number of "yes, it is a word" answers to nonwords when the patient believes she or he knows little (and perhaps does know little). In these cases one should be cautious about considering correct "yes" responses to real words as evidence for correct word recognition.

Design considerations. The design of this section is uncomplicated. As indicated in the contribution section above, however, interpretation of the results may not be a simple matter.

Cross-reference. Interpretation of the score for this section requires that the score be compared to the score for repetition of the same words (items 193–221). The score should also be compared to the score in the VAD subtest (48–65).

Finally, an examination of the score for multisyllabic lexical decision (224–252) may reveal that the interpretation of the patient's lexical decision ability would be aided by collapsing the two sections to yield a single lexical decision score.

Lexical Decision: Multisyllabic Words
15 items (224, 226, 228, 230, 232, 234, 236, 238, 240, 242, 244, 246, 248, 250, 252)

Task.   The patient hears a multisyllabic word and must repeat it. She or he must then decide whether that word is a real existing word of the language.

Stimuli.   Ten of the stimuli in this subtest are real words of the language. Five words are bisyllabic and five are trisyllabic. All stimuli are monomorphemic. They are the same stimuli as those used for real multisyllabic word repetition.

Five of the stimuli presented are nonwords. These are the same words used in the multisyllabic non-word repetition section. The nonwords are formed by taking a real bisyllabic monomorphemic word of the language and changing a single consonant or consonant cluster.

Contribution.   This test offers essentially the same information as the lexical decision subtest for monosyllabic words. It is expected, however, that this task would be more difficult. In many languages long monosyllabic words tend to be less common than shorter ones. This increases the probability that the patient may not recognize the real words, or that she or he may believe the nonword he does not recognize to be simply outside of his or her vocabulary.

Another reason for the greater difficulty of this section is that the multisyllabic stimuli are not taken from the VAD section (in most languages) as are the monosyllabic ones. Therefore this constraint of "picturability," presumably an aid in comprehension, is not placed on the multisyllabic words.

Design considerations.   Ideally, the words used in this section would be in the same frequency range as the monosyllabic words. It is difficult to meet this ideal, however, in languages like English which contain very few frequent monomorphemic trisyllabic words, or in languages that do not contain monosyllabic words (e.g., Oriya).

Cross-reference.   The patient's performance on this task must be compared to his or her performance in the repetition of multisyllabic words (223–251). The score should also be compared to the score for monosyllabic lexical decision.

SENTENCE REPETITION
7 items (253–259)

Task.   The patient hears a sentence and must then repeat it.

Stimuli.   The stimuli are sentences taken from the syntactic comprehension subtest. Each repetition sentence represents a different sentence type.

Contribution.   The performance of this task requires both that the patient be able to process the auditory stimulus and be able to correctly produce the sentence. The task therefore, although not difficult for a fluent speaker, is relatively complex. Sentence repetition may be sensitive to the patient's mnemonic ability, particularly in cases where the patient has comprehension difficulties.

Design considerations.   The selection of a variety of sentence types for this subtest was the major design consideration. The selectional criterion, therefore, was syntactic and not phonological.

Cross-reference.   This subtest is cross-referenced to the single word repetition subtest (193–251). It is also cross-referenced to the other subtests of the BAT which use sentences from the syntactic comprehension subtest (66–152). These include the grammaticality judgment subtest (173–182), the reading sentences aloud subtest (377–386), the sentence dictation subtest (403–407), and the sentence reading comprehension subtest (418–427).

Cross-language equivalence. The same type of sentence is used in all languages for each item as follows: 253 (S), 254 (P), 255 (NS2S), 256 (NS2O), 257 (NS1n), 258 (P), 259 (Sn). For each language, the sentences have been selected among the stimuli used in the syntactic comprehension section of that language.

SERIES
3 items (260–262)

```
SERIES


260.  Please name all the days of the week.      +   -   0   (260)
261.  Could you count from one to twenty-five?   +   -   0   (261)
262.  Could you name all the months of the year? +   -   0   (262)
```

Task.   The patient is asked to name the days of the week, to count to 25 and to name the months of the year.

Stimuli.   The only test stimuli that the patient is exposed to in this section are the requests for the members of a particular series. The three series used for each language test are commonly treated as series in each language. For most languages the patient is asked to name the days of the week, the months of the year, and to count to 25.

Contribution.   This subtest offers a measure of the patient's ability to produce highly formulaic and practiced speech.

Design considerations.   In designing this subtest it was necessary to insure that, for each language, it is culturally appropriate to recite the members of each series.

Cross-reference.   None.

Cross-language equivalence.   The same series are used in all languages except in those in which months do not have a specific name (e.g., in Japanese: the first month, the second month, etc., up to the twelfth month), some other similarly overlearned series has been substituted (e.g., in Vietnamese: the year of the mouse, the year of the ox, the year of the tiger, etc.). In some formerly occupied territories, native speakers know the names of days of the week or months of the year only in some more or less phonologically integrated form of Arabic, English, or French.

VERBAL FLUENCY
6 items (263–268)

```
VERBAL FLUENCY

In this section I will ask you to say as many words as you can that start with a certain

sound.  For example if I say "I would like you to give me words starting with the sound

"s," you would give me words like sit, cement, soap, sailor, salad, special, etc.

#33., ready?

I would like you to give me words that begin with the sound "p."

Try to say as many words as you can, as fast as you can.


263.                              All words begin with right sound?  +  -  0  (263)

                                  Number of acceptable words?       _____   (264)

O.K., now words that begin with "f."

265.                              All words begin with right sound?  +  -  0  (265)

                                  Number of acceptable words?       _____   (266)

O.K., now words that begin with "k."

267.                              All words begin with right sound?  +  -  0  (267)

                                  Number of acceptable words?       _____   (268)
```

Task.   The patient is presented with three consonant sounds and is asked to produce as many words as possible that begin with that sound.

Stimuli.   The stimuli are common word-initial sounds of the language. For most languages, the sound is a single consonant (see cross-language equivalence below). It should be noted that for languages such as English, the patient is instructed to produce as many words as she or he can that begin with the sound /tə/, not with the letter "t" /ti:/.

Contribution.   The verbal fluency subtest offers an accurate measure of performance on a task that is strongly correlated with other linguistic tasks and is used to characterize word-finding difficulty.

Design considerations. This subtest differs from most of the other subtests of the BAT in that the patient's response is not compared to an answer key. In this subtest there is no correct score. The patient's score in a particular language is only meaningful in comparison to the norm and to his verbal fluency performance in the other languages tested.

Cross-reference. None.

Cross-language equivalence. The sounds used are not identical across languages. Rather, sounds are selected on the basis of their use within each language—i.e., sounds are used which occur word initially in many common words. While a phoneme is provided in languages written alphabetically, a syllable is provided in Japanese (given the relatively small number of syllables in the language, each is as productive as a consonant in English), and an example with three syllables beginning with the same consonant is given in Tamil (because the writing system is syllabic but each syllable is not as productive as in Japanese).

NAMING
20 items (269–288)

Task. The patient is presented with 2 objects one at a time. The patient is asked to name each object.

Stimuli. The stimuli used in this subtest are small everyday objects which have common names. Of the 20 stimuli, 10 are presented to the patient for the first time in this subtest. The other 10 are presented in earlier sections of the BAT (see cross-reference below).

Contribution. The naming test is a test of single word-finding and production ability. It is designed to be the production counterpart of the pointing task and therefore shares with that task a very low ceiling on message length and vocabulary difficulty. The transparency of the task to the patient reduces the artificiality of the task and the need for special instructions.

The naming task is the easiest of all the production tasks in the BAT. A patient who does not obtain a satisfactory score on this subtest displays a very low level of word-finding and/or production ability. In this case the scores on the other more difficult tests involving production ability may be difficult to interpret.

Design considerations. The selection of the objects for this subtest was constrained by considerations of availability, portability, and cross-cultural famil-

```
NAMING

I will show you some things.  Tell me what the thing is called.
Ready?

    269.  (book)                    +   -   0   (269)

    270.  (glasses)                 +   -   0   (270)

    271.  (key)                      +   -   0   (271)

    272.  (cup)                      +   -   0   (272)

    273.  (tie)                      +   -   0   (273)

    274.  (scissors)                +   -   0   (274)

    275.  (spoon)                    +   -   0   (275)

    276.  (glove)                    +   -   0   (276)

    277.  (pencil)                   +   -   0   (277)

    278.  ([playing] card)           +   -   0   (278)

    279.  (thermometer)              +   -   0   (279)

    280.  (button)                   +   -   0   (280)

    281.  (cigarette)                +   -   0   (281)

    282.  (fork)                     +   -   0   (282)

    283.  (feather)                  +   -   0   (283)

    284.  (ring)                     +   -   0   (284)

    285.  (candle)                   +   -   0   (285)

    286.  (envelope)                 +   -   0   (286)

    287.  (toothbrush)               +   -   0   (287)

    288.  (watch)                    +   -   0   (288)
```

iarity. All the stimuli are small, common objects that are easily transported to the testing site.

Cross-reference. The score on the naming task is to be compared to the patient's performance on the pointing task (23–32).

The inclusion of 10 new stimuli and 10 stimuli from the pointing and/or commands section, was designed to enhance comparability between measures of word comprehension and word production in the BAT. The use of the same stimuli allows for strict comparison of the scores.

It is possible, however, that the patient's score on the production task is affected by his or her having been exposed to the names and the objects in the pointing subtest presented early in the BAT. If this were the case one would expect to find a difference, within the naming subtest, between the scores for the 10 new stimuli and the 10 old stimuli (old items: 270, 271, 276, 277, 280, 282, 284, 286, 288).

If a difference is found between the score for the new and the old stimuli, only the performance on the 10 new stimuli should be compared to the pointing score.

Cross-language equivalence.   In all languages, 10 of the stimuli are the objects which have already been used for pointing and/or commands. As in pointing, the 10 additional objects are the same in all languages, with only very few exceptions made, due to ethnic or climatic conditions. In these few cases, a similarly common object is substituted (e.g., a comb). Never more than 3 items have been substituted in any language.

SENTENCE CONSTRUCTION
25 items (289–313)

Task.   The patient is presented with 2, 3, or 4 words and is asked to make the simplest possible sentence with them.

Stimuli.   There are 5 sets of stimuli in this subtest. The first set contains 2 words, the second and third contain 3 words, and the fourth and fifth contain 4 words. Each set is made up of common words. The words are associates in the sense that they suggest semantically and pragmatically appropriate sentences.

Contribution.   The sentence construction task offers a view of many aspects of the patient's productive ability. Each stimulus set has 5 questions associated with it. In the first item the examiner records whether the patient is able to perform the task at all. If the patient does produce something, the grammaticality and semanticality of the utterance are recorded. Finally, the number of stimulus words used, and the total number of words in the utterance are recorded.

For each stimulus set, therefore, the sentence construction subtest offers diverse measures of the patient's linguistic ability. More specifically, the task is a measure of the patient's ability to organize words in an acceptable syntactic form.

Design considerations.   The stimulus words are provided to the patient in an order that differs from that of the corresponding simplest possible sentence that could be constructed with them.

SENTENCE CONSTRUCTION

I will give you some words. With these words make the simplest and shortest
sentence possible. So for example, if I give you the words: "door," "open,"
"nurse" you try to make a simple sentence that uses all the words, like "The
nurse opens the door." Ready?

289. house/cat	response obtained?	+	0	(289)
	correct English sentence?	+	-	(290)
	does it make sense?	+	-	(291)
	number of stimulus words used?		____	(292)
	total number of words		____	(293)
294. chair/doctor/sit	response obtained?	+	0	(294)
	correct English sentence?	+	-	(295)
	does it make sense?	+	-	(296)
	number of stimulus words used?		____	(297)
	total number of words?		____	(298)
299. desk/open/drawer	response obtained?	+	0	(299)
	correct English sentence?	+	-	(300)
	does it make sense?	+	-	(301)
	number of stimulus words used?		____	(302)
	total number of words?		____	(303)
304. tree/green/leaf/see	response obtained?	+	0	(304)
	correct English sentence?	+	-	(305)
	does it make sense?	+	-	(306)
	number of stimulus words used?		____	(307)
	total number of words?		____	(308)
309. pencil/write/blue/paper/	response obtained?	+	0	(309)
	correct English sentence?	+	-	(310)
	does it make sense?	+	-	(311)
	number of stimulus words used?		____	(312)
	total number of words?		____	(313)

Cross-reference.   This subtest is not explicitly cross-referenced to any particular subtest of the BAT. Because it is a complex task, however, sentence construction performance is best interpreted with reference to the patient's score on the simpler subtests of the BAT.

Cross-language equivalence.   The stimuli in this section are translation equivalents in all of the languages. The order of presentation of words in some items may be slightly modified in some languages to avoid successive nouns forming noun phrases in those languages (e.g., to avoid the equivalent of house/cat or dog/house).

SEMANTIC OPPOSITES
10 items (314–323)

Task.   The patient is presented with a word and is asked to say a different word that has the opposite meaning.

```
SEMANTIC OPPOSITES


I will give you a word.  You give me a different word that has the

opposite meaning.  So, for example, if I say "BIG" you would say

"SMALL" because "big" and "small" have opposite meanings.  Ready?


   314.  TRUE          + FALSE    OR _____    1  -  0   (314)

   315.  WIDE          + NARROW   OR _____    1  -  0   (315)

   316.  POOR          + RICH     OR _____    1  -  0   (316)

   317.  SLOW          + FAST     OR _____    1  -  0   (317)

   318.  TALL          + SHORT    OR _____    1  -  0   (318)

   319.  SHUT          + OPEN     OR _____    1  -  0   (319)

   320.  HEAVY         + LIGHT    OR _____    1  -  0   (320)

   321.  HIGH          + LOW      OR _____    1  -  0   (321)

   322.  SOFT          + HARD     OR _____    1  -  0   (322)

   323.  THICK         + THIN     OR _____    1  -  0   (323)
```

Stimuli. The words used in this subtest are all adjectives that have obvious and relatively frequent antonyms.

Contribution. To perform this task, the patient must be able to understand the stimulus word, must have access to the stimulus' antonym, and must be able to produce that antonym.

This task, therefore, provides a measure of lexical comprehension, word-finding ability, and production.

Design considerations. The major difficulty in this section is the selection of adjectives that have obvious and frequent antonyms in each language.

In many cases, there exists in the language more than one acceptable antonym. For this reason, next to each stimulus word on the test, the most probable correct response is provided. If the patient produces this response the examiner scores "+." Because it is possible that the patient will produce an antonym other than the one expected, space is provided to record that word and the examiner scores it as "1." This is also interpreted as a correct response.

Cross-reference. This subtest is directly comparable to the Antonym 1 subtest (163–167). In the Antonym 1 subtest the patient hears a common adjective and is required to select its antonym from a choice of four alternatives. The comparison of these two subtests allows the interpreter of the BAT to isolate the patient's production ability in this area.

The patient's score on this subtest should also be compared to his scores on the synonym subtest (158–162). It should be noted, however, that the synonym subtest uses nouns as stimuli and therefore is not strictly comparable to the antonym and semantic opposites subtests.

Cross-language equivalence. In all languages, translation equivalents are used as stimuli whenever possible. Only words that have an obvious, common, unambiguous opposite in the language are used. Therefore, in some languages, one or two stimuli may differ so as to ensure familiar pairs of opposites.

DERIVATIONAL MORPHOLOGY
20 items (324–343)

Note: The derivational morphology subtest is made up of 2 sections. Each section is made up of 10 items.

Task. The patient hears a word and is required to change that word to a morphologically related form of the same word.

```
DERIVATIONAL MORPHOLOGY


Now, you will hear a word.  Change the word to an adjective.  So,

for example, if I say "softness" you would say "soft."  If I say

"help" you would say "helpful."  Ready?


324.  POWER        + POWERFUL   OR _____   1  -  0   (324)

325.  NOBILITY     + NOBLE      OR _____   1  -  0   (325)

326.  WISDOM       + WISE       OR _____   1  -  0   (326)

327.  CARE         + CAREFUL    OR _____   1  -  0   (327)

328.  NATURE       + NATURAL    OR _____   1  -  0   (328)

329.  YOUTH        + YOUNG      OR _____   1  -  0   (329)

330.  CALMNESS     + CALM       OR _____   1  -  0   (330)

331.  PRIDE        + PROUD      OR _____   1  -  0   (331)

332.  SILENCE      + SILENT     OR _____   1  -  0   (332)

333.  NOISE        + NOISY      OR _____   1  -  0   (333)
```

The patient is required to produce two different types of morphological changes in each language tested (see language equivalence below). In English, for example, she or he is required to change nouns to adjectives for the first set of stimuli, and to change verbs and adjectives to their morphological opposites for the second set of 10 stimuli.

Stimuli. The stimuli are all single words. The stimuli differ across languages depending on the types of morphological changes that are required for the specific language test and the particular words that can undergo these changes for each language (see cross-language equivalence below).

Contribution. The primary value of this section of the test is that it allows the comparison of the patient's overall mastery of the morphological system the language with his or her ability to produce certain morphological forms on demand in this subtest. The derivational morphology subtest therefore provides a controlled enviornment for the observation of the patient's morphological ability. Information from the patient's performance can lead to a more comprehensive investigation of the patient's ability in this area.

114

```
MORPHOLOGICAL OPPOSITES


Now for the next set of words you DON'T need to find a DIFFERENT
word that means the opposite.  Just CHANGE the word so it has the
opposite meaning.  So, for example, if I say "POLITE" you would
say "IMPOLITE"; if I say "PACK" you would say "UNPACK."  Ready?


334.  TRUST       + DISTRUST      OR _____   1  -  0   (334)

325.  LEGIBLE     + ILLEGIBLE     OR _____   1  -  0   (335)

336.  JUST        + UNJUST        OR _____   1  -  0   (336)

337.  PROBABLE    + IMPROBABLE    OR _____   1  -  0   (337)

338.  VISIBLE     + INVISIBLE     OR _____   1  -  0   (338)

339.  REGARD      + DISREGARD     OR _____   1  -  0   (339)

340.  PRECISE     + IMPRECISE     OR _____   1  -  0   (340)

341.  LITERATE    + ILLITERATE    OR _____   1  -  0   (341)

342.  BELIEVABLE  + UNBELIEVABLE  OR _____   1  -  0   (342)

343.  COMPETENT   + INCOMPETENT   OR _____   1  -  0   (343)
```

The task is the most metalinguistic of all the BAT tasks, and therefore may be the most influenced by the patient's educational background. Although the instructions to the patient are designed to minimize the effect of educational background and his or her experience with metalinguistic tasks, the patient may fail to perform this task simply because she or he is not aware of what is required of him or her.

Design considerations.   The type of derivation must be selected so that two or three different productive rules are applied to stimuli with corresponding different properties (see cross-language equivalence).

Cross-reference.   This subtest is cross-referenced to the Antonyms II subtest. In that subtest, the patient is presented with a word and must select its opposite from three alternatives. All three alternatives are morphological forms of the same root (the root is the semantic opposite of the stimulus root). To perform this task correctly, the patient must be able to match the part of speech value of the stimulus to the correct alternative.

The Antonyms II subtest differs from the derivational morphology subtest in that it is a recognition rather than a production task.

Cross-language equivalence.   In each language the patient is required to perform two types of morphological changes. The first set of 10 items requires morphological changes of this type: noun—adjective, adjective—adverb, noun—verb, etc. For each language tested a productive type of change was selected (i.e., admitting of at least two forms).

For most languages, the second set of 10 items requires the patient to change a word to its morphological opposite. However, for languages in which morphological negation is too regular, i.e., in which there is only one affix for all words, a different morphological change (one of the above) is selected. For all languages the two sets require different types of morphological changes.

As in the first morphology subtest, the stimuli in the second subtest have been selected in accordance with language-specific criteria that nevertheless reflect the same general pattern across languages. In all languages that meet the requirement of having at least two or three different ways of morphologically marking an opposite (e.g., English: in-, un-, dis-), stimuli are selected so as to represent a mixed sample of each productive affixing type. For languages in which the formation of the morphological opposite is highly regular, involving, for example, the simple addition of one prefix for all words (as in Slavic languages), a different, more varied process has been selected on the pattern of the previous section (e.g., adjectives derived from nouns, nouns from verbs, or adverbs from adjectives).

DESCRIPTION
3 items (344–346)

```
DESCRIPTION


I am going to show you a set of six pictures.  All together the pictures make a little story.
Look at the pictures and tell me the story.


344.  Amount of speech:  0) nothing, 1) very little, 2) less than normal, 3) normal     (344)

345.  Did the patient go to the end?                                           +    -    (345)

346.  Did the patient:    1) simply describe the pictures, 2) tell a connected

                          story, 3) do neither?                                      (346)
```

Task. The patient is shown a sequence of 6 pictures and is asked to tell the story illustrated by these pictures. The pictures remain in full view of the patient throughout the task. The patient's production is tape-recorded.

Items 344–346 represent a multiple-choice assessment of the patient's performance. The scores are provided by the test administrator, who rates the amount of speech produced by the patient, records whether the patient proceeded to the end, and records whether the patient told a connected story (as opposed to a mere description of each picture without any attempt at telling a story). This provides a preliminary, quick, clinical assessment of the patient's descriptive speech.

The complete analysis of the Description section takes place after the BAT has been administered to the patient. The recording of his or her production is subjected to the posttest analysis (540–565). This analysis provides quantitative measures for the various components of the patient's verbal production.

117

Stimuli.   The stimuli are a series of 6 pictures that tell a sequential story.

1. A girl points to a bird's nest in a tree. In the nest, a bird is feeding its young. A boy looks on.

2. While the girl is watching, the boy climbs into the tree and reaches for the nest. The bird is scared away.

3. The branch on which the boy is leaning breaks. The nest and the boy fall to the ground. The boy breaks his leg in the process.

4. While the boy with a broken leg lies near the fallen nest, the girl seeks help from a nearby house.

5. The boy is carried on a stretcher to an ambulance.

6. The boy is on a hospital bed with his leg in a cast, while his mother sadly looks on. Outside, the mother bird cries over the loss of her young.

Contribution.   This section of the test allows the comparison of the patient's spontaneous speech production with his or her ability to tell a structured story. It also provides an extra sample of the patient's speech to be analyzed after the test for the presence of word-finding difficulty, neologisms, and paraphasias. The posttest analysis provides an additional measure of fluency, accuracy, and lexical diversity.

Design considerations.   The story had to be as culturally neutral as possible. The building of a snowman, for instance, would not have been appropriate for about half of the language versions of the BAT. The story had to be obvious from the captionless sequence of pictures. The drawings had to be clear and devoid of unnecessary details and distracting ornamentation.

Cross-reference.   The posttest analysis of descriptive speech should be compared to the posttest analysis of the Spontaneous Speech subtest (514–539) and the Writing subtest (8i3–835).

Cross-language equivalence.   The same set of 6 pictures is used in all language versions of the BAT. Their sequence is arranged from left to right, right to left, or top to bottom, depending on the cultural habits associated with each language. The dress of the girl has been adapted to suit specific religious and cultural exigencies.

MENTAL ARITHMETIC
15 items (347–361)

Task.   The patient is presented verbally with mental arithmetic problems. He must listen to the problem and then say the correct answer.

Stimuli.   The stimuli in this section are 4 addition problems, 4 subtraction problems, 4 multiplication problems, and 3 division problems. All the problems require arithmetic operations on two numbers. In all cases, the numbers to be operated on and the results of the operations are integers with a value of less than 100.

The problems vary in difficulty for each type of arithmetic operation. For example, in the addition problems, the first problem involves the addition of single digit numbers with a single-digit result, the second requires the addition of single-digit numbers with a double-digit result, the third requires the addition of double-digit numbers without carrying, and finally the fourth requires the addition of double-digit numbers where carrying is required.

In this subtest, the types of arithmetic operations are presented in random order, but within each type the first problems are the easiest and the last are the most difficult.

```
MENTAL ARITHMETIC

I am going to ask you some arithmetic questions.  Try to give me the correct
answer as quickly as you can.

347.  How much is FIVE plus FOUR?        NINE         +  -  0  (347)

348.               SEVEN minus TWO?       FIVE         +  -  0  (348)

349.               TWO times THREE?       SIX          +  -  0  (349)

350.               NINE divided by THREE? THREE        +  -  0  (350)

351.               SIX plus SEVEN?        THIRTEEN     +  -  0  (351)

352.               TWENTY-ONE minus NINE? TWELVE       +  -  0  (352)

353.               FOUR times SIX?        TWENTY-FOUR  +  -  0  (353)

354.               TWELVE divided by FOUR? THREE       +  -  0  (354)

355.               FOURTEEN plus TWENTY-TWO? THIRTY-SIX +  -  0  (355)

356.               FORTY-SIX minus TWENTY-ONE? TWENTY-FIVE + - 0 (356)

357.               THREE times TWELVE?    THIRTY-SIX   +  -  0  (357)

358.               SIXTY divided by FOUR? FIFTEEN      +  -  0  (358)

359.               SEVENTEEN plus EIGHTEEN? THIRTY-FIVE +  -  0  (359)

360.               THIRTY-TWO minus FIFTEEN? SEVENTEEN +  -  0  (360)

361.               THREE times FOURTEEN?  FORTY-TWO    +  -  0  (361)
```

Contribution.   This subtest measures the patient's ability to perform an essentially nonlinguistic cognitive operation. The problems are, however, presented to the patient in the language being tested and the patient must give the response in that language.

Therefore the test offers the possibility for controlled cross-linguistic comparison of the patient's language input and output performance in such an automatized task.

Design considerations.   In many languages, there exist alternative means of expressing arithmetic problems verbally. These alternative expressions are often correlated with socioeconomic status, and may change from generation to generation. In each language test therefore, the verbal expression of the problem is given on the test sheet and is simply read to the patient by the examiner. This offers a control for differences between examiners.

Cross-reference.   None.

Cross-language equivalence.   The same stimuli are used in each language.

120

TEXT LISTENING COMPREHENSION
5 items (362–366)

Task. The patient is told a story of approximately 40 words (3–4 sentences) in length. At the end of the story the patient is asked 5 comprehension questions.

Stimuli. The patient is exposed to two kinds of stimuli in this subtest. He is first exposed to the story and then to a set of questions about that story.

In each language test the structure of the story presented to the patient is the same, although the lexical items and hence the actual story differs in each language (see language equivalence below).

There are 5 questions that the patient is asked about the story. All of the questions are information questions (WH questions in English). All questions re independently related to the story. That is, no correct answer depends on the correct answer to another question.

Contribution. The text listening comprehension subtest offers a multifaceted view of the patient's ability to comprehend and produce connected discourse.

Design considerations. The major design problem in this section was to find a task that would allow for the objective measurement of text listening comprehen-

```
LISTENING COMPREHENSION


You are going to hear a little story.  Listen carefully to the story and then I
will ask you some questions about it.  Ready?


On Saturday afternoon the boy and his sister were at the
beach.  The boy bought an ice-cream for his sister because
it was very hot.  But before she could eat it, the girl
dropped the ice-cream on the sand.


362.  Where were the boy and his sister?            +   -   0   (362)

363.  What day of the week was it?                  +   -   0   (363)

364.  What did the boy buy her?                     +   -   0   (364)

365.  Why did the boy buy an ice-cream for his sister?  +  -  0  (365)

366.  Why didn't the girl eat the ice-cream?        +   -   0   (366)
```

sion. An additional problem was maintaining the comparability across languages and avoiding the practice effect that would result from hearing the same story in two languages. This was, to a large extent, achieved by the selection of a paragraph with a preset information load and structure and by varying the lexical items across languages (see language equivalence below).

Cross-reference.   This subtest is explicitly cross-referenced to the text reading comprehension subtest (387–392). That subtest differs from the text listening comprehension subtest in that the patient reads the story rather than listens to it. In both cases, the questions and answers are verbal. Comparison of the patient's performance on these two subtests should yield a good measure of the differences between text reading comprehension and text listening comprehension abilities for each language tested.

Cross-language equivalence.   A different story is used in each language. That is, because the patient will be given the test in another language the next day, paragraphs cannot be simple translation equivalents, for then it would not be possible to ascertain whether the patient is able to answer the questions because she or he has understood the story in one of the languages or because she or he remembers it from the previous day, when it was told in the other language. However, in every language the following features of the stories are the same: the number of referential noun phrases and predicates; the number of thematic roles; and the structure of the story. Only the lexical items and hence the actual stories differ. The information load is the same, though the information content is different. Each story is constructed on the following pattern:

At some time (day, month, season, or time of day) someone and someone (or some animal) are somewhere. One person does something because of some reason. Something happens which prevents something from being realized. The questions that follow are uniform across languages: (362) Where? (363) When? (364) What? (365) Why? (366) Why not? The number of items understood in one language can then be compared with the number understood in the other.

READING WORDS ALOUD
10 items (367–376)

Task.   The patient is presented visually with a word and is asked to read it aloud.

Stimuli.   The stimuli in this subtest are words that correspond to the foil pictures of the verbal auditory discrimination subtest (48–65). For all languages the words are picturable nouns or action verbs.

```
READING WORDS ALOUD


You will get some words to read.  Read each word aloud.  Ready?


367.  CAT                  read correctly?  +  -  0   (367)

368.  MALL                 read correctly?  +  -  0   (368)

369.  CHICK                read correctly?  +  -  0   (369)

370.  BEES                 read correctly?  +  -  0   (370)

371.  FAN                  read correctly?  +  -  0   (371)

372.  STAMP                read correctly?  +  -  0   (372)

373.  BEAR                 read correctly?  +  -  0   (373)

374.  SHIP                 read correctly?  +  -  0   (374)

375.  TRAIN                read correctly?  +  -  0   (375)

376.  DICE                 read correctly?  +  -  0   (376)
```

Contribution.   The subtest measures the patient's ability to read aloud single words.

Design considerations.   The words are minimal pairs of the auditory discrimination stimuli.

Cross-reference.   The subtest is cross-referenced to the other subtests that use stimuli and picture foils of the verbal auditory discrimination subtest (VAD). The words in this section are also used in the word reading comprehension subtest (408–417).

Ten of the stimuli from the VAD subtest are used in the repetition subtest and the judgment subtest (193–252).

Five words that represent VAD picture foils are used as stimuli in the copying (393–397) and dictation subtest (398–402), which integrates many of the skills tested in the other, less complex, subtests.

Cross-language equivalence.   The words in this section are selected from the foil pictures of the verbal auditory discrimination test. They therefore vary across languages. Their equivalence is due to the fact that, in each language, they are minimal pairs of the VAD stimuli for that language. Language equivalence, however, is limited by the ways in which writing systems vary. The complexity of spelling/sound correspondences differs across languages as do the perceptual demands of different writing systems.

READING SENTENCES ALOUD
10 items (377–386)

Task.   The patient is presented visually with a sentence and is asked to read it aloud.

Stimuli.   The stimuli in this subtest are sentences taken from the syntactic comprehension subtest (66–152). The stimuli were selected so that the patient is required to read a representative sample of the sentence types used in the syntactic comprehension section.

```
READING SENTENCES ALOUD


Now I would like you to do the same with the following sentences.  Read the
sentences aloud.  Ready?


377.  The boy holds the girl.           read correctly?   +   -   0   (377)

378.  He washes himself.                read correctly?   +   -   0   (378)

379.  The dog is bitten by the cat.     read correctly?   +   -   0   (379)

380.  It's the truck that pulls the car. read correctly?  +   -   0   (380)

381.  The boy does not push the girl.   read correctly?   +   -   0   (381)

382.  The truck is not pulled by the car. read correctly? +   -   0   (382)

383.  It's the dog that the cat bites.  read correctly?   +   -   0   (383)

384.  He holds her.                     read correctly?   +   -   0   (384)

385.  The girl is pushed by the boy.    read correctly?   +   -   0   (385)

386.  The woman is not kissed by the man. read correctly? +   -   0   (386)
```

Contribution.   The subtest measures the patient's ability to read a variety of sentence types aloud. The patient's baseline ability to read words is determined in the preceding word reading subtest (see cross-reference below). This more difficult subtest allows the comparison of the patient's ability across sentence types.

Design considerations.   Sentences from the Syntactic Comprehension section are selected in accordance with their structural type (S, A, NS1, NS2S, Sn, NS1n) and the place on the page of the picture that represents them in accordance with the answer key for items 418–427.

Cross-reference.   The patient's performance on this subtest should be compared to his or her performance on the test of reading words aloud (367–376).

The subtest is cross-referenced to the other subtests which use stimuli from the syntactic comprehension subtest (66–152). These include the grammaticality judgment subtest (173–182), the sentence repetition section (253–259), and the sentence reading comprehension subtest (418–427).

All these subtests are relevant in interpreting the patient's score on this subtest. Comparison with the sentence reading comprehension subtest, in particular, offers a means of isolating the production component in this subtest.

Cross-language equivalence.   The same type of sentence is used in all languages for each item, as follows: 377 (S), 378 (A), 379 (NS1), 380 (NS2S), 381 (Sn), 382 (NS1n), 383 (NS2O), 384 (P), 385 (NS1), 386 (NS1n). For each language, the sentences are selected among the stimuli used in the syntactic comprehension section of that language.

TEXT READING COMPREHENSION
6 items (387–392)

Task.   The patient reads a story of approximately 40 words in length. At the end of the story the patient is asked 6 comprehension questions.

Stimuli,   The patient is exposed to two kinds of stimuli in this subtest. She or he is first exposed to the story and then to a set of questions about that story.

In each language test the structure of the story presented to the patient is the same, although the lexical items and hence the actual story differ (see cross-language equivalence below). The structure of the story is as follows:

Someone went somewhere with another person or an animal. The person got something. Upon his or her return somewhere, she or he went to some specific place and exchanged whatever she or he had acquired for something else.

There are 6 questions that the patient is asked about the story. All of the questions are information questions (WH questions in English). All questions are independently related to the story. That is, no correct answer depends on the correct answer to another question. The 6 questions ask the following:

(387) With whom did X go?
(388) Where did X go?
(389) What did X do?
(390) Where did they bring whatever they got?
(391) What did they do with whatever they got?
(392) What did they receive in exchange?

```
READING COMPREHENSION


I will give you a little paragraph to read.  Read the paragraph
one time quietly to yourself.  Tell me when you have read it and I
will ask you some questions.  Ready?


The man left to go fishing by the river with his son.
They caught some trout.  When they returned to the
village, they went to the market and exchanged their
trout for a chicken.


387.  Who did the man go with?              +   -   0   (387)
388.  Where did the man and his son go?      +   -   0   (388)
389.  What did they do at the river?         +   -   0   (389)
390.  Where did they bring their trout?      +   -   0   (390)
391.  What did they do with the trout?       +   -   0   (391)
392.  What did they receive for the trout?   +   -   0   (392)
```

Contribution.   The text reading comprehension subtest tests both the patient's ability to understand written text and to verbally produce connected discourse. The number of items understood in one language can be compared with the number understood in another.

Design considerations.   The design problems in this section are identical to those of the text listening comprehension subtest (362–366). The problem was to find a task that would allow for the objective measurement of text listening comprehension. An additional problem was maintaining the comparability across languages and avoiding the practice effect that would result from reading the same story in two languages. This was, to a large extent, achieved by selecting a paragraph with a preset information load and structure and by varying the lexical items across languages (see language equivalence below).

Cross-reference.   This subtest is explicitly cross-referenced to the text listening comprehension subtest (362–366). That subtest differs from the text reading comprehension subtest in that the patient hears the story rather than reads it. In both cases, the questions and answers are verbal. Comparison of the patient's performance on these two subtests should yield a good measure of the differences

126

between his or her text reading comprehension and text listening comprehension abilities for each language tested.

Cross-language equivalence.   In this subtest, language equivalence is attained by keeping story structure and information load constant and by varying only information content across languages.

The number of thematic roles, referential noun phrases, and predicates are the same across languages. The number of words used in each story differs slightly across languages, as determined by the surface structure of each language.

The questions used are equivalent across languages, differing in information content but not in structure or information load.

COPYING
5 items (393–397)

Task.   The subject is visually presented with a word and is asked to write that word. The stimulus remains in view while the patient writes it.

Stimuli.   The stimuli are 5 words which correspond to picture foils from the verbal auditory discrimination subtest (i.e., minimal pairs of the VAD stimuli). The words used in this subtest are not used as stimuli in any other subtest of the BAT.

```
COPYING


I will give you a list of words to look at.  Here is a pencil.
Please copy each word on this sheet.


393.  THICK                    +   -   0   (393)

394.  CHIP                     +   -   0   (394)

395.  CRANE                    +   -   0   (395)

396.  PLATE                    +   -   0   (396)

397.  KNEES                    +   -   0   (397)
```

Contribution.   This subtest allows for the investigation of the patient's graphemic ability. The copying subtest is relatively simple in that it requires little linguistic processing. It is particularly useful, therefore, in establishing the patient's baseline ability in grapheme-to-grapheme conversion.

The patient's performance on this task serves to constrain the possible interpretations of a patient's text writing ability and his or her ability to write to dictation (see cross-reference below).

Design considerations.   The words are minimal pairs of VAD stimuli selected from among the foil pictures of that section.

Cross-reference.   The copying subtest is cross-referenced to the other subtests that use stimuli and minimal pairs of the stimuli of the verbal auditory discrimination subtest (48–65). These include the repetition subtest and judgment subtests (193–252), the reading words aloud subtest, and the word reading comprehension subtest (408–417).

Five minimal pairs of the VAD stimuli are also used as stimuli in the dictation subtest (398–402). Data for the copying subtest is most important in the interpretation of the patient's dictation performance.

Cross-language equivalence.   The words in this section, being selected from among the foil pictures of the Verbal Auditory Discrimination test, vary across languages. They are equivalent because, in each language, they are minimal pairs of the VAD stimuli in that language.

WORD DICTATION
5 items (398–402)

Task.   The patient hears a word and must then write it down.

Stimuli.   The stimuli are 5 words which correspond to minimal pairs of stimuli from the verbal auditory discrimination subtest. The words used in this subtest are not used as stimuli in any other subtest of the BAT.

Contribution.   Dictation is a complex task that requires both receptive and productive ability. In languages like English in which there exist many alternative means of converting sounds to graphemes, the dictation task is also a measure of auditory word recognition.

Design considerations.   The words are minimal pairs of VAD stimuli selected from among the foil pictures of that section.

Cross-reference.   The word dictation subtest is cross-referenced to the other subtests that use stimuli and picture foils of the verbal auditory discrimination subtest (48–65). These include the repetition subtest and judgment subtests

```
WORD DICTATION

Now I will read you some words.  You write them down.  Ready?

398.  FAT                              +    -    0   (398)

399.  GLUE                             +    -    0   (399)

400.  STICK                            +    -    0   (400)

401.  CHIN                             +    -    0   (401)

402.  TRAMP                            +    -    0   (402)
```

(193–252), the reading words aloud subtest (367–376), the copying subtest (393–397) and the word reading comprehension subtest (408–417).

The patient's performance on this subtest is particularly important in the interpretation of his or her performance in the more difficult sentence dictation subtest (403–407).

Cross-language equivalence.   As in the copying and reading of words sections, words for dictation are minimal pairs of Auditory Verbal Discrimination test stimuli in each language.

SENTENCE DICTATION
5 items (403–407)

```
SENTENCE DICTATION

Now you will hear some sentences.  Please write them down.  Ready?

403.  She pulls her.                    +    -    0   (403)

404.  He sprays himself.                +    -    0   (404)

405.  The man is kissed by the dog.     +    -    0   (405)

406.  The boy does not push the car.    +    -    0   (406)

407.  It's the girl that kisses her mother.  +    -    0   (407)
```

Task.   The patient hears a sentence and must then write it down.

Stimuli.   The stimuli used in this section are sentences that do not appear as stimuli in any other subtest of the BAT. They are constructed, however, on the pattern of stimuli from the syntactic comprehension subtest (66–152). Each sentence in the subtest represents a different sentence type.

Contribution.   The sentence dictation subtest, which requires sentence comprehension and production, presents a complex task to the patient. A posttest analysis of the patient's responses can yield highly detailed information about his or her abilities in this area.

Design considerations.   For this subtest, stimuli had to be created that were equivalent to the stimuli used in the syntactic comprehension subtest (66–152) but not identical to them. All the sentence types and lexical items used in this subtest are taken from the syntactic comprehension subtest. They are given to the patient in a new combination, so that each sentence is presented for the first time, but all the elements of the sentences are taken from the earlier subtest.

Cross-reference.   Because the sentence dictation task is dependent on the patient's graphemic output ability, the patient's performance must be interpreted in comparison with his or her performance on the copying subtest (393–397) and the word dictation subtest (398–402).

   This subtest is also cross-referenced to the other subtests of the BAT which use sentences from the syntactic comprehension subtest (66–152). These include the grammaticality judgment subtest (173–182), the sentence repetition subtest (253–259), the reading sentences aloud subtest (377–386), and the sentence reading comprehension subtest (418–427).

Cross-language equivalence.   Sentences that did not appear in the Syntactic Comprehension section but with the same words and type of sentence are used (P, A, NS1, Sn, NS2S).

WORD READING COMPREHENSION
10 items (408–417)

Task.   The patient is presented visually with a word. The patient has before him or her an array of 4 pictures. One of the 4 pictures represents the stimulus word and the other 3 pictures represent very similar sounding words. The patient is required to touch the correct picture.

Stimuli.   The stimuli used in this section are 10 words that correspond to picture foils (and hence minimal pairs of stimuli) from the verbal auditory discrimination subtest (48–65).

READING COMPREHENSION FOR WORDS

You will get some words to read. Touch the picture that shows the
meaning of the word. If the meaning of the word is not shown in
any of the pictures, then touch the "X." Ready?

408.	CAT	picture:	X	1	2	3	4	0	(408)
409.	MALL	picture:	X	1	2	3	4	0	(409)
410.	CHICK	picture:	X	1	2	3	4	0	(410)
411.	BEES	picture:	X	1	2	3	4	0	(411)
412.	FAN	picture:	X	1	2	3	4	0	(412)
413.	STAMP	picture:	X	1	2	3	4	0	(413)
414.	BEAR	picture:	X	1	2	3	4	0	(414)
415.	SHIP	picture:	X	1	2	3	4	0	(415)
416.	TRAIN	picture:	X	1	2	3	4	0	(416)
417.	DICE	picture:	X	1	2	3	4	0	(417)

408: cat

409: mall

Contribution.   The subtest provides a measure of the patient's visual word comprehension ability. It is therefore the visual counterpart of the verbal auditory discrimination subtest (48–65).

Design considerations.   The words are minimal pairs of VAD stimuli selected from among the foil pictures of that section and the place on the page of the

410: chick   411: bees

412: fan   413: stamp

414: bear 415: ship

416: train 417: dice

picture that represents them in accordance with the answer key for items 408–412.

Cross-reference. The stimuli used in this subtest are the same as those used in the reading words aloud subtest (367–376).

The subtest is also cross-referenced to the other subtests that use stimuli and minimal pairs of the stimuli of the verbal auditory discrimination subtest (48–

65). These include the repetition subtest, the judgment subtests (193–252), and the dictation subtest (398–402).

Cross-language equivalence.   In each language, words for this section are minimal pairs of the Auditory Verbal Discrimination test stimuli in that language. They are the same words as the ones read aloud earlier (367–376).

SENTENCE READING COMPREHENSION
10 items (418–427)

```
READING COMPREHENSION FOR SENTENCES

Now I would like you to do the same with the following sentences.  Read the
sentences silently and then touch the picture that shows the meaning of the
sentence.

418.  The boy holds the girl.          picture:  1   2   3   4   0   (418)

419.  He washes himself.               picture:  1   2   3   4   0   (419)

420.  The dog is bitten by the cat.    picture:  1   2   3   4   0   (420)

421.  It's the truck that pulls the car.  picture:  1   2   3   4   0   (421)

422.  The boy does not push the girl.  picture:  1   2   3   4   0   (422)

423.  The truck is not pulled by the car.  picture:  1   2   3   4   0   (423)

424.  It's the dog that the cat bites.  picture:  1   2   3   4   0   (424)

425.  He holds her.                    picture:  1   2   3   4   0   (425)

426.  The girl is pushed by the boy.   picture:  1   2   3   4   0   (426)

427.  The woman is not kissed by the man.  picture:  1   2   3   4   0   (427)
```

Task.   The patient has before him or her an array of 4 pictures. She or he is shown a sentence and must touch the picture that best represents the meaning of that sentence.

Stimuli.   The sentences used in this subtest are selected from the syntactic comprehension subtest (66–152). They are the same sentences that are used as stimuli in the sentence reading aloud subtest (377–386).

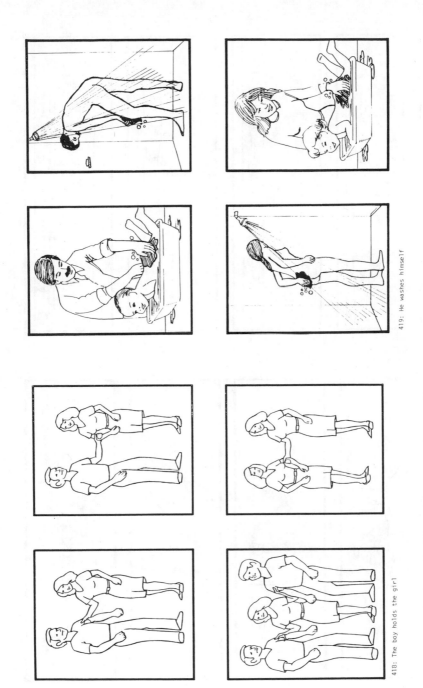

419: He washes himself

418: The boy holds the girl

135

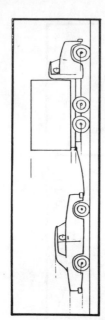
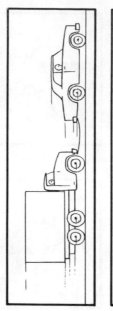
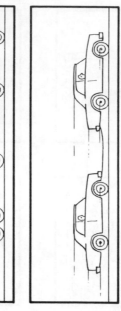
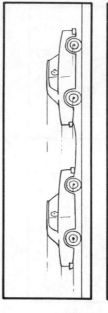
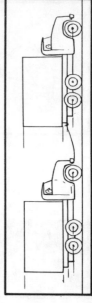

421: It's the truck that pulls the car

420: The dog is bitten by the cat

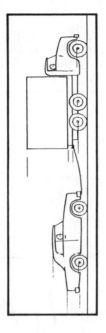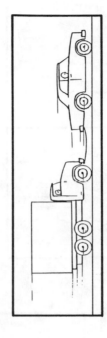

423: The truck is not pulled by the car

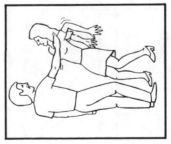

422: The boy does not push the girl

137

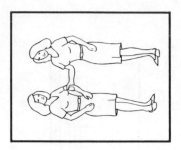

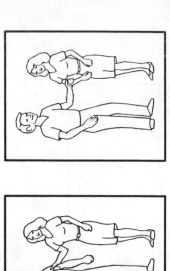

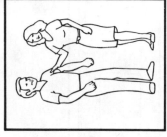
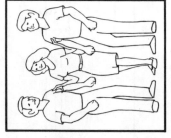

425: He holds her

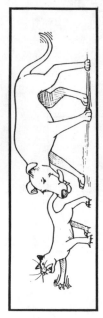

424: It's the dog that the cat bites

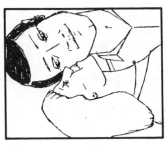

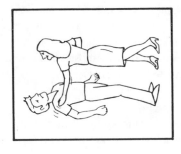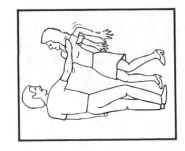

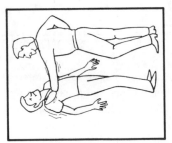

The stimulus sentences in this subtest all represent picturable actions. For each stimulus, one picture represents the meaning of the sentence, another represents the reverse situation, and the other two represent situations that are highly related to the meaning of the sentence (i.e., they share actors and/or actions), except for the negative sentences, which are represented by only two pictures, one that represents the meaning of the sentence, the other the reverse.

Contribution.   The subtest provides a measure of the patient's visual sentence comprehension ability. It is therefore the visual counterpart of the syntactic comprehension subtest (66–152).

Design considerations.   Sentences from the Syntactic Comprehension section are selected in accordance with their structural type (S, A, NS1, NS2S, Sn, NS1n) and the place on the page of the picture that represents them in accordance with the answer key.

Cross-reference.   The subtest is cross-referenced to all other subtests that use stimuli from the syntactic comprehension subtest (66–152). It is intended that comparison of the syntactic comprehension subtest and this subtest will reveal any modality-specific effects in the patient's sentence comprehension.

Careful comparison of the results of this subtest with those of the reading sentences aloud subtest (377–386) may serve to isolate specific components of the patient's reading difficulty.

Cross-language equivalence.   The sentences in this section are the same as those read aloud earlier (377–386) and hence are of the same structural type in all languages for each item.

SPONTANEOUS WRITING

In this section, which is administered at the end of Part B, the patient is given a pen and some paper and is asked to write for 5 minutes on the topic of his or her choice. The test administrator may suggest a topic to the patient. These topics can be the patient's illness, life in the hospital, family, work, etc.

There are no BAT items associated with the spontaneous writing task. The investigation of the patient's writing ability is carried out as part of the posttest analysis (813–835).

The posttest analysis involves a detailed quantitative study of the writing sample. The results of this analysis may be compared to the results of the posttest analysis of the patient's spontaneous speech production. Such comparisons, however, must take into account normal differences that exist between speaking and writing. These differences are most evident in the areas of sentence grammaticality and language register.

POSTTEST ANALYSIS
322 items (514–835)

Spontaneous speech, descriptive speech, reading aloud, copying, dictation, and spontaneous writing are further analyzed after the test has been administered.

Contribution.   The Posttest Analysis measures the patient's expressive ability. It provides data towards the assessment of the patient's fluency, the grammatical complexity and accuracy of his or her utterances, the richness of his or her vocabulary, the coherence and semantic acceptability of his or her discourse, as well as a measure of paraphasias, neologisms, and perseverations in his or her speech.

Design considerations.   Questions are objective and require quantitative answers. They are based on the tape-recorded portion of the patient's performance on Part B. The only two unavoidably subjective questions (535, 561) refer to the presence of a foreign accent in the patient's speech. These are to be rated by a minimum of three independent judges.

The questions have been selected in such a way that the quantitative data culled from the analysis may serve to derive a qualitative assessment toward the diagnosis of aphasic symptoms.

Cross-reference.   The score on the Spontaneous Speech subtest (514–539) should be compared to the score on the Descriptive Speech (540–565) and Spontaneous Writing subtests (813–835).

Cross-language equivalence.   The same analysis is performed in all languages. At present, the Posttest Analysis is available only in English and is presented in Chapter 4 (pp. 191–201). The word count for the type/token ratio has been adapted in such a way that it is equivalent across languages irrespective of language type (i.e., agglutinative languages as well as languages lacking articles and copulas—see Chap. 2, pp. 28–30). All other measures are identical and equally revealing.

PART C

Because each language may be spoken in combination with any of several others, this part of the test, which examines bilingual skills in a specific pair of languages, is available separately. At the time the present volume goes to press, the following combinations are available. Pairs of languages are listed alphabetically, each pair being listed only once, with the language that is prior in alphabetical order appearing first.

Arabic/French	English/Kannada
Armenian (Eastern)/Farsi	English/Latvian
Armenian (Eastern)/Russian	English/Mandarin
Armenian (Western)/English	English/Norwegian
Armenian (Western)/French	English/Oriya
Azari/Farsi	English/Polish
Azari/Russian	English/Portuguese
Basque/Spanish	English/Russian
Bulgarian/English	English/Spanish
Bulgarian/French	English/Swedish
Cantonese/English/Tamil	English/Tamil
Catalan/Spanish	English/Turkish
Czech/English	English/Urdu
Czech/Swedish	Finnish/Swedish
Danish/English	French/German
Dutch/English	French/Greek
Ducth/French	French/Hungarian
Dutch/German	French/Italian
English/Estonian	French/Malagasy
English/Farsi	French/Mandarin
English/French	French/Polish
English/German	French/Russian
English/Greek	French/Spanish
English/Gujarati	French/Vietnamese
English/Hebrew	Galician/Spanish
English/Hindi	German/Italian
English/Hungarian	German/Swedish
English/Icelandic	Greek/Turkish
English/Italian	Japanese/Mandarin
English/Japanese	Russian/Swedish

Part C comprises four tasks in each direction—recognition of translation equivalents, production of translation equivalents, translation of sentences, grammaticality judgments. Within each task, the patient's performance in one language may be compared with his or her performance in the other.

WORD RECOGNITION
10 items (428–432; 433–437)

Task. The patient is presented both visually and orally with words in one language and must identify their counterparts in a list of translation equivalents. The task is then repeated with the stimulus and list languages reversed.

語認知／WORD RECOGNITION

＊＊＊下記の単語を患者に１つずつ見せて，それを同時に，声に出して読みあげて下さい。

患者は10個の単語の表の中から，英語のそれに相当する単語を言うか，もしくは示さなければなりません。患者が選んだものに対応する番号を丸で囲んで下さい。

もし10秒たっても患者が何の反応も示さない場合は"０"を丸で囲んで，次の刺激語に進んで下さい。もし患者が単語が読めない場合は，選択が可能になるまで10個の単語を読んであげて下さい。もしその表を続けて３回読んだあとでも選ぶことができない場合は"０"を丸で囲んで次の刺激語に進んで下さい。

＊＊＊ここから読みはじめて下さい。

これから私は，あなたに日本語の単語を見せます。あなたは，この表の中のどの単語が英語のそれに相当するか私に言って下さい。

428. 木	1．apple	0	1	2	3	4	5	6	7	8	9	10	(428)
429. 雪	2．snow	0	1	2	3	4	5	6	7	8	9	10	(429)
430. 窓	3．lightning	0	1	2	3	4	5	6	7	8	9	10	(430)
431. 金づち	4．hammer	0	1	2	3	4	5	6	7	8	9	10	(431)
432. さかな	5．door	0	1	2	3	4	5	6	7	8	9	10	(432)
	6．fish												
	7．window												
	8．pliers												
	9．tree												
	10．sheep												

＊＊＊ Start reading here.

Now I am going to show you a word in English and you are going to tell me which of the words in the list means the same thing in Japanese. Ready?

433. milk	1．椅子	0	1	2	3	4	5	6	7	8	9	10	(433)
434. horse	2．牛乳	0	1	2	3	4	5	6	7	8	9	10	(434)
435. shirt	3．ワイシャツ	0	1	2	3	4	5	6	7	8	9	10	(435)
436. flower	4．テーブル	0	1	2	3	4	5	6	7	8	9	10	(436)
437. armchair	5．花	0	1	2	3	4	5	6	7	8	9	10	(437)
	6．水												
	7．ネクタイ												
	8．馬												
	9．葉												
	10．ろば												

Stimuli. The stimuli are 5 concrete nouns in one language to be matched with their translation equivalents pseudorandomly distributed within a list of 10 concrete nouns in the other language. They are printed on a separate page in 3mm × 3mm lower-case letters (or the equivalent in nonalphabetic scripts). The language of the first set of stimuli (428–432) becomes that of the list and vice versa in a second set (433–437) of different stimuli and choices, printed on a different page.

Contribution. The word recognition test is a test of the patient's ability to recognize translation equivalents in both directions. This section is the easiest test of cross-language ability. A patient who does not obtain a satisfactory score on this test displays a very low level of translation ability.

Design considerations. The words used as stimuli and as choices are common concrete nouns. The pseudorandom distribution of correct responses is different in the first (428–432) and second list (433–437).

Cross-reference. The patient's performance on the recognition of translation equivalents may be compared with his or her performance on the production of translation equivalents (438–442; 448–452). Though the words used in both sections are not identical, they are common concrete nouns in each.

Cross-language equivalence. In all languages, the same words (that is to say, their closest equivalent in each language) are used as stimuli and choices.

TRANSLATION OF WORDS
20 items (438–457)

Task. The patient is given a word orally and is required to provide its translation in the other language.

Stimuli. The stimuli are 5 common concrete nouns and 5 abstract nouns in each language.

Contribution. The word translation test is a test of the patient's ability to produce on command translation equivalents in both directions. It allows one to compare the patient's ability to translate from L_A to L_B and from L_B to L_A.

Design considerations. The words used as stimuli are, in each language, 5 common concrete nouns and 5 abstract nouns assumed to be part of every speaker's active vocabulary.

Cross-reference. The patient's performance on the word translation test may be compared with his or her performance on the recognition of translation equivalents test (428–437) and the sentence translation test (458–481).

Cross-language equivalence. The same stimulus words (i.e., their closest equivalent in each language) are used in all languages.

*** لغات زیر را یکی یکی و باصدای بلند برای بیمار بخوانید . اگر جواب داده شده لغتی است که در داخل پرانتز قرار دارد ، دور " + " دایره بکشید ، اگر لغت داده شده با لغت داخل پرانتز فرق دارد ولی قابل قبول است ، دور " ۱ " دایره بکشید ، اگر ترجمه اشتباه است دور " ـ " دایره بکشید . اگر در عرض ۵ ثانیه بیمار جوابی ندهد ، دور " ۰ " دایره کشیده و به لغت بعدی بروید .

*** در اینجا شروع به خواندن بکنید .

من یک لغت فارسی به شما میدهم و شما ترجمهٔ انگلیسی آن را به من بدهید . حاضرید ؟

(۴۳۸) +	۱	—	۰	(spoon)	۴۳۸ . قاشق
(۴۳۹) +	۱	—	۰	(door)	۴۳۹ . در
(۴۴۰) +	۱	—	۰	(ear)	۴۴۰ . گوش
(۴۴۱) +	۱	—	۰	(bread)	۴۴۱ . نان
(۴۴۲) +	۱	—	۰	(suitcase)	۴۴۲ . جمدان
(۴۴۳) +	۱	—	۰	(love)	۴۴۳ . عشق
(۴۴۴) +	۱	—	۰	(beauty)	۴۴۴ . زیبائی
(۴۴۵) +	۱	—	۰	(freedom)	۴۴۵ . آزادی
(۴۴۶) +	۱	—	۰	(short)	۴۴۶ . کوتاه
(۴۴۷) +	۱	—	۰	(happy)	۴۴۷ . خوشحال

*** Read aloud the following words, one at a time. If the patient's answer
is the word in parentheses, circle "+"; if the word is different but
acceptable, circle "1"; if the translation is incorrect, circle "-".
If the patient has given no anwwer after 5 seconds, circle "." and
read the next word.

(۴۴۸) +	۱	—	۰	(چنگال)	fork ۴۴۸ .
(۴۴۹) +	۱	—	۰	(دیوار)	wall ۴۴۹ .
(۴۵۰) +	۱	—	۰	(گردن)	neck ۴۵۰ .
(۴۵۱) +	۱	—	۰	(کره)	butter ۴۵۱ .
(۴۵۲) +	۱	—	۰	(کلاه)	hat ۴۵۲ .
(۴۵۳) +	۱	—	۰	(نفرت)	hatred ۴۵۳ .
(۴۵۴) +	۱	—	۰	(خوشی)	joy ۴۵۴ .
(۴۵۵) +	۱	—	۰	(ترس)	fear ۴۵۵ .
(۴۵۶) +	۱	—	۰	(دیوانگی)	madness ۴۵۶ .
(۴۵۷) +	۱	—	۰	(دانش)	knowledge ۴۵۷ .

145

TRANSLATION OF SENTENCES
12 items (458–481)

Task.   The patient is required to translate sentences read to him or her.

Stimuli.   There are 6 sentences in each language. The first 2 sentences in each language incorporate one reversible contrastive feature each, the next 2 sentences contain two reversible contrastive features each, the last 2 sentences comprise three reversible contrastive features each and each successive pair of sentences is thus assumed to increase in translation difficulty.

Contribution.   This subtest is an assessment of the patient's ability to translate sentences first in one, then in the other direction. Hence the patient's ability to translate from L_A to L_B (458–469) may be compared with his or her ability to translate from L_B to L_A (470–481). In addition, the translation of sentences may reveal which language is the stronger. All things being equal, one may expect the patient to be less likely to translate literally from his or her weaker to his or her stronger language than the reverse, and in general to be able to translate better into his or her stronger language. This test may also reveal whether there is a correlation between ease of access to a language (for spontaneous speech and other language tasks) and ability to translate into this language.

Design considerations.   This section is designed to compare the patient's relative ability to translate in each direction. It is therefore important that the difficulty of translation from L_B to L_A be equivalent to that from L_A to L_B. Hence, for each pair of languages, 18 reversible contrastive features have been selected. Two of these features are embedded in the first 2 sentences, a different one in each. Four features are incorporated in the next 2 sentences, two different ones in each. Six features are included in the last 2 sentences, three different ones in each. The remaining 6 reversible contrastive features are used in the following subtest (grammaticality judgments).

For every sentence in one language, a sentence incorporating the same contrastive feature is used in the other language. In this way, the sentences to be translated from L_A to L_B are assumed to contain the same number of translation difficulties of the same nature as sentences to be translated from L_B to L_A. For example, an English sentence containing a subordinate clause in the present tense that must be translated by the future in French in paired with a French sentence containing a subordinate clause in the future that must be translated by the present in English.

Cross-reference.   The patient's performance on the translation of sentences may be compared with his or her performance on the grammaticality judgments (482–497; 498–513) and in spontaneous speech.

ΜΕΤΑΦΡΑΣΗ ΦΡΑΣΕΩΝ / TRANSLATION OF SENTENCES

*** Διαβάστε τις φράσεις δυνατά στον ασθενή μέχρι τρεΐς φορές ανάλογα με την επιθυμία του ασθενή και βάλτε σε κύκλο τον αριθμό που αντιστοιχεί με τις φορές που διαβάσατε την φράση. Το σκόρ αντιστοιχεί στον αριθμό των ομάδων λέξεων (όπως φαίνεται στην ενδεικνυόμενη μετάφραση στην παρένθεση) σωστά μεταφρασμένων. Βάλτε σε κύκλο τον αριθμό που αντιστοιχεί στον αριθμό των λέξεων που μεταφράστηκαν σωστά. Μία παράλειψη μετράει σαν λάθος. Αν όλες οι ομάδες λέξεων έχουν ένα ή παραπάνω λάθη ή αν ο ασθενής δεν λέει τίποτε μετά από τρεΐς συνεχείς επαναλήψεις των φράσεων βάλτε σε κύκλο '0'. Αν η μετάφραση του ασθενή δεν είναι ίδια με αυτή στην παρένθεση αλλά παρ'όλα αυτά είναι σωστή βάλτε σε κύκλο '+'.

*** Αρχίστε να διαβάζετε δυνατά εδώ.

Θα σας δώσω μερικές προτάσεις στα Ελληνικά. Εσείς θα μου δώσετε την μετάφραση στα Αγγλικά. Έτοιμος;

458. Μπήκε στο δωμάτιο τρέχοντας.   Διαβάστηκε   1 2 3 φορές (458)

    (He entered the room running.)   Ομάδες χωρίς λάθη 0 1 2 3 (459)

460. Πουλάει το ψωμί 90 δραχμές το κιλό.   Διαβάστηκε   1 2 3 φορές (460)

    (He sells bread at 90 cents a kilo.)   Ομάδες χωρίς λάθη 0 1 2 3 (461)

462. Μου αρέσει να ταξιδεύω με το τρένο το βράδυ.   Διαβάστηκε   1 2 3 φορές (462)

    (I like travelling by train at night.)   Ομάδες χωρίς λάθη 0 1 2 3 (463)

464. Θα διορθώσω το ποδήλατό μου στις 10 Μαρτίου.   Διαβάστηκε   1 2 3 φορές (464)

    (I will have my bicycle repaired on the 10th of March.) Ομάδες χωρίς λάθη 0 1 2 3 (465)

466. Ο Γιάννης σταμάτησε να καπνίζει εδώ και δυό χρόνια. Διαβάστηκε   1 2 3 φορές (466)

    (John stopped smoking two years ago.)   Ομάδες χωρίς λάθη 0 1 2 3 (467)

468. Όταν θα έρθεις το καλοκαίρι θα πάμε στη θάλασσα. Διαβάστηκε   1 2 3 φορές (468)

    (When you come in the summer we will go to the Ομάδες χωρίς λάθη 0 1 2 3 (469)
    beach).

*** Read the sentences aloud to the patient up to three times in accordance with the patient's request for repetition and circle the digit corresponding to the number of the times that the text was read. The score corresponds to the number of word groups (as indicated in the suggested translation in parentheses) correctly translated. Circle the number corresponding to the number of word groups containing no error. An omission also counts as an error. If all groups contain one or more errors, or if the patient says nothing after three consecutive repetitions circle '0'. If the patient's translation is not the one suggested but nevertheless acceptable, circle '1'.

*** Begin reading aloud here.

    Now I am going to give you some sentences in English. You will translate them into Greek. Are you ready?

470. The teacher entered the class smiling.   Text read   1 2 3 times (470)

    (Η δασκάλα μπήκε στην τάξη χαμογελώντας.)   Groups without error 0 1 2 3 (471)

472. I bought the fruit for 10 cents a pound.   Text read   1 2 3 times (472)

    (Αγόρασα τα φρούτα 10 δραχμές το μισό κιλό.) Groups without error 0 1 2 3 (473)

474. At the beginning of our trip we travelled by boat. Text read   1 2 3 times (474)

    (Στην αρχή του ταξιδιού μας ταξιδέψαμε με πλοίο)Groups without error 0 1 2 2 (475)

476. I will have my hair cut on the 3rd of May. Text read   1 2 3 times (476)

    (Θα κόψω τα μαλλιά μου στις τρεΐς Μαΐου.)   Groups without error 0 1 2 3 (477)

478. Helen started jogging three days ago.   Text read   1 2 3 times (478)

    (Η Ελένη άρχισε να τρέχει εδώ και τρεΐς μέρες.) Groups without error 0 1 2 3 (479)

480. When you visit us in the winter we will go to the
    mountain.   Text read   1 2 3 times (480)

    (Όταν μας επισκεφθείς το χειμώνα θα πάμε στο Groups without error 0 1 2 3 (481)
    βουνό.)

Cross-language equivalence.   Of necessity, the structural distance between any two individual languages varies from pair to pair. The same distance does not exist between Basque and Spanish as between Catalan and Spanish, for instance. But because each sentence in one language has a corresponding sentence that incorporates the same contrastive feature(s) in the other language of a pair, each pair of languages is comparable to every other pair. The relation of Basque to Spanish (and the reverse) is equivalent to the relation of Catalan to Spanish (and the reverse), even though the actual contrastive features between Basque and Spanish and between Catalan and Spanish widely differ.

For some pairs of languages (e.g., English/Japanese) it is difficult to find sentences that differ in only one contrastive feature. Word order, for one, will always differ. Conversely, for other pairs of languages (e.g., Catalan/Spanish) it is difficult to find sentences whose structure differ at all, let alone by two or three features.

English locative prepositions and Japanese locative markers have but minimally overlapping contexts of use. Hence it will be difficult to find reversible contrasts. By comparison, such contrasts are much easier to find between English and French. For instance, the English preposition "at" usually translates as "*à*" in French, and preposition "in" generally translates as "*dans.*" Problems occur in cases when "in" is translated as "à" (as in "I live *in* Montreal": "Je demeure *à* Montréal"). In Japanese, however, there is no such "general" correspondence between a given English locative preposition and what would be its Japanese translation equivalent (locative suffix), and hence there is no possibility of systematic overgeneralization in both directions, and therefore no real reversibility.

The above are inherent properties of English/Japanese, Catalan/Spanish or English/French bilingualism. However, the same differences hold between English and Japanese as between Japanese and English, and between Catalan and Spanish as between Spanish and Catalan. Therefore, as long as the same contrasts are used in sentences to be translated from English to Japanese as in those to be translated from Japanese to English, the difficulty of translating from English to Japanese or from Japanese to English should be equal. The same is true for the recognition of sentences rendered ungrammatical by a surface feature of the other language, as long as the same feature is used in reverse. The same also holds true between Catalan and Spanish, English and French, and between any pair of languages, but only insofar as the contrastive features employed are truly reversible.

In order to consider a contrastive feature as reversible, it must be equally possible to translate the phrase involved word for word in each direction. Thus, consider two languages in which one possesses articles and the other does not: While it would be easy for a speaker of the language containing no articles to erroneously drop an article in the language in which they are obligatory, the reverse would not be possible, since there is no article in that language for the speaker to add inappropriately. On the other hand, if two languages both have definite and indefinite articles, but in some contexts L_A uses a definite article and L_B an indefinite article, then the contrastive feature is reversible because it is equally possible to erroneously use a definite article in L_B as to erroneously use an indefinite article in L_A in that context (e.g., "Ten cents *a* pound"/"Dix sous *la* livre").

The purpose of these tests is to determine whether a given language is recovered better than another, whether translation is easier for the patient in one direction than in the other, and whether interference errors are recognized in one language as readily as in the other. As long as English differs from Japanese in the same way that Japanese differs from English on any given task, the patient's performance may be expected to be equal for each language and for each direction in the translation task, provided that the two languages are of equal strength. Better performance in one language than in the other can therefore safely be interpreted as a sign of easier access to that language.

If the complexity of the tasks from L_A to L_B is the same as from L_B to L_A, and the complexity from L_C to L_D is the same as from L_D to L_C, then the ratio of L_A/L_B (the dominance pattern) may be compared to the ratio of L_C/L_D. In other words, as long as the linguistic complexity between members of any given pair of languages is equivalent, the dominance pattern is comparable between pairs, even though the structural distance between members of different pairs may widely vary. Hence the dominance pattern between English and Japanese may be validly compared to that between Catalan and Spanish.

GRAMMATICALITY JUDGMENTS
16 items (482–497; 498–513)

Task.   The patient is presented orally with a sentence and must report whether it is correct.

Stimuli.   There are 2 correct and 6 incorrect sentences in each language. Each incorrect sentence incorporates one interference error (i.e., one element of L_A grammar in an L_B sentence and the corresponding L_B element in an L_A sentence).

Design considerations.   For each incorrect sentence in one language, the same error in reverse is incorporated in a corresponding sentence in the other language. The order of correct and incorrect sentences is different in each language. The third and sixth sentences in the first language (486, 492) and the second and fourth sentences in the second language (500, 504) are correct.

Contribution.   The patient demonstrates whether she or he is capable of recognizing as incorrect a sentence in which a phrase is patterned after the other

***यहाँ से पढ़ना शुरू करें ।

मैं आपको कुछ हिन्दी के वाक्य दूँगी । आप मुझे बतायें कि वे सही हिन्दी के वाक्य हैं कि नहीं ।

अगर नहीं हैं तो आप उन्हें ठीक कर दें । मिसाल के तौर पर, अगर मैं कहूँ " कल रात को उसने

अपने बाप की बारे में सोचा" आप कहेंगे "गलत" और ठीक ऐसे करेंगे : " कल रात को उसने

अपने बाप के बारे में सोचा । " तैयार हैं ?

482. बाप बेटी को सुला रही है ।	क्या माना ?	+	–	0	(482)
	वाक्य ठीक किया ?	+	–	0	(483)
484. मैं मेरे हाथ धो रहा हूँ ।	क्या माना ?	+	–	0	(484)
	वाक्य ठीक किया ?	+	–	0	(485)
486. अब बारिश रुक गई है ।	क्या माना ?	+	–	0	(486)
	वाक्य ठीक किया ?	+	–	0	(487)
488. गिलास मुझसे टूट गया ।	क्या माना ?	+	–	0	(488)
	वाक्य ठीक किया ?	+	–	0	(489)
490. जब तक मां घर पहुँचती है, मैं उधर रहूँगा ।	क्या माना ?	+	–	0	(490)
	वाक्य ठीक किया ?	+	–	0	(491)
492. वह यहाँ चार सालों से रह रहा है ।	क्या माना ?	+	–	0	(492)
	वाक्य ठीक किया ?	+	–	0	(493)
494. लड़की बहुत लंबा है ।	क्या माना ?	+	–	0	(494)
	वाक्य ठीक किया ?	+	–	0	(495)
496. मैं दिल्ली से बंबई जायेगा ।	क्या माना ?	+	–	0	(496)
	वाक्य ठीक किया ?	+	–	0	(497)

***In this section the patient must indicate whether a sentence which is read to him/her
is a correct English sentence or not. If the patient judges the sentence to be ungra-
matical, he/she is asked to make it right. For the patient's judgment, circle "+" if
the patient considers the sentence to be correct, irrespective of whether the patient
is right or wrong, "-" if the patient considers the sentence to be incorrect, and "0"
if the patient gives no answer. Then score the corrected sentence as "+" if acceptable,
"-" if unacceptable, and "o" if the patient declares he/she is unable to make it right,
or has wrongly declared an incorrect sentence as "correct", in which case there is no
point in trying to make it right, or if the patient says nothing. When a correct sentence (500, 504) is declared incorrect, and subsequently made wrong, score "-" for
both judgment and correction. If the patient makes some change to the sentence which
does not make it incorrect, then score "+" for correction.

***Start reading aloud here.

     I am going to give you some sentences in English. Tell me if they are correct
English sentences. I will ask you to make them right. For example, if I say: "he
is thinking to his mother" you say "incorrect" and you correct it", "he is thinking
of his mother". Ready?

498. Where you are going?	Judgment	+	–	0	(498)
	Corrected Sentence	+	–	0	(499)
500. It has stopped snowing.	Judgment	+	–	0	(500)
	Corrected Sentence	+	–	0	(501)

language. This task may reveal which language is stronger. A patient may be expected to reject more readily an incorrect sentence in his or her strong language that contains a feature of his or her weaker language than the reverse (i.e., a sentence of the weaker language that incorporates a feature of the stronger language).

Cross-reference.   Scores on this section may be compared with those on the noninterference grammaticality judgment section for each language (173–182) to determine whether interference is a significant factor in accepting grammatically incorrect sentences. The patient's performance on the grammaticality judgments (482–497; 498–513) may also be compared with his or her performance on the translation of sentences (458–469; 470–481) and in spontaneous speech.

Cross-language equivalence.   Each incorrect sentence in one language (L$_A$) of a pair is made erroneous by incorporating a feature of the other language (L$_B$). For each such sentence in L$_A$, a sentence in L$_B$ is made incorrect by incorporating the corresponding feature of L$_A$. While the same structural distance does not exist between any pair of languages and any other pair, because of the reversibility of the errors within each pair, the dominance pattern is nevertheless comparable between pairs.

SHORT VERSION

When it is not possible to administer the whole test to a patient, the following sections will constitute the *short version* of the BAT.

Spontaneous speech (514–539)
Pointing (23–32)
Simple and semi-complex commands (33–42)
Verbal auditory discrimination (48–65)
Syntactic comprehension (66–70; 81–96; 121–124; 129–132; 137–144 only)
Synonyms (158–162)
Antonyms 1 (163–167)
Repetition of words (odd numbers only 193–251; 566–573)
Repetition of sentences (253–259; 574–622)
Series (260–262)
Naming (269–288)
Sentence construction (289–313)
Semantic opposites (314–323)
Listening comprehension (362–366)

For literate patients only:
Reading of words (367–376; 623–628)
Reading of sentences (377–386; 629–708)

Reading of paragraph (387–392)
Copying (393–397; 709–743)
Dictation of words (398–402; 744–783)
Dictation of sentences (403–407; 784–812)
Reading comprehension for words (408–417)
Reading comprehension for sentences (418–427)

Though less comprehensive, results obtained with the short version can nevertheless be compared across languages in the same patient. Cross-language patterns can be compared between patients who have been tested with the short version, as well as, to some extent, with patterns based on these items only in patients who have been administered the full test.

For clinical purposes, when the short test reveals deficits in a particular area (e.g., comprehension, lexical access, repetition; phonology, syntax, semantics), all sections of the test covering that aspect of performance (see *Profiles* in Chapter 4, pp. 215–227) may be administered to the patient.

INSTRUCTIONS TO TRANSLATORS

In order to adapt the *Bilingual Aphasia Test* to a new language (L_T), the following instructions are to be carried out. The translator uses the English or any other version as a model and proceeds as indicated below.

The Cross-Language Equivalence sections of the test description in the preceding pages may also help the translator adapt certain features of the test to L_T. All instructions to the test administrator and to the patient are simply to be translated into the most natural possible instructions in the target language (L_T).

A. PART COMMON TO ALL LANGUAGES

History of Bilingualism

Questions 1 to 50 require a straightforward translation into L_T. Make sure that yes/no questions (i.e., those with a "+ − 0" answer key) are phrased in such a way that an answer of "yes" in the target language corresponds to an answer of "yes" in the English version (or in whichever version is used as a model). For instance, questions 28, 34, 40, and 46, "Were there any other languages of instruction at that time?" should not be rendered in L_T as "Were all subjects taught in that language?" Though the same information might be obtained by asking either question, an answer of "yes" could be given in response to the first question, while an answer of "no" could be given in response to the second question. An answer of "yes" or "no" must refer to the same state of affairs in all languages in which this test is translated.

B. TEST OF A SPECIFIC LANGUAGE

English Background (1–17) becomes L_T Background. Questions 1–17 require a straightforward translation except that the name of L_T is to be substituted for the word "English" (or whatever langauge serves as a model). In cases in which L_T—unlike English, French or Spanish—is the official language in only one country (e.g., in Bulgaria or Czechoslovakia), the word "country" in Question 1 is to be replaced by the word meaning "community"; Question 2 should then read, "In what country was that L_T speaking community?

Spontaneous Speech (18–22). Straightforward translation of instructions and of items 18 to 22.

Verbal Comprehension. Straightforward translation of instructions.

Pointing (23–32). Straightforward translation of instructions and of items 23 to 32.

Simple and Semicomplex Commands (33–47). Straightforward translation of instructions and of items 33 to 47.

Verbal Auditory Discrimination (48–65). Straightforward translation of instructions. However, if in L_T the 4 pictures selected for the example which involves pointing to the X contain a bird or anything that could remind one of a bird, then a different concrete word—one that is not represented in the 4 pictures—is used instead.

Sixteen sets of 4 words in L_T that differ only in their initial consonantal sound (such as *man, pan, van,* and *fan* in English) are selected. The easiest way to come up with such minimal pairs is to write down in one column all the possible initial consonantal sounds in L_T (e.g., in English: b, d, f, g, h, d, k, l, m, n, p, r, s, t, v, z, š, č). When 2 or 3 words have been found, one goes down the list to see if a third and/or fourth word can be found. These words must be picturable. Hence, generally they are concrete nouns, action verbs, and occasionally adjectives. If 16 sets of 4 words cannot be constructed by varying a consonant, consonantal clusters may be used as contrasts (e.g., in English: bl, br; dr; fl, fr; gl, gr; kl, kr; pl, pr; sk, sl, sp, st; tr;).

If L_T is such that sets of 4 minimal pairs are rare, and 16 of them cannot be found, then a fourth word that differs in some way other than in the initial consonant (e.g., in addition, in vowel length), or words whose middle consonants differ (e.g., *chateau, chapeau,* in French) may be used to fill in incomplete sets. Such words will not be selected as stimuli in the VAD or in the word reading sections (i.e., they will be used as foils only).

When 16 sets of 4 picturable minimal pairs (or quasi-minimal pairs) have been identified, one word is selected from each set to serve as the stimulus, in such a way that as many of the stimuli as possible start with a different consonantal sound. Then each stimulus thus selected is assigned to items 48, 49, 51, 52, 53, 54, 55, 56, 58, 59, 60, 62, 63, 64, 65, and to the example. The set of minimal pairs considered to be the least good (i.e., the one in which there is the greatest distance between any of the foils and the stimulus, or for which one of the pictures is not compelling) is selected as the example.

Target pictures (i.e., those that correspond to the stimuli) are arranged in such a way that they are in the position indicated in the answer key. The numbers 1, 2, 3, and 4 refer to the position of the pictures on the page (top left, top right, bottom left, and bottom right, respectively). Note that items 50, 57, and 61 do not require minimal pairs but the translation of the word for "duck," "plate," and "rose," respectively. If any of these 3 words is used as a stimulus or as a foil elsewhere in this section, another word of the same category (e.g., "goose" for "duck"; "bowl" for "plate"; and "tulip" for "rose") is used.

Verbal Auditory Discrimination answer key:
Example: 3
   48: 2
   49: 1
   50: X (translation equivalent of "duck" in L_T)
   51: 1
   52: 2
   53: 4
   54: 4
   55: 3
   56: 2
   57: X (translation equivalent of "plate" in L_T)
   58: 3
   59: 1
   60: 2
   61: X (translation equivalent of "rose" in L_T)
   62: 4
   63: 3
   64: 3
   65: 1

Syntactic Comprehension (66–152). Whenever possible, the same pictures (i.e., the same situations) as those used in the English version (languages without arbitrary gender), the French version (languages with arbitrary gender), the Hungarian version (languages with animate/inanimate pronoun distinction), or the Oriya version (languages without marked gender) are to be used. The types of sentences are to be as follows, in the order given, with each sentence corresponding to the picture in the position indicated by the answer key.

66. S (standard, i.e., SVO, NVN in English)   2 (66)
67. S   1 (67)
68. P (animate gendered pronouns in English)   1 (68)
69. P   4 (69)
70. P   3 (70)
71. S   1 (71)
72. S   4 (72)
73. A (inanimate gendered pronouns as in French, or self-   1 (73)
    reference in English)
74. A   2 (74)
75. A   3 (75)
76. A   4 (76)
77. S   1 (77)
78. P   3 (78)
79. P   2 (79)
80. P   1 (80)
81. S   2 (81)
82. S   4 (82)
83. NS1 (nonstandard 1, i.e., passive in English)   2 (83)
84. NS1   4 (84)
85. NS2S (nonstandard 2, i.e., subject topicalized)   4 (85)
86. NS2S   2 (86)
87. NS2O (nonstandard 2, object topicalized)   2 (87)
88. NS2O   4 (88)
89. S   1 (89)
90. S   3 (90)
91. NS1   3 (91)
92. NS1   1 (92)
93. NS2S   1 (93)
94. NS2S   3 (94)
95. NS2O   1 (95)
96. NS2O   3 (96)
97. S   1 (97)
98. NS1   1 (98)
99. NS1   2 (99)
100. S   2 (100)
101. NS2S   1 (101)
102. NS2O   1 (102)
103. NS2S   2 (103)
104. NS2O   2 (104)
105. S   3 (105)
106. S   2 (106)
107. A   4 (107)
108. A   2 (108)
109. A   3 (109)
110. A   1 (110)
111. Sn   2 (111)

112. Sn	1 (112)
113. NS1n	1 (113)
114. NS1n	2 (114)
115. Sn	1 (115)
116. Sn	2 (116)
117. NS1	1 (117)
118. NS1n	1 (118)
119. NS1n	2 (119)
120. NS1	1 (120)
121. SN	2 (121)
122. NS1n	1 (122)
123. SN	1 (123)
124. NS1n	2 (124)
125. Sn	1 (125)
126. Sn	2 (126)
127. NS1n	2 (127)
128. NS1n	1 (128)
129. NS1n	1 (129)
130. NS1n	2 (130)
131. Sn	2 (131)
132. Sn	1 (132)
133. Sn	2 (133)
134. NS1n	2 (134)
135. Sn	1 (135)
136. NS1n	1 (136)
137. Reversible possessive type 1 ("'s" in English, masculine in French)	1 (137)
138. RP1	1 (138)
139. RP2 (reversible possessive type 2 ("of") in English, feminine in French	2 (139)
140. RP2	2 (140)
141. RP2	1 (141)
142. RP1	2 (142)
143. RP1	2 (143)
144. RP2	2 (144)
145. RP1 (reverse of 127)	2 (145)
146. RP1 (reverse of 138)	2 (146)
147. RP2 (reverse of 139)	1 (147)
148. RP2 (reverse of 140)	1 (148)
149. RP2 (reverse of 141)	2 (149)
150. RP1 (reverse of 142)	1 (150)
151. RP1 (reverse of 143)	1 (151)
152. RP2 (reverse of 144)	1 (152)

Semantic Categories (153–157).   Straightforward translation. However, if a word is not culturally or linguistically acceptable, it may be replaced by an equivalent word within the same category (e.g., "frog" → "toad"; "daisy" →

"buttercup"). The word that does not belong in the group must appear in the position indicated by the answer key.

153: 3
154: 1
155: 3
156: 4
157: 2

Synonyms (158–162). Whenever possible, items are translation equivalents. Words within the same semantic category may be substituted when necessary. In all cases, the target word must correspond to the answer key.

158: 3
159: 4
160: 1
161: 2
162: 2

Antonyms (163–172).   Whenever possible, items are translation equivalents. For items 168 to 172, word class may be systematically substituted when necessary (e.g., verb forms may replace adverbs for languages in which the adjective and adverb have the same form). In all cases, the target word must correspond to the answer key.

163: 2
163: 3
165: 2 Antonyms with high associates to the stimulus as foils.
166: 4
167: 1
168: 1
169: 3 Stimulus: adjective. Choices: its antonym among the noun and adverb
       formed with the same radical.
170: 3
171: 1
172: 1

Grammaticality Judgment (173–182).   Items in this section are sentences from the Syntactic Comprehension section made incorrect by adding, deleting, or substituting a grammatical morpheme (article, preposition, or inflection), or by changing the word order, except items 173, 177, and 181 which are correct sentences from the Syntactic Comprehension section.

Semantic Acceptability (183–192).   All sentences in this section are to be grammatically well formed. Items 184, 187, and 191 are also semantically acceptable sentences. The other sentences are semantically or pragmatically anomalous.

When translation results in a semantically acceptable sentence, a different, anomalous, sentence is substituted.

Repetition of Words and Nonwords (193–252).   The stimuli in this section are 20 real words—10 monosyllabic, 5 bisyllabic, 5 trisyllabic. (Ten of the real words [monosyllabic if possible; if not, a combination of mono- and bi-syllabic] are selected from the *stimuli* used in the verbal auditory discrimination test (48–65). Polysyllabic words are monomorphemic. Nonsense words are formed by taking a real word in the language and changing one consonant to form a phonologically acceptable nonword.

Monosyllabic real words: 193, 195, 197, 201, 207, 211, 213, 215, 217, 221
Bisyllabic real words: 223, 225, 229, 235, 237
Trisyllabic real words: 241, 243, 245, 249, 251
Monosyllabic nonwords: 199, 203, 205, 209, 219
Bisyllabic nonwords: 227, 231, 233, 239, 247

Sentence Repetition (153–159).   Sentences from the Syntactic Comprehension section (66–152) are selected in accordance with the following sentence types:

253. S
254. P
255. NS2S
256. NS2O
257. NS1n
258. P
259. Sn

Series (260–262).   Each item is to be translated, unless no such series exist in L_T, in which case a similarly overlearned sequence of words (e.g., "the seven colors" in Cantonese) is substituted. When the days of the week or the months of the year have no specific names but are given ordinal numbers, a different sequence of words is also used.

Verbal Fluency (263–268).   The instructions are translated. Three consonantal sounds that are productive in L_T are selected. These are not necessarily the same as the ones used in the version that serves as a model. In languages without an alphabet, several syllables (e.g., ka, ke, ki, ko, ku) may be given in the instructions instead of a single consonant.

Naming (269–288).   Whenever possible, the items are translation equivalents. Ten of the stimuli are the words already used in the pointing section (23–32) and/or in the commands (38–47). The 10 new words must be translation equivalents of the model unless an item is culturally inappropriate.

Sentence Construction (289–313).   Whenever possible, the stimulus words are translation equivalents. The order of the words in each item may be changed to ensure that the order of the words in each item does not correspond to the order of the words in the simplest sentence constructed with these words. The word "English" (or L_x) is replaced by the name of L_T in items 290, 295, 300, 305, and 310.

Semantic Opposites (314–323).   Whenever possible, translation equivalents are used. If necessary, words that have a more obvious and common lexical opposite in L_T are substituted.

Derivational Morphology (324–333).   Words of a given grammatical class (e.g., adverbs) are to be derived from morphologically related words of another grammatical class (e.g., adjectives). A derivation that admits of at least two or three different rules is selected. If the derivation in the language of the version that serves as a model is too regular in L_T (e.g., all adverbs are formed by addition of the same suffix to all adjectives), then a different derivation is selected (e.g., adjectives are derived from nouns) provided that there are at least two or three different rules depending on morphophonemic properties of the nouns (e.g., three different affixation rules depending on the final sound—or gender, or other property—of the noun from which the adjective is derived).

Morphological Opposites (334–343).   If, in L_T, all morphological opposites are derived in accordance with a single rule (e.g., the addition of the same prefix to all words), a different derivation is selected (e.g., agentive nouns from verbs). A morphological derivation different from the one selected in the previous section (324–333) is to be used.

Description (344–346).   A straightforward translation is required.

Mental Arithmetic (347–361).   A straightforward translation is required. Mathematical symbols ($+$, $-$, $\times$, $\div$) are not to be used. The type of operation is to be written in full in accordance with the most common way of saying it out loud (e.g., two *times* three, and not 2×3 which could also be read "two multiplied by three").

Listening Comprehension (362–366).   The story in the model version is not to be translated. A story on the following pattern is to be constructed in L_T:
At some time (day, month, season, or time of day) someone and someone (or animal) are somewhere (on the beach, in the forest, in the train, on a lake, etc.). One person does something with a view to achieving some goal for some reason. The goal cannot be reached because of some reason.

The pattern of the model story is to be followed, but the story must be different. The sentence structures and overall paragraph length must be roughly equivalent. The questions that follow the paragraph are adjusted to the story but keep the same pattern: 362: Where? 363: When? 364: What? 365: Why? 366: Why not?

Reading Words Aloud (367–376).   The words in this section are selected from those represented by foil pictures in the Verbal Auditory Discrimination section. They are selected on the basis of the answer key for the Reading Comprehension for Words section (408–417). Hence the words for items 408 to 417 are selected first. The same words are then used in this section.

Reading Sentences Aloud (377–392).   Sentences from the Syntactic Comprehension section (66–136) are selected on the basis of the place on the page occupied by the picture that illustrates them as determined by the answer key for items 418–427. These sentences must also conform to the following types:

377. S   2
378. A   2
379. NS1   3
380. NS2S   1
381. Sn   1
382. NS1n   1
383. NS2O   3
384. P   2
385. NS1   4
386. NS1n   2

Hence the translator is to select sentences of the above types that match pictures in the position indicated. The same sentences will then serve for the Reading Comprehension for Sentences section (418–427).

Reading of Paragraph for Comprehension (387–392).   The story in the version that serves as a model is not to be translated. Instead, a story on the following pattern is to be constructed in L_T:

Someone went somewhere with someone (or animal) to do something (hunt; fish; pick mushrooms, flowers, berries, driftwood; collect seashells, etc.). They did something (caught 2 birds, 5 fish, picked 2 pounds of mushrooms, etc.). Upon their return somewhere (village, city), they went somewhere (market-place, store, friend's house) and exchanged whatever they had (picked, caught) for something else (eggs, a cake, a bottle of wine, etc.).

The sentence structure and overall paragraph length must be roughly equivalent. The questions that follow the paragraph are adjusted to the story but keep the same pattern:

387. With whom did X go?
388. Where did X and Y go?
389. What did X and Y do?
390. Where did they bring what they brought back?
391. What did they do with what they brought back?
392. What did they receive in exchange?

Copying (393–397). The stimuli are 5 words from the Verbal Auditory Discrimination section foils in L_T not yet used (i.e., not used for items 362–366 which are then repeated as items 408–417).

Dictation of Words (398–402). The stimuli are 5 words from the Verbal Auditory Discrimination section foils in L_T not yet used (i.e., not for items 362–366 nor 393–397).

Dictation of Sentences (403–407). The stimuli are sentences that did NOT appear in the L_T Syntactic Comprehension section but that contain words used in that section and are constructed so as to conform to the following types:

403. P
404. A
405. NS1
406. Sn
407. NS2S

Reading Comprehension for Words (408–417). Foils from the L_T Verbal Auditory Discrimination section illustrated by pictures in the following positions:

408: 1
409: 4
410: 1
411. 3
412: 2
412. 2
413: 2
414: 4
415: 1
416: 1
417: 2

The above words, which are minimal pairs of the Visual Auditory Discrimination section (48–65) stimuli in L_T, and have been selected because they are illustrated in pictures 1, 4, 1, 3, 2, 2, 4, 1, 1, 2, respectively, must also be used in the Reading Aloud section (367–376).

Reading Sentences for Comprehension (418–427). The sentences in this section are selected from the Syntactic Comprehension section (66–136) in L_T because they are illustrated by pictures in the position indicated below:

418: 2 (S)
419: 2 (A)
420: 3 (NS1)
421: 1 (NS2S)
422: 1 (Sn)
423: 1 (NS1n)
424: 3 (NS2O)
425: 2 (P)
426: 4 (NS1)
427: 2 (NS1n)

These sentences must also conform to the structural type indicated in the Reading Aloud section (367–376) and must also be used in that section. The structural type is indicated above in parentheses as a reminder.

C.   TEST OF A SPECIFIC PAIR OF LANGUAGES

Part C tests a given pair of languages; in this case, the target language (L_T) and any other language (L_B). The title and headings appear in both languages concerned. The instructions appear alternately in L_T and L_B) in keeping with the language of the corresponding test items. Instructions relative to items in L_T are to be translated into L_T. Instructions relative to items in L_B appear in L_B. The order of presentation of the languages is as follows:

Word recognition.   Items 428–432 in L_T (their translation equivalent to be recognized among 10 choices in L_B). Items 433–437 in L_B (their translation equivalent to be recognized among 10 choices in L_T).
Word translation.   Items 438–447 in L_T (to be translated into L_B). Items 448–457 in L_B] (to be translated into L_T).
Sentence translation.   Items 458–469 in L_T (to be translated into L_B). Items 470–481 in L_B (to be translated into L_T).
Grammaticality judgments.   Items 482–497 in L_T and items 498–513 in L_B.

Word recognition (428–432).   Five concrete words in L_T to be recognized (in translation) within a list of 10 concrete words in L_B. (433–437) Five concrete words in L_B to be recognized (in translation) within a list of 10 concrete words in L_T. The stimulus words in L_T are to be the closest possible translation equivalent of the words in the English-French version or any other bilingual version that serves as a model. For the English-French version, see p. 167. The stimulus words in L_B are those already found in any version that contains L_B as one language of a pair. If no version including L_B is yet published, the closest possible translation equivalent of these items in any version is to be used. The stimuli and their translation are arranged as follows:

428. 9	1.	433. 2	1. 437
429. 2	2. 429	434. 8	2. 433
430. 7	3.	435. 3	3. 435
431. 4	4. 431	436. 5	4.
432. 6	5.	437. 1	5. 436
	6. 432		6.
	7. 430		7.
	8.		8. 434
	9. 428		9.
	10.		10.

Word Translation. In this section also, whenever possible, the stimulus words in L_T are to be the closest possible translation equivalent of the words in the English-French version or any other version that serves as a model. The stimuli are arranged as follows:

438–442. 5 concrete words of L_T to be translated into L_B.
443–447. 5 abstract words of L_T to be translated into L_B.
448–452. 5 concrete words of L_B to be translated into L_T.
453–457. 5 abstract words of L_B to be translated into L_T.

Reversible Contrastive Features. Before adapting the next two sections, the translator selects 20 reversible contrastive features between L_T and L_B. A contrastive feature is an element in L_T which differs from its usual translation equivalent in L_B. It is expected to lead to an interference error when translated word for word. In order to be reversible this interference must be equally possible in both directions. That is, it must be equally possible to use the L_T element in L_B and the L_B element in L_T, with the same ungrammatical result. A feature will not be reversible when there are two possible ways to realize it in one language but only one way in the other (see page 149). When a form F in L_T can be translated by either G or H in L_B, it is possible to erroneously translate F by H in a given context, but the reverse error is not possible because both G and H in L_B will correctly translate as F in L_T.

For example, a certain tense is to be used in a certain context in L_T and a different tense is to be used in the same context in L_B (e.g., present after *when* in English and future in French when the main clause is in the future), or a preposition is used in L_T but not in L_B in the same context, or a different preposition is used (e.g., in English: to ask *for* something; in French: demander Ø quelque chose). In order to avoid purely idiomatic (or lexicalized) expressions, at least two different contexts must be found in which a given contrast obtains (e.g., in English: *in* the evening—in French: O le soir; in English: *in* the morning—in French: O le matin). One context is then used in L_T, the other in L_B, so that the equivalent sentences are not translations of each other, though structurally identical.

Other common contrasts are difference in word order (e.g., adjective before/after the noun; adverb before/after the verb), verb aspect (e.g., perfective in L_T and imperfective in L_B), case (e.g., a dative in L_T and an accusative in L_B), and agreement (e.g., possessive adjective agreeing in gender with the possessor in L_T and with the object possessed in L_B). A preposition in L_T which, in a certain context, is not the usual or *dictionary* translation of the equivalent preposition in L_B (and the reverse) may also be used (e.g., in English: covered *with* - in French: couvert *de;* in English: filled *with* - in French: rempli *de*).

Once 20 reversible contrastive features have been identified, and once it has been ascertained that each feature could be used with at least two sets of different lexical items, sentences are constructed as follows:

Two correct sentences in L_T, each incorporating three of the selected features (466, 469 and their reverse in L_B, 478, 480); 2 correct sentences, each incorporating two features (462, 464 and their reverse, 474, 476), 2 correct sentences incorporating one feature each (458, 460 and their reverse, 470, 472); 6 sentences incorporating one feature each as an interference error, i.e., made ungrammatical by incorporating a surface feature of the other language (482, 484, 488, 490, 494, 496 and their mirror image in L_B, 498, 502, 506, 508, 510, 512); and 2 correct sentences incorporating one contrastive feature each (486, 492 and their reverse, 500, 504).

It is suggested that the translator start with items 466, 468 (and their reverse, 478, 480) because it is more difficult to incorporate three features in the same sentence than to incorporate one or two, and therefore it is better to do so while the largest number of features is available. Then one may proceed to items 462, 464 (and their reverse, 474, 476) which incorporate two features each. The remaining features can then easily be incorporated in the remaining sentences for it requires relatively little effort to construct sentences containing only one feature each. Sentences are to sound as natural (i.e., uncontrived) as possible.

Examples from the English/French version:
Sentences incorporating *one* feature each and their mirror image in the other language:

1a. Marc téléphonera dès qu'il *arrivera*.
French: future → English: present

1b. Melanie will write when she *gets* back.
English: present → French: future

2a. Elle travaille de bonne heure le matin.
French: Ø → English: in

2b. He eats late *in* the evening.
English: in → French: Ø

Sentences incorporating *two* features each:

3a. Louise had her hat cleaned.
had . . . cleaned → *a fait nettoyer*
her (feminine agreement with possessor) → *son* (masculine agreement with object possessed)

3b. Eric a fait réparer sa bicyclette.
a fait réparer → had . . . repaired
sa (feminine agreement with object
possessed) → his (masculine agreement with possessor)

4a. Paul *swam across* the river.
English V → French PP
English preposition → French verb

4b. Marie est entrée dans la chambre en
courant.
French verb → English preposition
French PP → English V

Sentences incorporating *three* features each:

5a. His brother *has been living in* Berlin
for 3 years.
English perfect progressive →
French simple present
English *in* → French *à* (and not
dans)
English *for* → French *depuis* (and
not *pour*)

5b. Mon ami *travaille à* Toronto *depuis*
2 mois.
French simple present → English
perfect progressive
French *à* → English *in* (not *at*)
French *depuis* → English *for* (not
since)

6a. *She was just told* where to go.
English *she* (subject) → French *lui*
(indirect object)
English passive → French active
English *just* → French *venir de* (not
juste)

6b. *On vient de lui* donner une robe.
French active → English passive
French indirect object (*lui*) → En-
glish subject (*she*)
French "*venir de*" → English
"*just*"

Sentences incorporating one feature each as an interference error:

7a. He went to work without to eat
breakfast.
(without + gerund → infinitive)

7b. Elle a passé la soirée sans buvant un
seul verre.
(*sans* + infinitive → gerund)

8a. The soldier asked a glass of water.
(for → Ø)

8b. Le boulanger a attendu pour l'auto-
bus.(Ø → *pour*)

9a. He earns a lot of money in working
hard. (*by* + gerund → *in*)

9b. Elle se désaltère par buvant de l'eau
fraîche. (*en* + gerund → *par*)

The translations of L_T stimulus sentences (458, 460, 462, 464, 466, 468) and
of L_B stimulus sentences (470, 472, 474, 476, 478, 480) are provided in parentheses under each sentence. For scoring purposes, the translation is divided into 3
word groups, indicated by curly brackets. Whenever possible each contrastive
feature contained in a sentence is isolated and forms one of these groups. In
sentences containing less than 3 contrastive features, the sentences are divided
according to phrases, one (458, 460; 470, 472) or two (462, 464; 474, 476) of

them containing a contrastive feature. These word groups are not strictly defina-ble and cannot be characterized formally. They are only a rough indication of the number of errors and hence a first approximation of the relative success on each sentence. It is then possible to check for the source of errors in a more thorough posttest analysis.

Translation of Sentences (458–481).   458–468. Sentences to be translated from L_T to L_B.
470–480. Sentences to be translated from L_B to L_T
Sentences are constructed as follows:

458, 460. L_T sentences differing from L_B by *one* reversible contrastive feature
462, 464. L_T sentences differing from L_B by *two* reversible contrastive features
466, 468. L_T sentences differing from L_B by *three* reversible contrastive features
470, 472. L_B sentences differing from L_T by *one* reversible contrastive feature
474, 476. L_B sentences differing from L_T by *two* reversible contrastive features
478, 480. L_B sentences differing from L_T by *three* reverisble contrastive features

Grammaticality Judgments (482–513).   Sentences 482–496 are in L_T and sen-tences 498–512 are in L_B as follows:

482–484.   Sentences incorporating one interference error
486.   A correct sentence incorporating one contrastive feature
488–490.   Sentences incorporating one interference error
491.   A correct sentence incorporating one contrastive feature
494–496.   Sentences incorporating one interference error

498.   Sentence incorporating one interference error
500.   A correct sentence incorporating one constrastive feature
502.   Sentence incorporating one interference error
504.   A correct sentence containing one contrastive feature
506–512.   Sentences incorporating one interference error

N.B. While words (428–457) can be the same in all languages, sentences are necessarily different due to the difference in surface structure between each given pair of languages (458–512).

English Translation of the L_T Instructions for Part C

English translation of the L_T instructions to the Word Recognition section (428–432).   ***Point out the words to the patient, one at a time and simultaneously read each word aloud. The patient must tell and/or show the word in the list of 10 words which is its equivalent in English (L_B). Circle the number corresponding to the patient's choice. If after 5 seconds the patient has given no response, circle "O" and go on to the next stimulus word. If the patient cannot read, read the 10 choices aloud until the patient has indicated a choice. If, after three consecutive readings of the list, the patient has not indicated a choice, circle "O" and go on to the next stimulus word.

***Start reading here.

I am going to show you a word in French (L_T) and you are going to tell me which of the words in the list has the same meaning in English (L_B). Are you ready?

English translation of the L_T instructions to the Word Translation section (438–447). ***Read the following words aloud, one at a time. If the answer is the word in parentheses, circle " − "; if the word is different, but acceptable, circle "1"; if the translation is wrong, circle " − ." If after 5 seconds the patient has given no response, circle "O" and go on to the next word.

***Start reading here.

I am going to say a word in French (L_T) and you will give me its English (L_B) translation. Are you ready?

EXAMEN DE L'APHASIE CHEZ LES BILINGUES
TEST OF APHASIA IN BILINGUALS

PARTIE C / PART C

Bilinguisme anglais-français   English-French bilingualism

RECONNAISSANCE DES MOTS/WORD RECOGNITION

***Montrez les mots un à la fois au patient et même temps lisez-les à haute voix. Le patient doit dire et/ou montrer le mot dans la liste de 10 mots qui est son équivalent en anglais. Encerclez le nombre correspondant au choix du patient. Si après 10 secondes le patient n'a donné aucune réponse, encerclez le "O" et passez au mot stimulus suivant. Si le patient est incapable de lire, lisez-lui les 10 choix jusqu'à ce qu'il ait formulé un choix. Si, après 3 lectures consécutives de la liste, le patient n'a pas indiqué de choix, encerclez le "O" et passez au mot stimulus suivant.

***Commencez à lire ici.
Je vais vous montrer un mot en français et vous allez me dire lequel des mots dans cette liste veut dire la même chose en anglais. Vous êtes prêt?

428. arbre	1. apple	0	1	2	3	4	5	6	7	8	9	10	(428)
429. neige	2. snow	0	1	2	3	4	5	6	7	8	9	10	(429)
430. fenêtre	3. lightning	0	1	2	3	4	5	6	7	8	9	10	(430)
431. marteau	4. hammer	0	1	2	3	4	5	6	7	8	9	10	(431)
432. poisson	5. door	0	1	2	3	4	5	6	7	8	9	10	(432)
	6. fish												
	7. window												
	8. pliers												
	9. tree												
	10. sheep												

***Start reading here.

Now I am going to show you a word in English and you are going to tell me which of the words in the list means the same thing in French. Ready?

433. milk	1. fauteuil	0	1	2	3	4	5	6	7	8	9	10	(433)
434. horse	2. lait	0	1	2	3	4	5	6	7	8	9	10	(434)
435. shirt	3. chemise	0	1	2	3	4	5	6	7	8	9	10	(435)
436. flower	4. table	0	1	2	3	4	5	6	7	8	9	10	(436)
437. armchair	5. fleur	0	1	2	3	4	5	6	7	8	9	10	(437)
	6. eau												
	7. cravate												
	8. cheval												
	9. feuille												
	10. âne												

TRADUCTION DE MOTS/TRANSLATION OF WORDS

***Lisez les mots suivants à haute voix, un à la fois. Si la réponse est le mot entre parenthèses, encerclez le signe "+," si le mot est différent mais acceptable, encerclez le chiffre "1," si la traduction est fausse, encerclez le signe "−." Si au bout de 5 secondes le patient n'a rien répondu, encerclez le "0" et passez au mot suivant.

***Commencez à lire ici.

Je vais vous dire un mot en français et vous allez me donner sa traduction en anglais. Vous êtes prêt?

438. couteau	(knife) + 1 − 0	(438)
439. porte	(door) + 1 − 0	(439)
440. oreille	(ear) + 1 − 0	(440)
441. sable	(sand) + 1 − 0	(441)

442.	valise	(suitcase)	+ 1 − 0	(442)
443.	amour	(love)	+ 1 − 0	(443)
444.	laideur	(ugliness)	+ 1 − 0	(444)
445.	courage	(courage)	+ 1 − 0	(445)
446.	tristesse	(sadness)	+ 1 − 0	(446)
447.	raison	(reason)	+ 1 − 0	(447)

***Read aloud the following words, one at a time. If the patient's answer is the word in parentheses, circle "+"; if the word is different but acceptable, circle "1"; if the translation is incorrect, circle "−." If the patient has given no answer after 5 seconds, circle "0" and read the next word.

***Begin reading aloud here.

I am going to say a word in English and you will give me its French translation. Are you ready?

448.	razor	(rasoir)	+ 1 − 0	(448)
449.	wall	(mur)	+ 1 − 0	(449)
450.	neck	(cou)	+ 1 − 0	(450)
451.	butter	(beurre)	+ 1 − 0	(451)
452.	hat	(chapeau)	+ 1 − 0	(452)
453.	hatred	(haine)	+ 1 − 0	(453)
454.	joy	(joie)	+ 1 − 0	(454)
455.	fright	(peur, effroi)	+ 1 − 0	(455)
456.	madness	(folie)	+ 1 − 0	(456)
457.	beauty	(beauté)	+ 1 − 0	(457)

TRADUCTION DE PHRASES/TRANSLATION OF SENTENCES

***Présentez les phrases à traduire à haute voix. Jusqu'à concurrence de trois fois, répétez la phrase autant de fois que le patient le demandera et encerclez le nombre de fois que la phrase aura été lue. Le score correspond au nombre de groupes de mots tels qu'indiqués dans la traduction suggérée entre parenthèses correctement traduits. Encerclez le chiffre qui correspond au nombre de groupes sans erreur; une omission compte également comme une erreur. Si tous les groupes contiennent au moins une erreur, ou si le patient ne dit rien après trois répétitions successives, encerclez le "0." Si la traduction du patient est autre que celle entre parenthèses mais acceptable, encerclez le "+."
Le score d'une phrase identique à la traduction entre parenthèses sera égal au nombre de groupes dans la phrase.

***Commencez à lire à haute voix ici.

Je vais vous donner des phrases en français. Vous m'en donnerez la traduction en anglais. Vous êtes prêt?

458. Marc téléphonera dès qu'il arrivera	texte lu	1 2 3 fois	(458)
(Mark will phone as soon as he arrives)	groupes sans erreur	+ 0 1 2 3	(459)
460. Elle travaille de bonne heure le matin	texte lu	1 2 3 fois	(460)
(She works early in the morning)	groupes sans erreur	+ 0 1 2 3	(461)
462. Marie est entrée dans la chambre en courant	texte lu	1 2 3 fois	(462)
(Mary ran into the room)	groupes sans erreur	+ 0 1 2 3	(463)
464. Eric a fait réparer sa bicyclette	texte lu	1 2 3 fois	(464)
(Eric had his bicycle repaired)	groupes sans erreur	+ 0 1 2 3	(465)
466. Mon ami travaille à Toronto depuis deux mois	texte lu	1 2 3 fois	(466)
(My friend has been working in Toronto for two months)	groupes sans erreur	+ 0 1 2 3	(467)
468. On vient de lui donner une robe	texte lu	1 2 3 fois	(468)
(She was just given a dress)	groupes sans erreur	+ 0 1 2 3	(469)

***Read the sentences aloud to the patient up to three times in accordance with the patient's request for repetition and circle the digit corresponding to the number of times that the text was read. The score corresponds to the number of word groups (as indicated in the suggested translation in parentheses) correctly translated. Circle the number corresponding to the number of word groups containing no error. An omission also counts as an error. If all groups contain one or more errors, or if the patient says nothing, after three consecutive repetitions, circle "0." If the patient's translation is not the one suggested but nevertheless acceptable, circle "+."

***Begin reading aloud here

Now I am going to give you some sentences in English. You will translate them into French. Are you ready?

470. Melanie will write when   text read   1 2 3 times   (470)
     she comes back
     (Mélanie écrira quand elle   groups without error   + 0 1 2 3   (471)
     reviendra)

472. He eats late in the evening   text read   1 2 3 times   (472)
     (Il mange tard le soir)   groups without error   + 0 1 2 3   (473)

474. Paul swam across the river   text read   1 2 3 times   (474)
     (Paul a traversé la rivière à groups without error   + 0 1 2 3   (475)
     la nage)

476. Louise had her hat cleaned   text read   1 2 3 times   (476)
     (Louise a fait nettoyer son   groups without error   + 0 1 2 3   (477)
     chapeau)

478. His brother has been living   text read   1 2 3 times   (478)
     in Berlin for three years
     (Son frère demeure à   groups without error   + 0 1 2 3   (479)
     Berlin depuis trois ans)

480. She was just told where to   text read   1 2 3 times   (480)
     go
     (on vient de lui dire où   groups without error   + 0 1 2 3   (481)
     aller)

JUGEMENTS DE GRAMMATICALITE
GRAMMATICALITY JUDGMENTS

***Dans cette section, le patient doit indiquer si une phrase qu'on lui dit est correcte ou non. Si le patient juge que la phrase n'est pas grammaticale, on lui demande de la corriger et ainsi de la rendre acceptable. Pour le jugement du patient, encerclez le signe ''+'' si le patient déclare que la phrase est correcte, ''−'' s'il la considère incorrecte, indépendamment du fait que son jugement soit effectivement juste ou erroné, et ''0'' s'il ne donne pas de réponse. Ensuite, encerclez le signe ''+'' si la phrase corrigée est acceptable, ''−'' si elle est inacceptable, ''0'' si le patient se déclare incapable de la rectifier, s'il a incorrectement déclaré la phrase comme étant correcte, auquel cas il n'y a pas lieu de la rectifier, ou si le patient ne dit rien. Lorsqu'une phrase correcte (486, 492) est jugée incorrecte par le patient, et ensuite rendue incorrecte par le patient dans sa tentative de correction, encerclez le signe ''−'' aux deux rubriques. Si le patient la change sans la rendre incorrecte, encerclez le signe ''+'' pour la correction.

***Commencez à lire à haute voix ici.

Je vais vous donner des phrases en français. Vous me direz si ces phrases sont correctes ou non. Si elles ne le sont pas, je vous demanderai de les corriger. Par exemple, si je dis "la nuit dernière il a pensé de son père" vous dites: "incorrect" et vous corrigez: "il a pensé *à* son père." Vous êtes prêt?

482. Le facteur a attendu pour	jugement	+ − 0	(482)
l'autobus	phrase corrigée	+ − 0	(483)
484. Il se désaltère par buvant de l'eau	jugement	+ − 0	(484)
fraîche	phrase corrigée	+ − 0	(485)
486. La statue est couverte de fleurs	jugement	+ − 0	(486)
	phrase corrigée	+ − 0	(487)
488. L'étudiant a emprunté un livre de	jugement	+ − 0	(488)
son ami	phrase corrigée	+ − 0	(489)
490. Elle a passé la soirée sans buvant	jugement	+ − 0	(490)
un seul verre	phrase corrigée	+ − 0	(491)
492. Georges va finir par casser son	jugement	+ − 0	(492)
verre	phrase corrigée	+ − 0	(493)
494. Il a neigé pendant les premiers	jugement	+ − 0	(494)
trois mois de son séjour	phrase corrigée	+ − 0	(495)
496. Frédéric arrivera de Madrid sur le	jugement	+ − 0	(496)
6 avril	phrase corrigé	+ − 0	(497)

***In this section the patient must indicate whether a sentence which is read to him/her is a correct English sentence or not. If the patient judges the sentence to be ungrammatical, she or he is asked to make it right. For the patient's judgment, circle "+" if the patient considers the sentence to be correct, irrespective of whether the patient is right or wrong, "−" if the patient considers the sentence to be incorrect, and "0" if the patient gives no answer. Then score the corrected sentence as "+" if acceptable, "−" if unacceptable, and "0" if the patient declares she or he is unable to make it right, or has wrongly declared an incorrect sentence as "correct," in which case there is no point in trying to make it right, or if the patient says nothing. When a correct sentence (500, 504) is declared incorrect, and subsequently made wrong, score "−" for both judgment and correction. If the patient makes some changes to the sentence which does not make it incorrect, then score "+" for correction.

***Start reading aloud here.

I am going to give you some sentences in English. Tell me if they are correct English sentences. If they are not, I will ask you to make them right. For example, if I say: "he is thinking to his mother" you say: "incorrect" and you correct it: "he is thinking *of* his mother." Ready?

498. The soldier asked a glass of water
judgment   +   −   0   (498)
corrected sentence   +   −   0   (499)

500. I can't help thinking he made a
mistake
judgment   +   −   0   (500)
corrected sentence   +   −   0   (501)

502. He earns a lot of money in working hard
judgment   +   −   0   (502)
corrected sentence   +   −   0   (503)

504. How far is London from here?
judgment   +   −   0   (504)
corrected sentence   +   −   0   (505)

506. He stole an apple to the farmer
judgment   +   −   0   (506)
corrected sentence   +   −   0   (507)

508. She went to work without to eat
breakfast
judgment   +   −   0   (508)
corrected sentence   +   −   0   (509)

510. They went swimming on the two
last days of summer
judgment   +   −   0   (510)
corrected sentence   +   −   0   (511)

512. Jack will go to Paris the 19th of
October
judgment   +   −   0   (512)
corrected sentence   +   −   0   (513)

4 Implementation, Scoring Procedures, and Interpretation

Most aphasia tests are too long and fatiguing to the patient and examiner.

—Kertesz (1979, p. 33)

IMPLEMENTATION

General instructions

An accepting and reassuring attitude is to be maintained throughout by the test administrator, whatever the patient's responses. In all questions and instructions to the patient, the gender of pronouns is to be adapted to the context (e.g., if the answer to question A18, "Did anyone else take care of you as a child?" is a man, question A19 is read: "What was *his* native language?"; if the answer is a woman, question A19 is read: "What was *her* native language?"). Similarly, when addressing a patient in a language with gendered nouns and adjective agreement, the test administrator is to use the masculine or feminine form in accordance with the sex of the patient. In languages where more than one form of address exists (formal, informal, and/or more than one degree of formality) the form appropriate to the cultural context will be used (e.g., *tu/vous* in French, *gij/U* in Dutch, or *tun/tuk* in Armenian, depending on age of patient and/or local custom).

No clues to the answers are to be given to the patient. The examiner is to refrain from looking at the correct picture or object in sections where such are displayed. All instructions to the patient are to be read clearly, exactly as given.

Inasmuch as possible, the patient's dialect should be used. Words of the patient's dialect may be substituted for test items whenever appropriate and feasible.

Additional explanations may be given when it is obvious that the patient has difficulties understanding *the nature* of the task, but not once the actual testing has begun. If such additional explanations or repetitions are given, except where specified, the score is recorded as ''0.'' Notes may be taken by the examiner with respect to type of facilitation provided and results subsequently obtained. These may prove useful for clinical assessment within the context of one hospital unit, but will not be considered for research purposes (i.e., for comparison across patients from different research centers around the world).

Any associated deficit disclosed by previous neuropsychological assessment will be reported, and tasks drawing on affected skills will not be performed (e.g., visual agnosia will exempt the patient from tasks requiring pictures and object recognition; apraxia, from pointing, etc.). When a patient is not literate, reading and writing exercises are omitted.

Language of test administration

Part A (History of bilingualism) is administered in the language of the hospital or in the language best spoken by the patient. Information may also be obtained from relatives, friends, or colleagues. Part B is administered in each of the patient's languages, and Part C for each pair of languages spoken by the patient.

Part B is administered by a native speaker of the language. Native speakers of each language of the relevant pair are present for Part C. Each examiner reads the instructions in his or her native language. The patient translates for the apparent benefit of the other examiner. Grammaticality judgment sentences (482–513) are read by the native speaker of the language of the item (i.e., the speaker of L_e reads the instructions in L_e and L_e items 482–497, whereas the speaker of L_f reads the instructions in L_f and L_f items 498–513).

Parts A, B, and C are administered on separate occasions. Part B is to be administered in each of the patient's languages at the same time of day on successive days. If the patient tires easily or is nonfluent and takes a long time to go through each item, Part B (test of each specific language) may be divided into two or three sessions on the same day, as long as the test for each language is divided in the same manner and each portion is administered at the same time of day in both or all languages. Part C is administered after both languages of a pair have been tested.

Materials

The following objects must be available before the testing begins: a button, a glove, a pair of scissors, an envelope, a ring (not a wedding band but a ring with a crown or setting such as a stone, a pearl, or some other ornament that gives it a ''front''), a clothes brush, a drinking glass, a booklet of matches, a door key, a wrist watch, a pencil, a fork, three pieces of paper of increasing sizes, a blue, a yellow, and a red pencil, three coins of different sizes (the value of which increases with the size of the coin), three sticks of increasing lengths, three books, a pair of eye-glasses, a cup, a neck-tie, a spoon, a playing card, a thermometer, a cigarette, a feather, a candle, and a toothbrush.

In addition to the *Bilingual Aphasia Test* booklet for each appropriate language, a book of visual stimuli for each language is needed, containing the pictures for the verbal auditory discrimination section (48–65), syntactic comprehension (66–152), description (344–346), reading of words (408–417), and sentences (418–427) for comprehension, as well as the written stimuli for reading aloud words (367–376) and sentences (377–386), for copying (393–397), and for comprehension of words (408–417) and sentences (418–427).

The test may be administered by hand, by portable computer, or by microcomputer. If by hand or portable computer, it can be administered at bedside. If by microcomputer, the patient is to be taken to the room where the computer is installed. If the test is administered by hand, the examiner circles the appropriate responses (+, −, 0, 1, 2, 3, 4, 5, 6, 7, 8, 9, X) or enters the required information (number or language 3-letter code); if by computer, the examiner presses the corresponding keys. In either case, all of the patient's verbal productions are audiotaped. Manual scores may later easily be entered into a computer. The advantage of scoring directly by computer is that it automatically gives reaction times for every item tested. The portable computer program also automatically starts and stops the cassette tape-recorder at the appropriate junctures. It also saves a step in the compilation of data for research purposes.

Performance on spontaneous (514–539) and descriptive (540–565) speech as well as on reading of words (566–571) and sentences (572–651) is subsequently further analyzed from the tape.

Tasks

Language Background (1–17).   As for the previous questions of Part A, information relating to questions 1 to 17 may be obtained from relatives if the patient is unable to supply the required details. A "0" score is entered when the information is altogether unavailable.

Spontaneous Speech (18–22).   "Spontaneous speech" refers to the patient's open ended, unconstrained quasi-monologue, with no directives from the examiner other than an initial question such as "Tell me about your accident." If the patient stops before the 5 minutes are up, the examiner may prompt him or her with a short question but should try to keep interventions to a minimum. The more the examiner has to prompt the patient, the longer the recording has to be so as to ensure a 5-minute sample from the patient, once the examiner's interventions have been deducted.

Questions 18–22 are a subjective assessment of (18) quantity, (19) fluency, (20) pronunciation, (21) grammar, and (22) vocabulary. This assessment can be useful in gaining a quick clinical impression when administered by an experienced person. To these indications, additional remarks on any aspect of the patient's performance not covered by the standardized questions may be recorded in the space provided at the end of the test. They may be valuable for diagnostic and/or prognostic purposes but will not be used in intercenter research where only strictly objective quantified data can be compared.

Pointing (23–32).   The objects are placed in front of the patient so that she or he is able to touch each item, arranged in the following way from left to right: a button, glove, scissors, envelope, ring, brush, glass, matches, key, watch. If the word must be repeated, the examiner may record that the item was correctly touched after x number of repetitions, but enters the score "−." If the patient points successively at more than one object, the examiner scores only the first item that the patient *touches*. All commands should be read slowly and clearly with normal intonation.

Simple and Semi-Complex Commands (33–42).   So that she or he can easily manipulate them, the following objects are placed in front of the patient, arranged in the following way from left to right: a ring (as described above in *Materials*), a booklet of matches, a drinking glass, a pencil, and a fork.

Patients may be told that the simple commands (33–37) are not cumulative, i.e., that they may open their eyes before the next command, "Open your mouth," is performed (so that patients do not remain with closed eyes and open mouth when raising hand). For semicomplex commands (38–42) the examiner is to place objects in their original position after each command has been performed.

Complex Commands (43–47).   For each set of commands the relevant materials are placed within reach in front of the patient: (43) three pieces of paper, (44) three colored pencils, (45) three coins of increasing size and value, (46) three sticks and a glass, (47) three books. The examiner points to the book farthest to the left of the patient when speaking the first command, "Open the first one," to indicate that this is the "first" book. The order of the objects referred to in this section is always left to right.

The entire command (i.e., all three subcommands) should be read as a single sentence to the patient. If the patient's answer is perfect (all correct in the right order) score "+." If it is not perfect, the examiner scores the number of commands that were performed correctly, irrespective of the order.

Verbal Auditory Discrimination (48–65).   The patient should have in front of him or her the section of the picture booklet titled "Verbal Auditory Discrimination'' so that it is easy to point to any picture on the page or the X on the opposite page by touching it. For each item, the patient's response is recorded by circling the number of the picture (1–4 or X) that he or she touches. If the patient does not touch any picture or the ''X,'' then ''0'' is circled in the area provided.

Each word is read once. If the stimulus must be repeated, the score is ''0'' but the examiner may record for internal (clinical) purposes the number of times the stimulus word was repeated and the ensuing choice of the patient. In this, as in all subsequent tasks, the patient should be encouraged to respond without asking for repetition.

Syntactic Comprehension (66–152).   The patient should have in front of him or her the section of the picture booklet titled ''Syntactic Comprehension'' so that it is possible to point easily to any one of the pictures on the page by touching it. The sentences are to be read by the examiner with normal intonation. Several sentences, as indicated by groups numbered ***page 1 to ***page 13, correspond to the same set of 4 (pages 1–7) or of 2 (pages 8–13) pictures. From pages 14 to 29 (137–152) each sentence corresponds to a different picture on a separate page. The patient's response is recorded by circling, in the area provided, the number of the picture that he or she touches. If the patient gives no response after 5 seconds, the examiner scores ''0'' and moves on to the next sentence.

As in the Verbal Auditory Discrimination section, in languages in which reading goes from left to right, the sets of 4 pictures are numbered in this order: (1) top left, (2) top right, (3) bottom left, (4) bottom right. For languages in which reading goes from right to left (e.g., Arabic, Azari, Farsi, Hebrew, Urdu), pictures are numbered accordingly: (1) top right, (2) top left, (3) bottom right, (4) bottom left. In Japanese, the pictures are arranged in accordance with the traditional order: (1) top right, (2) bottom right, (3) top left, (4) bottom left. In all languages, sets of 2 pictures (negative sentences) are numbered (1) top, (2) bottom; and in single pictures (possessives) the item above or to the left is numbered (1) and the item below or to the right is numbered (2).

Semantic Categories (153–157).   In this and all following sections with multiple choices, the examiner does not read the number in front of each choice.

After having read the instructions and provided an example, the examiner reads the 4 words for each item, one after the other, with a very short pause in between.

Synonyms (158–162).   Between this and the previous section, as well as between this and the next section, it is important for the examiner to pause and to ensure a change of set in the patient. Because they have multiple choice items, the various sections are somewhat similar in their format, but different in their specific task and the patient may have a tendency to perseverate from one task to the next. Additional examples may be provided before starting with item 158 to ensure that the patient has understood the nature of the task.

Antonyms (163–172).   Again here it is important to pause and to ensure a change of set in order to avoid perseveration. More than one example may be provided to ensure that the patient understands the new task.

Grammaticality Judgment (173–182).   The examiner scores what the patient says, not whether the patient's answer is right or wrong. To the question whether the sentence is correct or not, the examiner scores "+" when the patient says "yes" and "−" if the patient says "no."

Semantic Acceptability (183–192).   A pause and a change of set are necessary because the previous section dealt with grammatical acceptability, whereas this section investigates semantic acceptability. The patient is to be made quite aware of the difference. Additional contrastive examples may be given to ensure comprehension of the task and avoid confusion with the previous task. Here again, what is scored is what the patient says, not whether the patient's response is right or wrong.

Repetition of Words and Non-Words, and Lexical Decision (193–251).   Because the patient is required to do two things in succession with each item, namely repeat what she or he heard and tell whether it is a word or not, sometimes she or he may have a tendency to forget the repetition and say "yes" (it is a word) or "no" (it is not a word) immediately upon having heard the stimulus. Until the routine is well mastered by the patient (and subsequently whenever the patient fails to repeat an item), it is advisable to remind him or her of the task by saying, "Repeat," followed by a very short pause before the stimulus. If the patient has severe expressive problems and cannot repeat the stimulus, score "0" and accept nods of the head or other means of signifying "yes" or "no" in answer to the judgment of whether the item is a word or not.

Repetition of Sentences (253–259).   In this section the patient is asked to simply repeat the sentences spoken by the examiner.

Series (260–262).   In this section the patient is simply asked to recite 3 series, one at a time, exactly as stated.

Verbal Fluency (263–268).   In this section, the patient is asked to say as many words as she or he can that start with a certain sound. If the example that is provided is not sufficient, more examples with other sounds may be given until it is clear that the patient has understood the nature of the task. In languages where alphabets are used, a consonant is provided, not as it is read in the alphabet, but with a /ə/. In languages with a syllabic writing system one or more syllables are provided, as indicated. But it should be clear that it is the *sound* that matters, and not the written letter. Thus words that begin with the same sound, though they may be represented by different letters, are perfectly acceptable, as the examples try to illustrate (i.e., in English, "cement," "soap").

Naming (269–288).   The objects, kept in a box or in a bag out of the patient's sight, are presented to the patient one at a time so that she or he can easily see them. Each object is removed from the patient's sight once it has been named, and the next object is presented.

Sentence Construction (289–313).   The instructions are read to the patient exactly as provided. A second example may be given to make it clear that the verb need not remain in the infinitive or in whatever unmarked form that it is supplied in.

Semantic Opposites (314–323) *and Derivational Morphology* (324–343).   The following 3 sections have the same format. The patient is required to provide an oral response to the stimulus word. However, the nature of the response is different for each task and it is therefore important to pause and change the patient's set between sections. If the patient shows a tendency to perseverate and give the same type of response as in the previous section (e.g., a semantic opposite for item 324 or 334), the instructions should be explained again to the patient and an additional example given. For semantic opposites, derivational morphology, and morphological opposites (or other morphological task in some languages), the most probable correct response(s) to each item is/are given. If the patient produces exactly that response (or one of the suggested responses), the test administrator circles "+" and goes on to the next item. If the patient produces some other response, the examiner writes that response in the space provided and circles "1" if it is correct (i.e., acceptable in accordance with the criteria given for each section, taking into account the patient's dialect and regional usage), and "−" if it is incorrect. As usual, if the patient produces no response within 5 seconds, the examiner circles "0" and goes on to the next item.

Description (344–346).   The degree of familiarity with cartoon strips varies among individuals and, because in some bilingual (and even unilingual) communities, a page can be scanned in more than one direction depending on context, the examiner, in presenting the cartoon strip to the patient and while giving the instructions ("look at the pictures"), should move his or her hand across the page to indicate the sequence in which the pictures are to be looked at (i.e., left to right, starting with the top leftmost picture; right to left, starting with the top rightmost picture; or top to bottom, starting with the rightmost column). The pictures should remain visible to the patient during the story telling.

The patient is not to be interrupted and may speak for as long as she or he wishes, but if little or nothing is produced after 2 minutes, the examiner moves on to the next section.

Mental Arithmetic (347–361).   There is often more than one way of phrasing a sum (3 and 4; 3 plus 4), a multiplication (2 times 3; 2 multiplied by 3), or a division (9 divided by 3; 3 into 9). Therefore, to ensure uniformity across patients, each question should be read exactly as it appears. The test administrator is not to react to erroneous responses or to inform the patient in any way of whether the answer is right or wrong. The examiner simply nods approvingly after each answer, circles "+" or "−" and goes on to the next question. After 5 consecutive errors or failures to respond, the examiner circles "0" for the remaining questions in this section and moves on to the next one (Listening Comprehension).

Listening Comprehension (362–366).   After having read the instructions to the patient, the examiner reads the paragraph in a clear voice at a normal pace and intonation generally associated with story telling, pausing appropriately at commas and periods. Then the examiner reads the questions to the patient, one at a time. The information requested in these questions is not cumulative. Therefore, when a question is not answered after 5 seconds (or is incorrectly answered), the examiner proceeds to the next one. The answer to the previous question is either irrelevant or is given in the formulation of the question.

If the patient is illiterate in the language being tested, Part B of the test ends here for this patient.

Reading Aloud (367–386).   The patient should have in front of him or her the sections of the book of stimuli containing the words (5 to a page) and sentences (2 to a page) to be read aloud. The examiner ensures that the patient wears corrective glasses when appropriate.

Reading Comprehension (387–392).   The test administrator reads the instructions to the patient. The paragraph in the book of stimuli is placed in front of the patient so that she or he can read the passage quietly to him or herself. Some patients may insist on reading the paragraph out loud, not because they have not understood the instructions, but because they are used to vocalizing everything they read. They are to be allowed to do so, though the instructions are clear that they are to read the passage quietly to themselves. After 90 seconds or as soon as the patient has signaled that she or he is ready (whichever comes first), the text is removed from the patient's sight and the examiner reads the questions one at a time. As in the listening comprehension task, the information requested in these questions is not cumulative. Therefore, when a question is not answered after 5 seconds or is answered incorrectly, the examiner proceeds to the next one. The answer to the previous question is either irrelevant or is given in the formulation of the question.

Copying (393–397).   The patient is given a sheet of paper and a pencil. The page of the book of stimuli containing the 5 stimulus words for copying is placed in front of the patient. The instructions are read to him or her as provided. Throughout the written section, the patient will use his or her preferred or available hand. If the patient could read but not write in this language before his or her illness or has lost the use of both hands, the test examiner goes on to reading comprehension (408) and stops testing at item 427.

If the patient has made no attempt at copying after 1 minute, the examiner goes on to the next section (398).

Dictation (398–407).   The patient is given another sheet of paper and after the instructions are read to him or her the words are dictated one at a time. As soon as the word is written, or after 5 seconds if no attempt at writing is made, the next word is read. If the patient has failed to write any word correctly (or has made no attempt at writing) the examiner goes on to reading comprehension for words (408).

Reading Comprehension for Words (408–417).   The book of stimuli is open in front of the patient so that it is easy for him or her to read the word printed on the left-hand page and to touch the picture on the right-hand page or the x under the printed word. During the reading of the instructions, while saying, ''Then touch the x,'' the examiner touches the x to show the patient its location.

Reading Comprehension for Sentences (418–427).   The sentence stimuli follow the words in the booklet which should remain before the patient. Both the sentence and the pictures should be easy to see. Each item appears on a separate page. In this section, there is no x. As with the paragraph, some patients may choose to vocalize what they read although the instructions are to read the sentences silently.

Spontaneous Writing (813–835).   The patient is given a sheet of paper and a pencil and is asked to write something about his or her illness. The paper is collected after 5 minutes and the patient's production is analyzed in accordance with the criteria outlined in 813–835.

Part C

Two examiners are to be simultaneously present, each speaking only one of the languages of the pair being tested. Each examiner reads the instructions in his or her language and the patient translates for the apparent benefit of the other examiner. Examiners alternate in accordance with the language of the instructions for each subsection, which corresponds to the language of the stimulus items. Responses for items 428–481 are in the other language while those for items 482–513 are in the same language as the stimulus.

Before starting the administration of the test, the examiner removes the central sheet from the booklet by pulling it away from its staples. The first page of this sheet containing items 428–432 is placed in front of the patient so that it is easy to read.

Word Recognition (428–437).   The examiner whose language corresponds to the stimulus words 428–432 reads the instructions to the patient, then points to one word at a time, beginning with item 428, and reads it aloud. For each item, the patient is asked to point to the word in the list on the right which is its equivalent in the other language. If the patient has given no response after 10 seconds, the examiner circles "0" and goes on to the next stimulus word.

If the patient is unable to read, the examiner reads aloud the 10 choices at a regular pace, allowing for a mental repetition of each word before reading the next choice, until the patient has selected a response. If the patient has made no choice after 3 consecutive readings of the list, the examiner circles "0" for that item and moves on to the next stimulus word.

After the first section (428–432) is completed, the second page containing the stimuli in the other language is placed before the patient. The second examiner reads aloud the stimulus words in his or her language, as before, allowing the patient 10 seconds to find its translation equivalent in the list. The number corresponding to the response item selected by the patient is circled.

Translation of Words (438–457).   The first examiner takes over and reads the instructions relative to the translation of words (438–447), as given. Then she or he reads each stimulus word and allows 5 seconds for a response. If no response has been produced after 5 seconds, the examiner reads the next stimulus word.

After this subsection (438–447) is completed, the second examiner reads the instructions in his or her language, then reads each stimulus word, as above.

Translation of Sentences (458–481).   Each sentence of the first subsection (458–468) is read aloud by the first examiner. If necessary each sentence may be read up to 3 times. Sentences are repeated either at the patient's request or after 5 seconds if the patient has made no successful attempt.

After completion of item 468, the second examiner reads the sentences of the next subsection (470–480) in the same manner as earlier.

Grammaticality Judgments (482–513).   The first examiner reads aloud sentences 482–496, one at a time, and the second examiner reads sentences 498–512. Each sentence is to be read clearly once. When a patient declares that a sentence is incorrect, she or he is asked to make it right, whether in fact the sentence is correct or not. The examiner scores what the patient says, not whether the patient's answer is right or wrong. The examiner scores "+" when the patient signifies that the sentence is correct, "−" when the patient signifies that the sentence is incorrect.

SCORING

Because different examiners administer different language versions of the *Bilingual Aphasia Test* to the patients, it is especially important that the tests be objective and standardized. That is why, whenever possible, a "+/−" scoring method is adopted. Nevertheless, qualitative assessment is not lost, since it can be deduced from the profile and the answers to the post-test analysis (which are themselves quantified and strictly objective).

Most items are easy to score. They do not require an opinion or a judgment on the part of the examiner. They are scored rather mechanically: For the most part, the examiner simply circles "+," "−," "0," or digits corresponding to the patient's choice (or punches the corresponding computer key). For maximum ease in scoring, the number of each item is repeated next to the symbols to be circled. On rare occasions, the examiner is to write (or to enter in the computer) a number which corresponds to the number of responses produced by the patient for a given item.

Except for items 290, 295, 300, 305, and 310, which may require subjective judgment as to whether a sentence is grammatical, and for items 291, 296, 301, 306, and 311, which may require subjective judgment as to whether a sentence makes sense, scores require no decision on the part of the examiner. What is entered is what the patient says, not whether the patient's response is right or wrong. The examiner is not called upon to evaluate complex performance on a scale, except for 5 questions following the recording of spontaneous speech (18–22) and one question following the description of the cartoon strip (344), which are subjective assessments of the patient's performance. These scores, however, are not included in the quantitative data from which the patient's profile is derived. They may nevertheless be of use for a quick clinical appraisal of the patient's condition. For spontaneous and descriptive speech, only those objective quantitative data obtained from the posttest analysis (514–565) are computed.

In order to eliminate the need to interpret the patient's possibly imprecise gesture (or to decide which of successive directions to select) pointing is replaced by touching in all relevant tasks, namely, pointing (23–32), verbal auditory discrimination (48–65), syntactic comprehension (66–152), and reading comprehension for words (408–417) and for sentences (418–427). Only the first item actually touched by the patient is scored. In all multiple-choice questions (48–192 and 408–427), the patient's choice is scored (not whether the patient is right or wrong), thereby further objectifying the scoring procedure.

In most other sections, there is hardly any reasonable room for varied interpretation. Either the patient obviously does what she or he is requested to do, or does it incorrectly, or does nothing relevant, and his or her performance is respectively scored "+," "−," or "0." For example, in the pointing section (23–32), the patient either does or does not touch the appropriate object. In the simple and semicomplex commands section (33–42), the patient clearly does or does not perform the appropriate command. In the complex commands section (43–47), if all 3 commands are carried out in the right order, the examiner scores "+"; if they are not, the examiner circles the number of commands carried out, irrespective of order. Thus a score of "3" indicates that all commands were performed, but in the wrong order.

In the repetition of words and nonwords section (odd-numbered items 193–251), each item is either repeated or it is not. (That is, the patient either says the same word as the examiner, albeit in his or her own dialect, possibly with some systematic distortion caused by a congenital or acquired articulatory impediment or the patient produces a different word, or a nonword, or a paraphasia which alters the word so that it is no longer the same word as the target.) The response is scored "+" or "−" accordingly. (There is an objectively observable difference between a systematic distortion caused by a lisp or other speech defect and a paraphasia.) The patient's production is later further analyzed for paraphasias (566–573). In the lexical decision task of the section (even-numbered items 194–252) the patient's answer is simply recorded as "+" ("yes"—i.e., it is a word) or "−" ("no"—i.e., it is not a word). The examiner does not have to decide whether the patient's answer is right or wrong.

For the repetition of sentences (253–259), the examiner scores whether a sentence has been repeated *verbatim*, without addition, omission, or substitution of syllables or words, without paraphasias (though, again, taking into consideration the patient's dialect and possible systematic distortions such as lisps). A "+" indicates a sentence correctly repeated, and a "−" indicates some discrepancy which is to be analyzed after the test has been administered (574–622).

In the series recitation section (260–262), the examiner scores "+" only if a series is recited completely and correctly. If the patient makes any error, leaves any items out, adds incorrect items, or changes the order of items in the list, the examiner scores "−."

In the verbal fluency section (263–268), the examiner records whether all words produced begin with the right sound ("+" or "−") and the number of acceptable words. For naming (269–288), the examiner records as "+" or "−" whether the patient has named the object presented to him or her. Any acceptable name for the object is recorded as "+." The word does not have to be the one suggested on the test, provided that it is a name by which the object is called, taking into account dialectal or regional usage—including foreign words as in former colonies or where two languages have been in contact for a long time. Only the first name proposed by the patient is scored.

As mentioned earlier, in the sentence construction section (289–313), it is conceivable that for some borderline cases the sentence produced by the patient may be difficult to categorize as acceptable or not and hence examiners may differ in what they consider grammatical or meaningful. Whenever the examiner is in doubt, she or he should record a question mark and at least two independent judges (native speakers of the patient's dialect) should be consulted. (The criterion for acceptability is that of ordinary spoken language, not prescriptive grammar books.) A homophone of a stimulus word (e.g., see/sea, write/right in English) is accepted as if it were a stimulus word. The sentence thus produced is then independently scored as a (correct) grammatical and/or meaningful sentence, as appropriate. The other scores in this section are quantitative and objective: For each item the examiner indicates whether a response is obtained and she or he records the number of stimulus words and the total number of words used.

In the semantic opposites section (314–323), the examiner scores "+" if the expected response is given. If a different word is given it is written in the space provided and the examiner scores "1" if it is an acceptable response, "−" if it is not. It is assumed that the examiner can tell whether a word means the opposite of the stimulus or not. In cases of doubt, since words other than the expected response are written down, it is possible to check with other native speakers.

In the derivational morphology section (324–343), the same procedure as above applies. In this case, there are even fewer chances of ambiguity. Seldom will a word other than the one suggested be acceptable as a response. But for those few languages in which there might be a correct response other than the one suggested, a space is provided to write the response when it differs from the target word.

As mentioned previously, item 344 in the cartoon description section is a subjective assessment of the amount of speech produced and does not contribute to the analysis. Rather, the patient's production is analyzed after the administration of the test in accordance with the same objective quantitative criteria as spontaneous speech (540–565). The next two questions are objective: The patient did or did not go to the end (i.e., the 6th frame) and the examiner is asked to record whether the patient (1) simply described each picture, (2) told a connected story, or (3) did neither.

In the section on mental arithmetic (347–361) the examiner scores the response as "+" or "−." There is no possible correct response other than the one provided.

In the listening comprehension section (362–366) the patient provides either a correct response (scored "+") or an incorrect response (scored "−") or no response (scored "0"). Whether a response is correct or not should be easy to assess. Any appropriate (i.e., plausible) response to the question where?, when?, what?, why?, and why not? is accepted and scored "+." Single words or isolated phrases are accepted as correct as long as they are accurate.

In the reading of words section (367–376) the word is either read correctly in the patient's dialect, taking into account any systematic distortion in production, such as a lisp (i.e., it is recognizable as the target word, free of paralexias), or it is not read correctly, and is scored ''+'' or ''−'' accordingly. The patient's recorded responses are later further analyzed for paralexias (623–628).

In the reading of sentences section (377–386) the examiner indicates whether each sentence has been read correctly (i.e., without addition, omission, or substitution of syllables or words, albeit in the patient's dialect, with possible systematic distortions such as lisps). A ''+'' indicates a sentence correctly read while a ''−'' indicates some discrepancy that is to be further specified in the posttest analysis (629–708).

In the reading comprehension section (387–392), the patient provides a correct response (scored ''+''), an incorrect response (scored ''−''), or no response (scored ''0''). Any appropriate response to the questions who?, where?, what did they do?, where did they bring x back?, what did they do with what they brought back?, they exchanged it for what? is accepted and scored ''+.'' Some patients may occasionally give for question 388 the response expected for question 390. This should not be scored wrong. The answer to 392 may be given at the same time as that for 391, in which case both are scored and 392 need not be asked. Single words or isolated phrases are accepted as correct as long as they are accurate.

In the copying section (393–397), if the word is a recognizable copy of the stimulus it is scored ''+''; if there is anything wrong with it, it is scored ''−.'' The words are further analyzed after the administration of the test (709–743) to ascertain whether the patient's production is legible, whether the word is a servile copy or is written in the patient's handwriting, and to record the number of neologistic segments, letter substitutions, perseverations, and superfluous and/or missing letters.

In the dictation of words section (398–402), each word is scored ''+'' when it is correctly spelled or ''−'' if there is anything wrong with it. After the test, the dictated words are further analyzed (744–783) for number of spelling errors, neologistic intrusions, letter substitutions, perseverations, superfluous or missing letters, and letters substituted from the other alphabet, when applicable.

In the dictation of sentences section (403–407), if the patient writes the stimulus sentence correctly it is scored ''+.'' If there are errors, the examiner records the number of correctly spelled words in each sentence. The sentences are further analyzed for number of missing and/or superfluous words, neologisms, letter substitutions, and letters from the other alphabet, when applicable (784–812).

In the reading comprehension for words (408–417) what the patient touches is scored (X, 1, 2, 3, 4, 0). Likewise for the comprehension of sentences (418–427) section (1, 2, 3, 4, 0). Spontaneous writing is not scored until after the test (813–835).

TABLE 4.1
Answer Key For All Languages

1. +	56. 2	111. 2	166. 4	225. +
2. country code	57. X	112. 1	167. 1	226. +
3. #	58. 3	113. 1	168. 1	227. +
4. 3	59. 1	114. 2	169. 3	228. -
5. #	60. 2		170. 3	229. +
6. + (-)	61. X	115. 1	171. 1	230. +
7. + (-)	62. 4	116. 2	172. 1	231. +
8. + (-)	63. 3	117. 1		232. -
9. 1-5	64. 3	118. 1	173. +	233. +
10. + (-)	65. 1	119. 2	174. -	234. -
11. #		120. 1	175. -	235. +
12. 1-3	(Ex. 2)		176. -	236. +
12. 1-5	66. 2	121. 2	177. +	237. +
14. + (-)	67. 1	122. 1	178. -	238. +
15. #	68. 1	123. 1	179. -	239. +
16. 1-3	69. 4	124. 2	180. -	240. -
17. 1-5	70. 3		181. +	241. +
		125. 1	182. -	242. +
18. 1-4	71. 1	126. 2		243. +
19. 1-4	72. 4	127. 2	183. -	244. +
20. 1-4	73. 1	128. 1	184. +	245. +
21. 1-4	74. 2		185. -	246. +
22. 1-4	75. 3	129. 1	186. -	247. +
	76. 4	130. 2	187. +	248. -
23. +		131. 2	188. -	249. +
24. +	77. 1	132. 1	189. -	250. +
25. +	78. 3		190. -	251. +
26. +	79. 2	133. 2	191. +	252. +
27. +	80. 1	134. 2	192. -	
28. +		135. 1		253. +
29. +	81. 2	136. 1	193. +	254. +
30. +	82. 4		194. +	255. +
31. +	83. 2	137. 1	195. +	256. +
32. +	84. 4	138. 1	196. +	257. +
	85. 4	139. 2	197. +	258. +
33. +	86. 2	140. 2	198. +	259. +
34. +	87. 2	141. 1	199. +	
35. +	88. 4	142. 2	200. -	260. +
36. +		143. 2	201. +	261. +
37. +	89. 1	144. 2	202. +	262. +
38. +	90. 3	145. 2	203. +	
39. +	91. 3	146. 2	204. -	263. +
40. +	92. 1	147. 1	205. +	264. #
41. +	93. 1	148. 1		265. +
42. +	94. 3	149. 2	206. -	266. #
	95. 1	150. 1	207. +	267. +
43. +	96. 3	151. 1	208. +	268. #
44. +		152. 1	209. +	
45. +	97. 1	153. 3	210. -	269. +
46. +	98. 1	154. 1	211. +	270. +
47. +	99. 2	155. 3	212. +	271 +
	100. 2	156. 4	213. +	272. +
(Ex. 3)	101. 1	157. 2	214. +	273. +
48. 2	102. 1		215. +	274. +
49. 1	103. 2	158. 3	216 +	275. +
50. X	104. 2	159. 4	217. +	276. +
51. 1		160. 1	218. +	277. +
52. 2	105. 3	161. 2	219. +	278. +
53. 4	106. 2	162. 2	220. -	279. +
54. 4	107. 4		221. +	280. +
55. 3	108. 2	163. 2	222. +	281. +
	109. 3	164. 3	223. +	282. +
	110. 1	165. 2	224. +	283. +

188

(TABLE 4.1 continued)

284. +	336. + (1)	393. +	451. + (1)
285. +	337. + (1)	394. +	452. + (1)
286. +	338. + (1)	395. +	453. + (1)
287. +	339. + (1)	396. +	454. + (1)
288. +	340. + (1)	397. +	455. + (1)
	341. + (1)		456. + (1)
289. +	342. + (1)	398. +	457. + (1)
290. +	343. + (1)	399. +	
291. +	344. 3	400. +	458. #
292. #	345. +	401. +	459. 3
293. #	346. 2	402. +	460. #
			461. 3
294. +	347. +	403. + (#)	462. #
295. +	348. +	404. + (#)	463. 3
296. +	349. +	405. + (#)	464. #
297. #	350. +	406. + (#)	465. 3
298. #	351. +	407. + (#)	466. #
	352. +		467. 3
299. +	353. +	408. 1	468. #
300. +	354. +	409. 4	469. 3
301. +	355. +	410. 1	470. #
302. #	356. +	411. 3	471. 3
303. #	357. +	412. 2	472. #
	358. +	413. 2	473. 3
304. +	359. +	414. 4	474. #
305. +	360. +	415. 1	475. 3
306. +	361. +	416. 1	476. #
307. #		417. 2	477. 3
308. #	362. +		478. #
	363. +	418. 2	479. 3
309. +	364. +	419. 2	480. #
310. +	365. +	420. 3	
311. +	366. +	421. 1	481. 3
312. #		422. 1	482. -
313. #	367. +	423. 1	483. +
	368. +	424. 3	484. -
314. + (1)	369. +	425. 2	485. +
315. + (1)	370. +	426. 4	486. +
316. + (1)	371. +	427. 2	487. 0
317. + (1)	372. +		488. -
318. + (1)	373. +	428. 9	489. +
319. + (1)	374. +	429. 2	490. -
320. + (1)	375. +	430. 7	491. +
321. + (1)	376. +	431. 4	492. +
322. + (1)		432. 6	493. 0
323. + (1)	377. +	433. 2	494. -
	378. +	434. 8	495. +
324. + (1)	379. +	435. 3	496. -
325. + (1)	380. +	436. 5	497. +
326. + (1)	381. +	437. 1	498. -
327. + (1)	382. +		499. +
328. + (1)	383. +	438. + (1)	500. +
329. + (1)	384. +	439. + (1)	501. 0
330. + (1)	385. +	440. + (1)	502. -
331. + (1)	386. +	441. + (1)	503. +
332. + (1)		442. + (1)	504. +
333. + (1)	387. +	443. + (1)	505. 0
	388. +	444. + (1)	506. -
334. + (1)	389. +	445. + (1)	507. +
335. + (1)	390. +	446. + (1)	508. -
	391. +	447. + (1)	509. +
	392. +	448. + (1)	510. -
		449. + (1)	511. +
		450. + (1)	512. -
			513. +

Part C

Word Recognition (428–437).   In this section the patient is to either say or point to the word in the list that is the translation equivalent of the stimulus word. The examiner circles the number that corresponds to the patient's choice for each item.

If the test results are to be scored on a computer, the "+" key is pressed for a choice of "10" because the program can accept a response of only one digit or symbol in this section.

If the patient is able to read but gives no response after 10 seconds, a score of "0" is given and the examiner goes on to read the next stimulus word. If the patient is unable to read, a score of "0" is given if the patient has provided no response after the third consecutive reading of the list of choices.

Translation of Words (438–457).   In this section the patient is required to provide one translation of the stimulus word. If the patient produces the response suggested, the examiner circles "+" and goes on to the next item. If the patient produces some other response, the examiner writes that response in the space provided and circles "1" if it is an acceptable translation of the stimulus word or "−" if it is incorrect. If the patient produces no response within 5 seconds the examiner circles "0" and goes on to the next stimulus word.

Translation of Sentences (458–481).   The sentences to be translated are read to the patient up to three times, and the examiner circles in the appropriate number of times that the sentence was read. The patient's response is tape-recorded and after the test a score of "3" is given if all word groups are translated as suggested, "2" if only 2 word groups are error-free, "1" if only one word group is error-free, and "0" if all groups contain errors or if the patient said nothing. If the translation is considered acceptable but is not the one suggested, the examiner circles "+."

Grammaticality Judgments (482–513).   In this section the patient must indicate whether a sentence read to him or her is grammatically correct or not. The examiner circles "+" next to "judgment" if the patient considers the sentence to be correct, "−" if the patient considers the sentence to be incorrect, and "0" if the patient gives no answer after 5 seconds. When the patient considers a sentence to be correct, the examiner circles "0" for "corrected sentence" and goes on to the next sentence. When the patient considers a sentence to be incorrect, she or he is asked to make it right and the examiner circles "+" next to "judgment." If the patient's correction results in an acceptable sentence, the examiner circles "+" next to "corrected sentence." If the amended sentence is not correct, the examiner circles "minus," and if the patient declares she or he is unable to make it right, or has declared the sentence "correct" (whether it is so or not), the examiner circles "0" next to "corrected sentence." The patient's responses are tape recorded and it is possible to check later whether his or her responses were correct.

In all sections, scores are assigned before any facilitation is provided. If the patient succeeds after facilitation, type and frequency of facilitation may be recorded on the last page of the test. However, for comparative research purposes, only scores obtained without facilitation (or repetition of the stimulus) are to be recorded.

Since the only purpose of the Naming and the Verbal Fluency tasks is to assess the patient's lexical access capacity, phonemic paraphasias and articulatory mishaps are not to affect the score on these sections as long as the target word is obvious. A foreign accent is not to be taken into consideration in scoring any production task during the administration of Parts B and C. It will be noted where specifically requested in the posttest analysis.

When the patient produces approximations of the target responses, if a computer is used for scoring, the timer is kept "on" until the patient has finished autocorrections, then a score of "+" is given if the final production is correct or a score of "−" if it is incorrect. If the scoring is done by hand, the administrator waits until the end of the autocorrections, then circles "+" if the final production is correct and "−" if it is incorrect.

The answer key is identical for all languages in which the BAT has been transposed (Table 4.1, pp. 188–189).

Test and Posttest Scoring

There are two phases in the scoring of the Bilingual Aphasia Test. (1) During the administration of the test, a (possibly nonspecialized) examiner simply scores by reporting the absence or presence and type of response from the patient. Test items and scoring charts appear throughout Chapter 3. (2) After the test, an in-depth analysis of spontaneous and descriptive speech, reading, copying, dictation and spontaneous writing is performed by (or at least with the help of) a professional (i.e., an aphasiologist, linguist, neurolinguist, psycholinguist, speech pathologist, or speech therapist). Operational definitions of the terms used in the posttest analysis are provided at the end of the posttest below.

Posttest Analysis of Part B

Spontaneous speech

514. Number of utterances	_____	(514)
515. Total number of words	_____	(515)
516. Mean length of utterance	_____	(516)
517. Mean length of the 5 longest utterances	_____	(517)
518. Number of different words	_____	(518)
519. Type/token ratio	_____	(519)

520. Number of neologisms _____ (520)
521. Number of phonemic paraphasias resulting in nonwords _____ (521)
522. Number of phonemic paraphasias resulting in words _____ (522)
523. Number of semantic paraphasias _____ (523)
524. Number of verbal paraphasias (not similar in sound or _____ (524)
     meaning)
525. Number of perseverations _____ (525)
526. Number of paragrammatisms _____ (526)
527. Number of missing obligatory grammatical morphemes _____ (527)
528. Number of word-order errors _____ (528)
529. Number of verbs per utterance _____ (529)
530. Number of subordinate clauses _____ (530)
531. Number of intraphrasal pauses _____ (531)
532. Number of circumlocutions _____ (532)
533. Number of stereotypic phrases _____ (533)
534. Evidence of word-finding difficulty _____ (534)
535. Detection of foreign accent (0:none; 5:very strong)   0 1 2 3 4 5 (535)
536. Number of inappropriate foreign words _____ (536)
537. Number of individual sentences that are semantically _____ (537)
     deviant
538. The discourse is cohesive   + − 0 (538)
539. The discourse is pragmatically sound (makes sense)   + − 0 (539)

Descriptive speech
540. Number of utterances _____ (540)
541. Total number of words _____ (541)
542. Mean length of utterance _____ (542)
543. Mean length of the 5 longest utterances _____ (543)
544. Number of different words _____ (544)
545. Type/token ratio _____ (545)
546. Number of neologisms _____ (546)
547. Number of phonemic paraphasias resulting in nonwords _____ (547)
548. Number of phonemic paraphasias resulting in words _____ (548)
549. Number of semantic paraphasias _____ (549)
550. Number of verbal paraphasias (not similar in sound or _____ (550)
     meaning)
551. Number of perseverations _____ (551)
552. Number of paragrammatisms _____ (552)
553. Number of missing obligatory grammatical morphemes _____ (553)
554. Number of word order errors _____ (554)
555. Number of verbs per utterance _____ (555)
556. Number of subordinate clauses _____ (556)
557. Number of intraphrasal pauses _____ (557)
558. Number of circumlocutions _____ (558)
559. Number of stereotypic phrases _____ (559)
560. Evidence of word-finding difficulty _____ (560)
561. Detection of foreign accent (0:none; 5:very strong)   0 1 2 3 4 5 (561)

562. Number of inappropriate foreign words   _____ (562)
563. Number of individual sentences that are semantically   _____ (563)
     deviant
564. The discourse is cohesive   + − 0 (564)
565. The discourse is pragmatically sound (makes sense)   + − 0 (565)

Repetition of real words (193-197, 201, 207, 211-217, 221-225,
                 229, 235, 237, 241-245, 249, 251)
566. Number of neologisms   _____ (566)
567. Number of phonemic paraphasias resulting in non-   _____ (567)
     words
568. Number of phonemic paraphasias resulting in words   _____ (568)
569. Number of semantic paraphasias   _____ (569)
570. Number of perseverations   _____ (570)

Repetition of non-words (199, 203, 205, 209, 219, 227, 231, 239, 247)
571. Number of neologisms (unrecognizable target)   _____ (571)
572. Number of phonemic paraphasias resulting in other   _____ (572)
     non-words
573. Number of phonemic paraphasias resulting in real   _____ (573)
     words

Repetition of sentences (253-259)
574. Number of phonemic paraphasias resulting in non-   _____ (574)
     words in the 1st sentence
575. Number of phonemic paraphasias resulting in non-   _____ (575)
     words in the 2nd sentence
576. Number of phonemic paraphasias resulting in non-   _____ (576)
     words in the 3rd sentence
577. Number of phonemic paraphasias resulting in non-   _____ (577)
     words in the 4th sentence
578. Number of phonemic paraphasias resulting in non-   _____ (578)
     words in the 5th sentence
579. Number of phonemic paraphasias resulting in non-   _____ (579)
     words in the 6th sentence
580. Number of phonemic paraphasias resulting in non-   _____ (580)
     words in the 7th sentence
581. Number of phonemic paraphasias resulting in words in   _____ (581)
     the 1st sentence
582. Number of phonemic paraphasias resulting in words in   _____ (582)
     the 2nd sentence
583. Number of phonemic paraphasias resulting in words in   _____ (583)
     the 3rd sentence
584. Number of phonemic paraphasias resulting in words in   _____ (584)
     the 4th sentence
585. Number of phonemic paraphasias resulting in words in   _____ (585)
     the 5th sentence

586. Number of phonemic paraphasias resulting in words in   _____ (586)
      the 6th sentence

587. Number of phonemic paraphasias resulting in words in   _____ (587)
      the 7th sentence

588. Number of semantic paraphasias in the 1st sentence   _____ (588)

589. Number of semantic paraphasias in the 2nd sentence   _____ (589)

590. Number of semantic paraphasias in the 3rd sentence   _____ (590)

591. Number of semantic paraphasias in the 4th sentence   _____ (591)

592. Number of semantic paraphasias in the 5th sentence   _____ (592)

593. Number of semantic paraphasias in the 6th sentence   _____ (593)

594. Number of semantic paraphasias in the 7th sentence   _____ (594)

595. Number of perseverations in the 1st sentence   _____ (595)

596. Number of perseverations in the 2nd sentence   _____ (596)

597. Number of perseverations in the 3rd sentence   _____ (597)

598. Number of perseverations in the 4th sentence   _____ (598)

599. Number of perseverations in the 5th sentence   _____ (599)

600. Number of perseverations in the 6th sentence   _____ (600)

601. Number of perseverations in the 7th sentence   _____ (601)

602. Number of missing words in the 1st sentence   _____ (602)

603. Number of missing words in the 2nd sentence   _____ (603)

604. Number of missing words in the 3rd sentence   _____ (604)

605. Number of missing words in the 4th sentence   _____ (605)

606. Number of missing words in the 5th sentence   _____ (606)

607. Number of missing words in the 6th sentence   _____ (607)

608. Number of missing words in the 7th sentence   _____ (608)

609. Number of missing grammatical morphemes in the 1st   _____ (609)
      sentence

610. Number of missing grammatical morphemes in the 2nd   _____ (610)
      sentence

611. Number of missing grammatical morphemes in the 3rd   _____ (611)
      sentence

612. Number of missing grammatical morphemes in the 4th   _____ (612)
      sentence

613. Number of missing grammatical morphemes in the 5th   _____ (613)
      sentence

614. Number of missing grammatical morphemes in the 6th   _____ (614)
      sentence

615. Number of missing grammatical morphemes in the 7th   _____ (615)
      sentence

616. Number of neologisms in the 1st sentence   _____ (616)

617. Number of neologisms in the 2nd sentence   _____ (617)

618. Number of neologisms in the 3rd sentence   _____ (618)

619. Number of neologisms in the 4th sentence   _____ (619)

620. Number of neologisms in the 5th sentence   _____ (620)

621. Number of neologisms in the 6th sentence   _____ (621)

622. Number of neologisms in the 7th sentence   _____ (622)

Reading words aloud (367-376)

623. Number of neologisms   _____ (623)
624. Number of phonemic paralexias resulting in nonwords   _____ (624)
625. Number of phonemic paralexias resulting in words   _____ (625)
626. Number of semantic paralexias   _____ (626)
627. Number of grapheme-phoneme correspondence errors   _____ (627)
628. Number of perseverations   _____ (628)

Reading sentences aloud (377-386)

629. Number of phonemic paralexias resulting in nonwords   _____ (629)
     in the 1st sentence
630. Number of phonemic paralexias resulting in nonwords   _____ (630)
     in the 2nd sentence
631. Number of phonemic paralexias resulting in nonwords   _____ (631)
     in the 3rd sentence
632. Number of phonemic paralexias resulting in nonwords   _____ (632)
     in the 4th sentence
633. Number of phonemic paralexias resulting in nonwords   _____ (633)
     in the 5th sentence
634. Number of phonemic paralexias resulting in nonwords   _____ (634)
     in the 6th sentence
635. Number of phonemic paralexias resulting in nonwords   _____ (635)
     in the 7th sentence
636. Number of phonemic paralexias resulting in nonwords   _____ (636)
     in the 8th sentence
637. Number of phonemic paralexias resulting in nonwords   _____ (637)
     in the 9th sentence
638. Number of phonemic paralexias resulting in nonwords   _____ (638)
     in the 10th sentence
639. Number of phonemic paralexias resulting in words in   _____ (639)
     the 1st sentence
640. Number of phonemic paralexias resulting in words in   _____ (640)
     the 2nd sentence
641. Number of phonemic paralexias resulting in words in   _____ (641)
     the 3rd sentence
642. Number of phonemic paralexias resulting in words in   _____ (642)
     the 4th sentence
643. Number of phonemic paralexias resulting in words in   _____ (643)
     the 5th sentence
644. Number of phonemic paralexias resulting in words in   _____ (644)
     the 6th sentence
645. Number of phonemic paralexias resulting in words in   _____ (645)
     the 7th sentence
646. Number of phonemic paralexias resulting in words in   _____ (646)
     the 8th sentence
647. Number of phonemic paralexias resulting in words in   _____ (647)
     the 9th sentence

648. Number of phonemic paralexias resulting in words in   _____ (648)
      the 10th sentence
649. Number of semantic paralexias in the 1st sentence   _____ (649)
650. Number of semantic paralexias in the 2nd sentence   _____ (650)
651. Number of semantic paralexias in the 3rd sentence   _____ (651)
652. Number of semantic paralexias in the 4th sentence   _____ (652)
653. Number of semantic paralexias in the 5th sentence   _____ (653)
654. Number of semantic paralexias in the 6th sentence   _____ (654)
655. Number of semantic paralexias in the 7th sentence   _____ (655)
656. Number of semantic paralexias in the 8th sentence   _____ (656)
657. Number of semantic paralexias in the 9th sentence   _____ (657)
658. Number of semantic paralexias in the 10th sentence   _____ (658)
659. Number of grapheme-phoneme correspondence errors   _____ (659)
      in the 1st sentence
660. Number of grapheme-phoneme correspondence errors   _____ (660)
      in the 2nd sentence
661. Number of grapheme-phoneme correspondence errors   _____ (661)
      in the 3rd sentence
662. Number of grapheme-phoneme correspondence errors   _____ (662)
      in the 4th sentence
663. Number of grapheme-phoneme correspondence errors   _____ (663)
      in the 5th sentence
664. Number of grapheme-phoneme correspondence errors   _____ (664)
      in the 6th sentence
665. Number of grapheme-phoneme correspondence errors   _____ (665)
      in the 7th sentence
666. Number of grapheme-phoneme correspondence errors   _____ (666)
      in the 8th sentence
667. Number of grapheme-phoneme correspondence errors   _____ (667)
      in the 9th sentence
668. Number of grapheme-phoneme correspondence errors   _____ (668)
      in the 10th sentence
669. Number of perseverations in the 1st sentence   _____ (669)
670. Number of perseverations in the 2nd sentence   _____ (670)
671. Number of perseverations in the 3rd sentence   _____ (671)
672. Number of perseverations in the 4th sentence   _____ (672)
673. Number of perseverations in the 5th sentence   _____ (673)
674. Number of perseverations in the 6th sentence   _____ (674)
675. Number of perseverations in the 7th sentence   _____ (675)
676. Number of perseverations in the 8th sentence   _____ (676)
677. Number of perseverations in the 9th sentence   _____ (677)
678. Number of perseverations in the 10th sentence   _____ (678)
679. Number of missing words in the 1st sentence   _____ (679)
680. Number of missing words in the 2nd sentence   _____ (680)
681. Number of missing words in the 3rd sentence   _____ (681)
682. Number of missing words in the 4th sentence   _____ (682)
683. Number of missing words in the 5th sentence   _____ (683)

684. Number of missing words in the 6th sentence   _____ (684)
685. Number of missing words in the 7th sentence   _____ (685)
686. Number of missing words in the 8th sentence   _____ (686)
687. Number of missing words in the 9th sentence   _____ (687)
688. Number of missing words in the 10th sentence   _____ (688)
689. Number of missing grammatical morphemes in the 1st   _____ (689)
     sentence
690. Number of missing grammatical morphemes in the 2nd   _____ (690)
     sentence
691. Number of missing grammatical morphemes in the 3rd   _____ (691)
     sentence
692. Number of missing grammatical morphemes in the 4th   _____ (692)
     sentence
693. Number of missing grammatical morphemes in the 5th   _____ (693)
     sentence
694. Number of missing grammatical morphemes in the 6th   _____ (694)
     sentence
695. Number of missing grammatical morphemes in the 7th   _____ (695)
     sentence
696. Number of missing grammatical morphemes in the 8th   _____ (696)
     sentence
697. Number of missing grammatical morphemes in the 9th   _____ (697)
     sentence
698. Number of missing grammatical morphemes in the 10th   _____ (698)
     sentence
699. Number of neologisms in the 1st sentence   _____ (699)
700. Number of neologisms in the 2nd sentence   _____ (700)
701. Number of neologisms in the 3rd sentence   _____ (701)
702. Number of neologisms in the 4th sentence   _____ (702)
703. Number of neologisms in the 5th sentence   _____ (703)
704. Number of neologisms in the 6th sentence   _____ (704)
705. Number of neologisms in the 7th sentence   _____ (705)
706. Number of neologisms in the 8th sentence   _____ (706)
707. Number of neologisms in the 9th sentence   _____ (707)
708. Number of neologisms in the 10th sentence   _____ (708)

Copying (393-397)
709. The 1st word is (1) an unrecognizable scribble; (2)   0 1 2 (709)
     legible
710. The 2nd word is (1) an unrecognizable scribble; (2)   0 1 2 (710)
     legible
711. The 3rd word is (1) an unrecognizable scribble; (2)   0 1 2 (711)
     legible
712. The 4th word is (1) an unrecognizable scribble; (2)   0 1 2 (712)
     legible
713. The 5th word is (1) an unrecognizable scribble; (2)   0 1 2 (713)
     legible

If the word is recognizable as a word,

714. The 1st word is (1) a servile copy; (2) in patient's handwriting ⸺ 1 2 (714)

715. The 2nd word is (1) a servile copy; (2) in patient's handwriting ⸺ 1 2 (715)

716. The 3rd word is (1) a servile copy; (2) in patient's handwriting ⸺ 1 2 (716)

717. The 4th word is (1) a servile copy; (2) in patient's handwriting ⸺ 1 2 (717)

718. The 5th word is (1) a servile copy; (2) in patient's handwriting ⸺ 1 2 (718)

719. Number of paragraphias in the 1st word ⸺ (719)
720. Number of paragraphias in the 2nd word ⸺ (720)
721. Number of paragraphias in the 3rd word ⸺ (721)
722. Number of paragraphias in the 4th word ⸺ (722)
723. Number of paragraphias in the 5th word ⸺ (723)
724. Number of neologistic segments in lieu of letters in the 1st word ⸺ (724)
725. Number of neologistic segments in lieu of letters in the 2nd word ⸺ (725)
726. Number of neologistic segments in lieu of letters in the 3rd word ⸺ (726)
727. Number of neologistic segments in lieu of letters in the 4th word ⸺ (727)
728. Number of neologistic segments in lieu of letters in the 5th word ⸺ (728)
729. Number of perseverations in the 1st word ⸺ (729)
730. Number of perseverations in the 2nd word ⸺ (730)
731. Number of perseverations in the 3rd word ⸺ (731)
732. Number of perseverations in the 4th word ⸺ (732)
733. Number of perseverations in the 5th word ⸺ (733)
734. Number of superfluous letters in the 1st word ⸺ (734)
735. Number of superfluous letters in the 2nd word ⸺ (735)
736. Number of superfluous letters in the 3rd word ⸺ (736)
737. Number of superfluous letters in the 4th word ⸺ (737)
738. Number of superfluous letters in the 5th word ⸺ (738)
739. Number of missing letters in the 1st word ⸺ (739)
740. Number of missing letters in the 2nd word ⸺ (740)
741. Number of missing letters in the 3rd word ⸺ (741)
742. Number of missing letters in the 4th word ⸺ (742)
743. Number of missing letters in the 5th word ⸺ (743)

Dictation of words (398-402)

744. The 1st word is (1) an unrecognizable scribble; (2) legible ⸺ 0 1 2 (744)

745. The 2nd word is (1) an unrecognizable scribble; (2) legible ⸺ 0 1 2 (745)

746. The 3rd word is (1) an unrecognizable scribble; (2)   0 1 2   (746)
     legible
747. The 4th word is (1) an unrecognizable scribble; (2)   0 1 2   (747)
     legible
748. The 5th word is (1) an unrecognizable scribble; (2)   0 1 2   (748)
     legible

     If the word is recognizable as a word,
749. Number of spelling errors in the 1st word   _____   (749)
750. Number of spelling errors in the 2nd word   _____   (750)
751. Number of spelling errors in the 3rd word   _____   (751)
752. Number of spelling errors in the 4th word   _____   (752)
753. Number of spelling errors in the 5th word   _____   (753)
754. Number of neologistic intrusions in the 1st word   _____   (754)
755. Number of neologistic intrusions in the 2nd word   _____   (755)
756. Number of neologistic intrusions in the 3rd word   _____   (756)
757. Number of neologistic intrusions in the 4th word   _____   (757)
758. Number of neologistic intrusions in the 5th word   _____   (758)
759. Number of paragraphias in the 1st word   _____   (759)
760. Number of paragraphias in the 2nd word   _____   (760)
761. Number of paragraphias in the 3rd word   _____   (761)
762. Number of paragraphias in the 4th word   _____   (762)
763. Number of paragraphias in the 5th word   _____   (763)
764. Number of perseverations in the 1st word   _____   (764)
765. Number of perseverations in the 2nd word   _____   (765)
766. Number of perseverations in the 3rd word   _____   (766)
767. Number of perseverations in the 4th word   _____   (767)
768. Number of perseverations in the 5th word   _____   (768)
769. Number of superfluous letters in the 1st word   _____   (769)
770. Number of superfluous letters in the 2nd word   _____   (770)
771. Number of superfluous letters in the 3rd word   _____   (771)
772. Number of superfluous letters in the 4th word   _____   (772)
773. Number of superfluous letters in the 5th word   _____   (773)
774. Number of missing letters in the 1st word   _____   (774)
775. Number of missing letters in the 2nd word   _____   (775)
776. Number of missing letters in the 3rd word   _____   (776)
777. Number of missing letters in the 4th word   _____   (777)
778. Number of missing letters in the 5th word   _____   (778)
779. Number of letters substituted from the other alphabet in   N/A__   (779)
     the 1st word
780. Number of letters substituted from the other alphabet in   N/A__   (780)
     the 2nd word
781. Number of letters substituted from the other alphabet in   N/A__   (781)
     the 3rd word
782. Number of letters substituted from the other alphabet in   N/A__   (782)
     the 4th word

783. Number of letters substituted from the other alphabet in   N/A___   (783)
the 5th word

Dictation of sentences (403-40)
784. The 1st sentence is (1) not legible; (2) legible   0 1 2   (784)
785. The 2nd sentence is (1) not legible; (2) legible   0 1 2   (785)
786. The 3rd sentence is (1) not legible; (2) legible   0 1 2   (786)
787. The 4th sentence is (1) not legible; (2) legible   0 1 2   (787)
788. The 5th sentence is (1) not legible; (2) legible   0 1 2   (788)
789. Number of legitimate words correctly spelled in the 1st   _____   (789)
sentence
790. Number of legitimate words correctly spelled in the   _____   (790)
2nd sentence
791. Number of legitimate words correctly spelled in the 3rd   _____   (791)
sentence
792. Number of legitimate words correctly spelled in the 4th   _____   (792)
sentence
793. Number of legitimate words correctly spelled in the 5th   _____   (793)
sentence
794. Number of missing words in the 1st sentence   _____   (794)
795. Number of missing words in the 2nd sentence   _____   (795)
796. Number of missing words in the 3rd sentence   _____   (796)
797. Number of missing words in the 4th sentence   _____   (797)
798. Number of missing words in the 5th sentence   _____   (798)
799. Number of superfluous words in the 1st sentence   _____   (799)
800. Number of superfluous words in the 2nd sentence   _____   (800)
801. Number of superfluous words in the 3rd sentence   _____   (801)
802. Number of superfluous words in the 4th sentence   _____   (802)
803. Number of superfluous words in the 5th sentence   _____   (803)
804. Number of non-words (neologisms) in the 1st sentence   _____   (804)
805. Number of non-words (neologisms) in the 2nd sentence   _____   (805)
806. Number of non-words (neologisms) in the 3rd sentence   _____   (806)
807. Number of non-words (neologisms) in the 4th sentence   _____   (807)
808. Number of non-words (neologisms) in the 5th sentence   _____   (808)
809. Total number of paragraphias (substitution of letters)   _____   (809)
810. Total number of missing grammatical morphemes   _____   (810)
811. Total number of spelling errors   _____   (811)
812. Total number of letters substituted from the other   N/A___   (812)
alphabet

Spontaneous writing
813. Number of sentences   _____   (813)
814. Total number of words   _____   (814)
815. Mean length of sentence   _____   (815)
816. Number of different words   _____   (816)
817. Type/token ratio   _____   (817)
818. Number of neologisms   _____   (818)
819. Number of literal paraphasias resulting in non-words   _____   (819)

820. Number of literal paraphasias resulting in words   _____ (820)
821. Number of semantic paraphasias   _____ (821)
822. Number of verbal paraphasias   _____ (822)
823. Number of spelling errors   _____ (823)
824. Number of perseverations   _____ (824)
825. Number of paragrammatisms   _____ (825)
826. Number of missing obligatory grammatical morphemes   _____ (826)
827. Number of word-order errors   _____ (827)
828. Number of verbs per sentence   _____ (828)
829. Number of subordinate clauses   _____ (829)
830. Number of circumlocutions   _____ (830)
831. Number of stereotypic phrases   _____ (831)
832. Number of intrusions from the other writing system   _____ (832)
833. Number of individual sentences that are semantically   _____ (833)
      deviant
834. The text is cohesive   _____ (834)
835. The text is pragmatically sound (makes sense)   _____ (835)

Scoring of Spontaneous and Descriptive Speech

514/540.   Number of utterances: For the purpose of this analysis an utterance is defined as a self-contained segment of speech conveying its own independent meaning. A sentence is one utterance. However, an utterance may be shorter than a complete sentence. It is generally marked by falling intonation, followed by a short pause. An utterance may be a single word or phrase. A false start is scored as one utterance. A sentence with an intrasentential pause is nevertheless scored as one utterance. Any segment shorter than a sentence which stands by itself, i.e., does not form a syntactic unit with what follows, is scored as one utterance. In short, an utterance is a sentence (including compound sentences) or a sentence fragment (word or phrase) that stands on its own (i.e., does not form a syntactic unit with what follows). For example, "The smoke was . . . there was a fire in the chimney" counts as 2 utterances.

515/541.   Total number of words: the total number of words in a 5-minute sample of sustained spontaneous speech (for descriptive speech, the duration of the description). Reductions count as two words ("wanna" → "want to"). In agglutinative languages, compound words that are not listed as such in the dictionary are decomposed into those parts that are, and each such part is counted as one word.

516/542.   Mean length of utterance: the total number of words in the sample divided by the number of utterances.

517/543.   Mean length of the 5 longest utterances: the total number of words contained in the 5 longest utterances divided by 5.

517/544.   Number of different words: the number of different lexical items (types) occurring in a 5-minute sample (or during the description). Different inflected forms count as tokens of the same type provided their radical remains unchanged and they are not represented as a separate entry in the dictionary (i.e., plural by adding ''s,'' past tense by adding ''ed,'' gerund by adding ''ing'').

Inflected forms count as different types when the form of the radical is changed (e.g., ''man'' → ''men''; be, am, is, are, was, were) and they appear as a separate entry or are specified next to the uninflected form in the dictionary. Derived forms count as different types (e.g., ''nation,'' ''national,'' ''possible,'' ''impossible'').

Closed class words (i.e., articles, particles, prepositions, conjunctions, demonstrative and possessive adjectives, the copula ''be,'' and pronouns) are deleted from the word count for the purpose of obtaining the type/token ratio.

519/545.   Type/token ratio: the number of different words (types) divided by the total number of words (tokens). Every time a given word is used in the sample, it is a token of the same type. Grammatical words (i.e., the closed class words listed above) are not computed.

520/546.   Number of neologisms: number of wholly uninterpretable nonwords, i.e., forms that do not resemble a word in the language, and that cannot be interpreted as a word containing one or even two phonemic paraphasias.

521/547.   Number of phonemic paraphasias resulting in nonwords: number of forms in which one or two phonemes have been substituted so that the result is a nonword, although it is possible to guess the target word from the context, and to identify the phonemic substitution(s).

522/548.   Number of phonemic paraphasias resulting in words: number of words that are inappropriate in the context but that are obvious distortions of the target word by the substitution of one or two phonemes.

523/549.   Number of semantic paraphasias: number of words inappropriate in the context but related semantically to the target (same semantic field, close associate, semantic opposite, etc.).

524/550.   Number of verbal paraphasias (not similar in sound or meaning): number of words inappropriate in the context, and having no phonemic resemblance with, or semantic relation to, the target (i.e., not a phonemic or a semantic paraphasia).

525/551.   Number of perseverations: number of inappropriate successive repetitions of syllables, words, or phrases.

526/552.   Number of paragrammatisms: number of syntactic/morphological erroneous grammatical inflections (substitutions of function words, wrong tense or aspect or person); any deviant use of grammatical morphemes (except omission).

527/553.   Number of missing obligatory grammatical morphemes: number of function words (e.g., articles, prepositions, postpositions, conjunctions, particles, pronouns, auxiliary verbs, demonstratives and possessives) and inflectional affixes (e.g., person, tense, aspect markers, gender, plural, case markers) missing in an obligatory context. The above examples refer to English. In some languages articles and prepositions are realized as inflectional affixes. What is realized as a preposition in one language may be realized as a postposition or a suffix in another.

528/554.   Number of word-order errors: number of times that words appear in the wrong place in the phrase, or phrases appear in the wrong place in the sentence. (Phrases and clauses may reflect the word order in the patient's other language(s).)

529/555.   Number of verbs per utterance: the total number of verbs found in the 5-minute sample (or description) divided by the number of utterances.

530/556.   Number of subordinate clauses: the total number of subordinate clauses found in the 5-minute sample or description (clauses introduced by a subordinative conjunction (because, if, since, that, etc.) or relative pronouns (who, (to) whom, (from) which, that)).

531/557.   Number of intraphrasal pauses: number of (undue) pauses within a phrase, in places not in keeping with the normal flow of speech (as evidence of word-finding difficulty).

532/558.   Number of circumlocutions: number of times that phrases descriptive of the referent or pertinent to its function are used instead of the target word (the name of the referent).

533/559.   Number of Stereotypic phrases: number of automatic filler phrases that can be used independently of the context and are not factually informative (e.g., "you know"; "as far as I am concerned"; "if you ask me").

534/560.   Evidence of word-finding difficulty: 17, 18, 19 plus any other obvious clue to word-finding difficulty (such as empty words, e.g., "the thing").

535/561.   Detection of foreign accent. This is an unavoidably subjective judgment. However, the mean score obtained by three independent native speaking judges listening to the speech sample, scoring 0 for no trace of foreign accent, 1 for a very mild trace, 2 for a mild accent, 3 for a moderate accent, 4 for a strong accent, 5 for a very strong accent, should be an acceptable measure.

For purposes of comparison (group studies) scores of 1 and 2, 4 and 5 will be collapsed.

536/562.   Number of inappropriate foreign words: number of foreign words that cannot be considered words which, as standard borrowings, the patient would have used premorbidly when she or he spoke to a unilingual.

537/563.   Number of individual sentences that are semantically deviant: number of sentences that are nonsensical, even if all the words are real words, and the grammatical structure of the sentence is correct.

538/564.   The discourse is cohesive: The discourse is not incoherent. The patient follows an acceptable line of exposition: She or he is *saying* something intelligible.

539/565.   The discourse is pragmatically sound: What the patient says is plausible, on the whole reasonable, not extravagant with respect to content.

Scoring of Spontaneous Writing

813.   Number of sentences: Any isolated segment, separated from the rest by a period, or beginning on a different line and forming a grammatically and/or semantically self-contained unit (irrespective of whether it is well-formed or not) is counted as one sentence.

814.   Total number of words: the total number of recognizable word forms (including those containing paragraphias, but excluding neologisms and scribbles) produced by the patient in the 5 minutes allotted. In agglutinative languages, compound words that are not listed as such in the dictionary are decomposed into those parts that are, and each part is counted as one word.

815.   Mean length of sentence: the total number of words in the sample divided by the number of sentences.

816.   Number of different words: the number of different lexical items (types) occurring in the sample. Different inflected forms are counted as tokens of the same type provided their radical remains unchanged and they are not represented as a separate entry in the dictionary.

Inflected forms count as different types when the form of the radical is changed and they appear as a separate entry or are specified next to the uninflected form in the dictionary. Derived forms count as different types. Closed class words are deleted from the word count for the purpose of obtaining the type/token ratio.

817.   Type/token ratio: the number of different words (types) divided by the total number of words (tokens). Closed class words are not computed.

818.   Number of neologisms: number of wholly uninterpretable nonwords, i.e., forms that do not resemble a word in the language, and that cannot be interpreted as a word containing one or even two paragraphias.

819.   Number of literal paraphasias resulting in nonwords: number of written forms in which one or two letters have been substituted so that the result is a nonword, although it is possible to guess the target word from the context, and to identify the letter substitution(s).

820.   Number of literal paraphasias resulting in words: number of words that are inappropriate in the context but that are obvious distortions of the target word by the substitution of one or two letters.

821.   Number of semantic paraphasias: number of words inappropriate in the context but related semantically to the target (same semantic field, close associate, semantic opposite, etc.).

822.   Number of verbal paraphasias: number of words inappropriate in the context, and having no phonemic resemblance with, or semantic relation to, the target (i.e., not a literal or semantic paraphasia).

823.   Number of spelling errors: number of recognizable words violating spelling conventions. The substitution of a homophone for the target word (e.g., their→therc) is to be counted as a spelling error, not as a verbal paraphasia.

824.   Number of perseverations: number of inappropriate successive repetitions of letters, syllables, words, or phrases.

825.   Number of paragrammatisms: number of syntactic/morphological erroneous grammatical inflections (substitution of function words, wrong tense or aspect or person); any deviant use of grammatical morphemes (except omission).

826.   Number of missing obligatory grammatical morphemes: number of function words (e.g., articles, particles, prepositions, postpositions, conjunctions, pronouns, auxiliary verbs, demonstratives, and possessives) and inflectional affixes (e.g., person, tense, aspect markers; gender, plural, case markers) missing in an obligatory context.

827. Number of word-order errors: number of times that words appear in the wrong place in the phrase, or phrases in the wrong place in the sentence.

828. Number of verbs per sentence: the total number of verbs found in the sample divided by the number of sentences.

829. Number of subordinate clauses: the total number of subordinate clauses found in the sample.

830. Number of circumlocutions: number of times that phrases descriptive of the referent or pertinent to its function are used instead of the target word (the name of the referent).

831. Number of stereotypic phrases: number of automatic filler phrases that can be used independently of the context and are not factually informative.

832. Number of intrusions from the other writing system: number of intruding features of the writing system of another language (e.g., Cyrillic letters replaced by their equivalent Roman letters).

833. Number of individual sentences that are semantically deviant: number of sentences that are nonsensical, even if all the words are real words, and the grammatical structure of the sentence is correct.

834. The text is cohesive: The text is not incoherent. The patient follows an acceptable line of exposition: His or her text is intelligible.

835. The text is pragmatically sound: What the patient writes is plausible, on the whole reasonable, not extravagant with respect to content.

COMPUTER CODES FOR LANGUAGES

In order to avoid possible errors in coding languages, instead of giving each language a number, the code has been divided so that no two languages share any consecutive letters or differ only in the middle letter. Erroneous combinations of letters will be rejected by the computer. The code is based on the first 3 letters of the name of the language in the languages concerned, with modification to prevent near-homographicity when necessary.

List by Language

Arabic (Maghrebian)	ARM	Japanese	NIP
Armenian (Eastern)	HAE	Kannada	KAN

Armenian (Western)	WHA	Korean	KRN
Azari (Azerbaijani)	AZE	Kinyawranda	KWR
Basque	EUS	Latvian	LAV
Bulgarian	BUL	Lithuanian	LIT
Cantonese	YUE	Norwegian	NOR
Catalan	CAT	Mandarin (Standard Modern Chinese)	SMC
Czech	CZE	Oriya	ORI
Danish	DNK	Polish	POL
Dutch	NED	Portuguese (Brazilian)	PRT
English	ENG	Russian	RUS
Estonian	EES	Serbo-Croatian	CRO
Farsi (Persian)	PER	Spanish	ESP
Finnish	SUO	Swedish	SVE
French	FRA	Swiss German	SWD
Galician	GAL	Tamil	TAM
German	DEU	Telegu	TEL
Greek	ELL	Turkish	TUR
Gujarati	GUJ	Urdu	URD
Hebrew	IVR	Valaque	VAL
Hindi	HIN	Vietnamese	VIE
Hungarian	MAG	Yiddish	YID
Icelandic	ISL		
Italian	ITA	Other	OTH

List by Code

ARM	Arabic (Maghrebian)	LIT	Lithuanian
AZE	Azari (Azerbaijani)	MAG	Hungarian
BUL	Bulgarian	NED	Dutch
CAT	Catalan	NIP	Japanese
CRO	Serbo-Croatian	NOR	Norwegian
CZE	Czech	ORI	Oriya
DEU	German	PER	Farsi (Persian)
DNK	Danish	POL	Polish
EES	Estonian	PRT	Portuguese
ELL	Greek	RUS	Russian
ENG	English	SMC	Mandarin (Standard Modern Chinese)
ESP	Spanish	SUO	Finnish
EUS	Basque	SVE	Swedish
FRA	French	SWD	Swiss German
GAL	Galician	TAM	Tamil
GUJ	Gujarati	TEL	Telegu
HAE	Armenian (Eastern)	TUR	Turkish
HIN	Hindi	URD	Urdu
ISL	Icelandic	VAL	Valaque
ITA	Italian	VIE	Vietnamese
IVR	Hebrew	WHA	Armenian (Western)
KAN	Kannada	YID	Yiddish

KRN	Korean	YUE	Cantonese
KWR	Kinyawranda		
LAV	Latvian	OTH	Other

NEUROPSYCHOLOGICAL ASSESSMENT

Since the effects of associated deficits on linguistic performance are considered to be identical in all of the patient's languages, visual recognition, short-term memory span, and other cognitive functions need not be assessed separately when the purpose is to compare performance in the two languages. However, when the results on the BAT are also to function as part of a diagnosis of aphasia, the capacities listed below must be independently assessed. The result of these assessments must also be reported for research purposes, since the presence of some associated deficit may be correlated with a particular pattern of language recovery in bilinguals.

1. Handedness
2. Presence of familial left-handedness
3. Visual and auditory acuity
4. Neurological findings (including pyramidal and extrapyramidal signs, cranial nerves semiology, homonymous quadri- or hemianopia, peripheral motor and sensory deficits)
5. Site and size of lesion (supported by CT scan, scintegraphy or other means)
6. Orientation in time and space
7. Short-term memory span
8. Presence and degree of agnosia and apraxia
9. Presence and degree of construction apraxia
10. Presence and degree of retrograde and/or anterograde amnesia.

It is assumed that each hospital routinely administers its own neurological and neuropsychological test batteries. The above information should therefore be available from the patient's file. If this information is not available, relevant portions of standard tests (e.g., the PIENC) should be administered (Peña i Casanova, 1986).

INTERPRETATION

In order to ensure that differential performance in the two languages does not stem from differential knowledge and/or use of the languages before insult, the aphasic patient's linguistic performance on the BAT must be interpreted in the light of his or her premorbid competence in each language. This premorbid competence is rarely objectively documented, except in cases when the patient is tested preoperatively or when tapes of the patient's speech are available. Most of the time, previous competence must be deduced from the information provided by the answers to the 50 questions of Part A (History of Bilingualism) and to the first 17 questions in Part B (Language Background), supplemented by whatever information can be obtained from relatives, friends, and colleagues.

Test results are of course most revealing for patients who had a good and roughly equal knowledge of the two languages before insult, or who score lower on their formerly dominant language. When degree of premorbid linguistic competence in each language can only be estimated or cannot be assessed at all, only a minimal interpretation will be made. That is, if the language known to have been premorbidly weaker is more impaired than the premorbidly dominant language, not much can be said, except that the premorbid pattern of dominance is unchanged. As long as the previous degree of proficiency is not known it is not possible to measure whether the difference in competence between the two languages has increased, has remained the same, or has decreased. However, if the premorbidly dominant language is weaker after insult, then the difference in proficiency must be attributed to pathology (and not to premorbid bilingual imbalance).

A patient's poorer performance on tasks in a language in which she or he was not educated and/or which was decidedly his or her weaker language before insult may nevertheless be interpreted as a result of pathological processes so long as it can be ascertained that his or her premorbid competence exceeded that of a person who had studied this language for a minimum of 400 hours or who had been living at least 3 years in a community in which it was the habitual language.

It is probably in writing abilities that the premorbid discrepancy between the two languages is most likely to be most apparent. In fact, some patients may be literate in only one of their languages. Even if they can read, they may rarely have had occasion to write. Many patients may be more proficient in reading and/or writing in one of their languages. However, as long as a patient is at all literate in a language, she or he should have no difficulty in meeting criterion on the reading and writing tasks of the BAT, because of their low complexity. (See Table 4.2 for the permissible number of errors in each section.)

As with any other test battery, the presence of agnosia or apraxia will affect the scores on certain tasks, thus obscuring the diagnosis of specific language deficits. However, the effects of associated deficits will have no bearing on the comparison between two languages of a same patient since these effects will be equal on both languages. In fact, differential scores will eliminate the possibility of attributing to agnosia or apraxia an influence on the score of the most impaired language: if a particular task is performed well in one language and poorly in another, the poor performance must be attributable to linguistic factors, and not

TABLE 4.2
Error Range for Normal Subjects Broken Down by Subtest

Item Range	Subtest Name	N of Items	N of Errors in Normal Range
18-22	Spontaneous Speech	5	*
23-32	Pointing	10	0
33-37	Simple Commands	5	0
38-42	Semicomplex Commands	5	1
43-47	Complex Commands	5	2**
48-65	Verbal Auditory Discrimination	18	3
66-110	Syntactic Comprehension (S)	13	0
66-110	Syntactic Comprehension (P)	6	1
66-110	Syntactic Comprehension (A)	8	1
66-110	Syntactic Comprehension (NS1)	8	1
66-110	Syntactic Comprehension (NS2)	12	2
111-136	Syntactic Comprehension (Sn)	12	2
111-136	Syntactic Comprehension (NS1n)	12	3
137-152	Syntactic Comprehension (RP)	16	1
153-157	Semantic Categories	5	1
158-162	Synonyms	5	1
163-167	Antonyms I	5	1
168-172	Antonyms II	5	1
173-182	Grammaticality Judgment	10	1
183-192	Semantic Acceptability	10	1
193-252	Repetition	30	0
193-252	Judgment	30	1
253-259	Sentence Repetition	7	1
260-262	Series	3	0
263-268	Verbal Fluency	6	***
269-288	Naming	20	0
289-313	Sentence Construction	25	***
314-323	Semantic Opposites	10	1
324-333	Derivational Morphology	10	2
334-343	Morphological Opposites	10	2
344-346	Description	3	*
347-351	Mental Arithmetic	5	0
352-361	Mental Arithmetic	10	2
362-366	Listening Comprehension	5	1
367-376	Reading (words)	10	0
377-386	Reading (sentences)	10	1
387-392	Reading (text)	6	1
393-397	Copying	5	0
398-402	Dictation (words)	5	0
403-407	Dictation (sentences)	5	1
408-417	Reading Comprehension (words)	10	1
418-427	Reading Comprehension (sentences)	10	1

*   The patient's performance is evaluated in the Post-Test Analysis.
**   Two complete items or the equivalent of 8/20.
*** Norms on these items are given at the end of each version of the BAT.

to language-independent contaminating variables, since the latter would have equally affected performance in the other language. For example, good performance in one language on a picture pointing task would rule out visual agnosia and apraxia as a cause of failure in the other language.

The purpose of the BAT is to reveal differential ability in two languages. By measuring the level of performance in each language, one can objectively determine whether one language is less impaired or better recovered than another. Since it is to be used with aphasic patients, tasks sensitive to various types of aphasia have been selected: It is in these areas that there is a greater likelihood of finding deficits, and hence that differences between languages are likely to appear. For this reason, and only secondarily, the BAT may serve as a test of aphasia, especially in cases where no standardized test is available in a particular language.

Many types of deficit (especially word-finding difficulty, paraphasias, and lexical semantic deterioration) are not systematically associated with any particular clinical type of aphasia and yet are clearly symptomatic of aphasia per se (as opposed to normal performance) and are thus capable of differentiating between degrees of impairment in each of a patient's languages. Specific syntactic comprehension deficits have also been shown not to be necessarily correlated with classical aphasic syndromes (not even expressive agrammatism), lesion site or lesion size (Caplan, Baker, & Dehaut, 1985).

Should a patient exhibit a different pattern of deficits in each language (i.e., relatively high scores in one language and low scores in the other on some tasks, but the reverse pattern on other tasks), and should this difference not be explicable in terms of differences in premorbid competence, then a diagnosis of differential aphasia (Silverberg & Gordon, 1979) or of differential processing strategies (Gordon & Weide, 1983) might be considered.

The theoretical status of classical syndrome types in aphasia has been increasingly challenged in recent years. One criticism is that the structure of the classical aphasia categories is "polytypic" (Schwarz, 1984): Members of a taxonomic category do not necessarily share any single symptom or even any pattern of symptoms, and any particular symptom may be represented in more than one category. And yet, in spite of this inherent indefiniteness, more than half the cases of aphasia seen routinely in a clinical practice are reported not to fit any of the descriptions of classical syndromes (Benson, 1979:136). The status of "standard" and "non-standard" syndromes and of "modality-specific" deficits is still a matter of debate. Moreover, patient groupings based on clinical intuition do not necessarily coincide with linguistic or neuropsychological theoretical categories. There is at present no consensus on how to characterize most aphasic syndromes. Researchers disagree about the very essence of the syndromes. Some authors even go so far as to deny that they exist and argue that the elimination of the use of the classical categories of aphasia would be to the benefit of neurolinguistic and cognitive neuropsychological research (Badecker & Caramazza, 1985, p. 124).

Hence, for the sake of theoretical neutrality, no steadfast classification of patients' syndromes or aphasic types on the basis of their scores on the BAT is provided. Each clinician may use his or her taxonomy in accordance with his or her theoretical framework and can infer syndromes on the basis of the patient's relative scores on some specific tasks considered to be characteristic of a specific aphasia type. Each research center is free to classify its patients in keeping with the collective clinical intuition its researchers have developed over years of working with aphasic patients.

However, scores can be grouped by affinity into clusters, depending on whether one is interested in obtaining a patient's profile for performance in the various linguistic skills (Table 4.3) or for levels of linguistic structure (Table 4.4). From these profiles a sufficient number of symptoms will emerge to allow one to assign a patient to a specific aphasia type group in accordance with whatever classificatory framework one happens to use.

TABLE 4.3
Profiles for Linguistic Skills

COMPREHENSION

Auditory Comprehension (23-152; 362-366)   Reading Comprehension (408-427; 387-392)
Pointing (23-32)   Words (408-417)
Simple Commands (33-37)   Sentences (418-427)
Semicomplex Commands (38-42)   Paragraph (387-392)
Complex Commands (43-47)
Auditory Verbal Discrimination (48-65)
Syntactic Comprehension (66-152)
Listening Comprehension (362-366)

JUDGMENT

Grammaticality Judgments (173-182)
Semantic Acceptability (183-192)
Lexical Decision (194-252, even numbers only)

LEXICAL ACCESSIBILITY

Spontaneous Speech (519, 534)
Naming (269-288)
Verbal Fluency (263-268)
Semantic Opposites (314-323)
Description of Pictures (545, 560)

REPETITION

Repetition of Words (193-251, odd numbers only)   Copying (393-397)
Repetition of Sentences (253-259)

READING

Words (aloud) (367-376; 566-571)   Words (for comprehension) 408-417)
Sentences (aloud) (377-386; 572-651)   Sentences (for comprehension) (418-427)

WRITING

Copying (393-397; 652-686)
Dictation of Words (398-402; 687-726)
Dictation of Sentences (403-407; 727-755)
Spontaneous Writing (756-835)

SPELLING

Dictation of Words (398-402; 687-726)   Spontaneous Writing (756-835)
Dictation of Sentences (403-407; 727-755)

TRANSCODING TASKS

Repetition of Words and Nonwords   Reading Words Aloud (367-376;566-571)
  (193-251, odd numbers only)   Reading Sentences Aloud (377-386;
Repetition of Sentences (253-259)   572-651)
Dictation of Words (398-402; 687-726)   copying (393-397; 652-686)
Dictation of Sentences (403-407; 727-755)

TABLE 4.4
Profiles for Levels of Linguistic Structure

PHONOLOGY

Phonemic Discrimination (48-65)

Spontaneous Speech (521-524, 535)
Repetition of Words (193-251, odd numbers only)
Repetition of Sentences (253-259)
Description (547-550, 561)
Reading Words Aloud (367-376; 566-571)
Reading Sentences Aloud (377-386; 572-651)

MORPHOLOGY

Derivational Morphology (324-333)
Morphological Opposites (334-343)
Antonyms (168-172)

SYNTAX

Comprehension of Syntactic Forms

Syntactic Comprehension (66-152)
SemiComplex Commands (38-42)
Grammaticality Judgments (173-182)
Reading Comprehension for Sentences
(418-427)

Production of Syntactic Forms

Spontaneous Speech (516, 517, 526-530)
Sentence Construction (289-313)
Description (542, 543, 552-556)

SEMANTICS

Semantic Categories (153-157)
Synonyms (158-162)
Antonyms (163-172)
Semantic Acceptability (183-192)
Listening Comprehension (362-366)
Reading Comprehension* (387-392)

Semantic Opposites (314-323)
Spontaneous Speech (537-539)
Description (563-565)

*If reading comprehension for words and sentences is poor, impaired performance on reading comprehension of the paragraph is not revealing. On the other hand, if reading comprehension for words and sentences is good and reading comprehension for the paragraph is poor, then it can be interpreted as a semantic deficit.

Each task may not represent an equally important aspect of language use and hence, in the elaboration of a patient's profile, each task can be weighted in accordance with the researcher's theoretical presuppositions. Score groupings and relative weights of various sections are determined by the purpose of the analysis. The patient's performance in one language is simply noted and compared section by section to his or her performance in the other language. In this way, the final comparison between the languages of a patient's performance features will not be lost amid classificatory problems. For example, a fluent aphasic who omits closed class items does not have to be categorized as agrammatic. Nor is this patient to be described in terms of having a more or less severe agrammatic component in one of his or her languages, but as omitting, for example, 45% more obligatory morphemes in one language than in the other. (Other discrepancies can also be described in quantitative terms.)

Part B of the BAT provides a strictly quantitative assessment through numerical scores on each subtest and on the test as a whole. An objective qualitative assessment may be obtained by comparing the relative scores on various sections of the test, and those on various skills as reflected in the groupings suggested in

Table 2.1. Also, the error pattern on some subtests (e.g., a consistent interpretation of passive sentences as active sentences vs. random error in the Syntactic Comprehension section) reveals important information about the processing strategies employed by the patient. A quantified qualitative assessment is supplied in the Posttest Analysis through the report of the number of qualitatively discriminating features found in critical sections of the BAT.

A comparison of scores on specific tasks in different modalities (e.g., listening/speaking, reading/writing, comprehension/production) allows one to verify whether a deficit is modality-specific or central. For example, a comprehension deficit per se will appear in auditory as well as reading comprehension tasks (and in any task in which comprehension is a prerequisite or a component). A comprehension deficit limited to the auditory modality, on the other hand, will be revealed by the discrepancy between a low score on Commands (33-47), Verbal Auditory Discrimination (48-65), Syntactic Comprehension (66-152), and Listening Comprehension (362-366), and a relatively higher score on reading words (408-417), sentences (418-427) and a paragraph (387-392) for comprehension. Impairment in phonemic discrimination (48-65) may entail deficits in the Repetition of Words (193-251) and in Dictation (398-407). However, poor repetition in the absence of deficits in verbal auditory discrimination is indicative of an output deficit (or at least of a deficit in the process from input to output, but not involving input).

From spontaneous and descriptive speech, a score may be obtained for FLUENCY, based on richness of vocabulary (519/545), total number of words (515/541), sentence length (516, 517/542, 543), and pauses (531/557); ACCURACY, based on use of neologisms (520/546), paraphasias (521-524/-547-550), paragrammatisms (526/552), agrammatisms (527/553), perseverations (525/551), and deviant word order (528/554); LEXICAL ACCESSIBILITY, based on richness of vocabulary (519/545), pauses (531/557), circumlocutions (532/558), evidence of word-finding difficulty (534/560); and COMPLEXITY, based on sentence length (516, 517/542, 543), number of verbs per utterance (529/555), and number of subordinate clauses (530, 556). Additional information on complexity is available from scores on Sentence Construction (289-313), and on lexical accessibility from scores on naming (269-288), verbal fluency (263-267), and semantic opposites (314-323). These parameters are well suited for a comparison between performance in each of a patient's languages.

The data collected from the test and the posttest analysis may be grouped in accordance with level of linguistic structure (phonology, morphology, syntax, lexicon, semantics), linguistic skill (comprehension, repetition, expression, judgment, reading, writing), scope (word, sentence, paragraph), and modality (auditory, visual, cross-modal). There are four types of tasks relying on cross-modal linguistic processing: Oral reading (visual stimulus—oral response), dictation (auditory stimulus—digitomanual response), copying (visual stimulus—

digitomanual response), and repetition. Also relying on cross-modal processing is any task requiring an oral response to auditory instructions (auditory stimulus—oral response). Sections particularly relevant to specific levels of linguistic structure are indicated in Table 2.1. Sections assessing specific skills are mentioned in Table 2.2. In Table 3.1 tasks are identified by unit of speech and modality involved.

Thus, from the results on the BAT, one may derive either a syndromatic profile for clinical purposes, or a linguistic profile for research purposes. The linguistic profile is used to compare the various languages of the same patient. But, by determining in this way which language is more appropriate for communication, it is also of clinical use in helping to decide which language should undergo therapy and what aspects of language should be treated.

Even though the purpose of the BAT is not to assess aphasia but to compare the residual capacities of aphasic patients in one language to those in another language, it may nevertheless serve as a useful diagnostic tool because it contains most of the tasks generally regarded as discriminating among the principal clinically meaningful types of aphasia (cf. Boller & Hécaen, 1969; Boller, Kim, & Mack, 1977; Goodglass & Kaplan, 1983; Kertesz, 1979).

The following profiles are not intended to be limiting. They are provided only as general suggestions consistent with broadly defined and currently used typologies. Relative levels of function according to fluency, auditory comprehension, and repetition, based on Davis's (1983, p. 144) decision matrix reflecting Kertesz's (1979) criteria, serve as a guideline to differential diagnosis of the aphasias proposed below. Each type of aphasia is listed alphabetically according to its most current appellation.

Anomic Aphasia

Amnesic aphasia (Hécaen & Dubois, 1971; Lecours, 1974; Weisenburg & McBride, 1935), Anomia (Brown, 1972; Goodglass & Kaplan, 1983), Anomic aphasia (Benson, 1979; Geschwind, 1965; Kertesz, 1979), Nominal aphasia (Brain, 1965; Brown, 1977).

Fluent speech with good comprehension and good repetition (but poor confrontation-naming). The anomic patient is expected to show evidence of word-finding difficulty in spontaneous (534) and descriptive (545) speech (and in spontaneous writing). Because of his or her difficulty in accessing the lexicon, the number of circumlocutions (532, 558, 830) and intraphrasal pauses (531, 557) is likely to be high. Because of the use of empty words, the type/token ratio (519, 545, 817) is expected to be low.

The anomic patient's deficit is most evident in confrontation naming (269-288) and may also affect performance on tasks requiring the production of single words, namely, in Verbal Fluency (263-267) and Semantic Opposites

TABLE 4.5
Anomic Aphasia

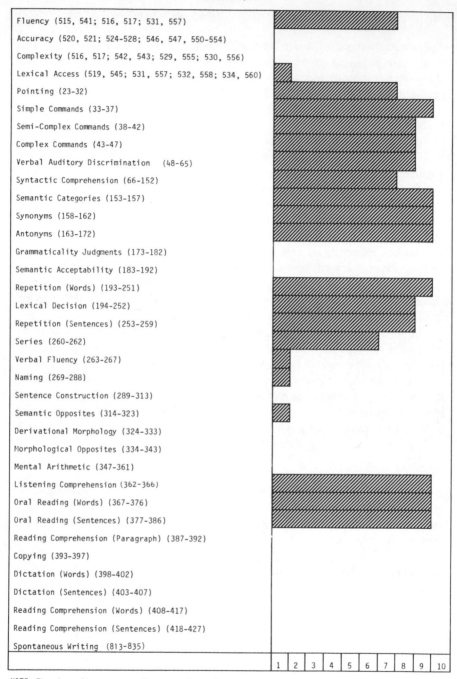

	1	2	3	4	5	6	7	8	9	10
Fluency (515, 541; 516, 517; 531, 557)										
Accuracy (520, 521; 524-528; 546, 547, 550-554)										
Complexity (516, 517; 542, 543; 529, 555; 530, 556)										
Lexical Access (519, 545; 531, 557; 532, 558; 534, 560)										
Pointing (23-32)										
Simple Commands (33-37)										
Semi-Complex Commands (38-42)										
Complex Commands (43-47)										
Verbal Auditory Discrimination (48-65)										
Syntactic Comprehension (66-152)										
Semantic Categories (153-157)										
Synonyms (158-162)										
Antonyms (163-172)										
Grammaticality Judgments (173-182)										
Semantic Acceptability (183-192)										
Repetition (Words) (193-251)										
Lexical Decision (194-252)										
Repetition (Sentences) (253-259)										
Series (260-262)										
Verbal Fluency (263-267)										
Naming (269-288)										
Sentence Construction (289-313)										
Semantic Opposites (314-323)										
Derivational Morphology (324-333)										
Morphological Opposites (334-343)										
Mental Arithmetic (347-361)										
Listening Comprehension (362-366)										
Oral Reading (Words) (367-376)										
Oral Reading (Sentences) (377-386)										
Reading Comprehension (Paragraph) (387-392)										
Copying (393-397)										
Dictation (Words) (398-402)										
Dictation (Sentences) (403-407)										
Reading Comprehension (Words) (408-417)										
Reading Comprehension (Sentences) (418-427)										
Spontaneous Writing (813-835)										

NOTE: The above figures are only suggestive. Expected scores are indicated for each task as a ratio of performance relative to other tasks. The value of absolute scores is a function of severity. Only tasks considered to be contributing to the symptomatic picture of Anomic aphasia are given a hypothetical relative score.

216

(314-323) sections. In severe cases, even the recitation in the Series section (260-262) may be affected. The patient may also have problems in the comprehension of isolated words (23-32; 48-65).

The anomic patient does not have difficulties in repetition. She or he will also do well on multiple-choice tasks. Reading and writing may be either good or defective, and hence are not symptomatic (Table 4.5).

Broca's Aphasia

Agrammatic aphasia (Brown, 1977), Broca's aphasia (Brain, 1965; Brown, 1972; Geschwind, 1965; Goodglass & Kaplan, 1983; Kertesz, 1979), efferent motor aphasia (Luria, 1964), expressive aphasia (Weisenburg & McBride, 1935), motor aphasia (Goldstein, 1948).

Nonfluent speech with relatively good comprehension but poor repetition. The production of a Broca's aphasic is typically reduced and nonfluent, with frequent perseverations (525, 551), many pauses (531, 557), awkward articulation with some phonemic paraphasias (521, 522, 547, 548) and stereotypic expressions (533, 559). One may expect a low mean length of utterance (516, 517; 542, 543), with a grammar restricted to the simplest forms—i.e., few verbs (529, 555), and subordinate clauses (530, 556) per utterance.

Oral reading (367-386) is likely to be affected by poor pronunciation. One may expect better repetition (193-251) and recitation (260-262) than spontaneous production (although repetition is still defective). Also, the patient usually exhibits better naming (269-288) than narration (540-565).

The patient may exhibit expressive agrammatism, which may or may not be accompanied by difficulties in syntactic comprehension (66-152). The number of missing obligatory morphemes (527, 543, 826) will be particularly revealing of an agrammatic component. Repetition of sentences (253-259; 609-615) may then be affected. In this case, the patient may also be expected to do poorly on the Reading Sentences Aloud (679-688), Semicomplex (38-42) and Complex Commands (43-47) sections, and in more severe cases of agrammatism, on the Grammaticality Judgment (173-182) and Reading Comprehension for Sentences (417-428) tasks. Derivational Morphology (324-343) may also prove to be difficult.

Written language is usually as impaired as spoken language and may be characterized by perseverations and metatheses. Reading is generally less affected. The Pointing (23-32), Simple Commands (33-37), Verbal Auditory Discrimination (48-65), Listening Comprehension (362-366), and Reading Comprehension (387-392; 408-417) tasks should be relatively spared. In general, the patient should obtain relatively good scores on tasks not requiring a verbal response (Table 4.6).

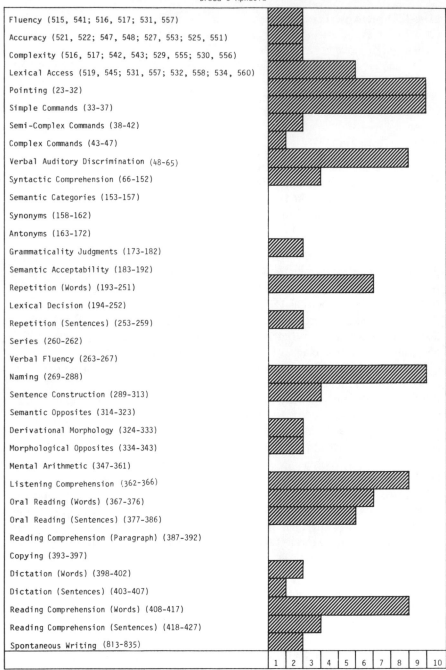

TABLE 4.6
Broca's Aphasia

	1	2	3	4	5	6	7	8	9	10

Fluency (515, 541; 516, 517; 531, 557)
Accuracy (521, 522; 547, 548; 527, 553; 525, 551)
Complexity (516, 517; 542, 543; 529, 555; 530, 556)
Lexical Access (519, 545; 531, 557; 532, 558; 534, 560)
Pointing (23-32)
Simple Commands (33-37)
Semi-Complex Commands (38-42)
Complex Commands (43-47)
Verbal Auditory Discrimination (48-65)
Syntactic Comprehension (66-152)
Semantic Categories (153-157)
Synonyms (158-162)
Antonyms (163-172)
Grammaticality Judgments (173-182)
Semantic Acceptability (183-192)
Repetition (Words) (193-251)
Lexical Decision (194-252)
Repetition (Sentences) (253-259)
Series (260-262)
Verbal Fluency (263-267)
Naming (269-288)
Sentence Construction (289-313)
Semantic Opposites (314-323)
Derivational Morphology (324-333)
Morphological Opposites (334-343)
Mental Arithmetic (347-361)
Listening Comprehension (362-366)
Oral Reading (Words) (367-376)
Oral Reading (Sentences) (377-386)
Reading Comprehension (Paragraph) (387-392)
Copying (393-397)
Dictation (Words) (398-402)
Dictation (Sentences) (403-407)
Reading Comprehension (Words) (408-417)
Reading Comprehension (Sentences) (418-427)
Spontaneous Writing (813-835)

NOTE: The above figures are only suggestive. Expected scores are indicated for each task as a ratio of performance relative to other tasks. The value of absolute scores is a function of severity. Only tasks considered to be contributing to the symptomatic picture of Broca's aphasia are given a hypothetical relative score.

Conduction Aphasia

Conduction aphasia (Benson, 1979; Brown, 1972; Geschwind, 1965; Goodglass & Kaplan, 1983; Kertesz, 1979; Lecours, 1974), phonemic aphasia (Brown, 1977).

Fluent speech with good comprehension but poor repetition. Conduction aphasia is characterized by a discrepancy between clearly impaired repetition and relatively well-preserved comprehension and expression. The patient exhibits more paraphasias in repetition (567, 568; 574-587) than in fluent paraphasic conversational speech. Oral reading may be rendered abnormal by numerous phonemic paraphasias (624, 625; 629-648) but reading comprehension should be comparatively good.

Performance should also be relatively less impaired on judgment tasks (173-192; 194-252 even numbers only) and on the tasks of Pointing (23-32), Simple and Semicomplex Commands (33-42), Verbal Auditory Discrimination (48-65), Syntactic Comprehension (66-152), Semantic Categories (153-157), Synonyms (158-162), Antonyms (163-172), and Listening Comprehension (362-366). (Table 4.7.)

Global Aphasia

Global aphasia (Benson, 1979; Goodglass & Kaplan, 1983; Kertesz, 1979).

Nonfluent speech with poor comprehension and poor repetition. All major language functions are severely impaired in all modalities. Since global aphasia is unlikely to represent a single, consistent syndrome, patients will demonstrate significant variations. Ability in the Series task (260-262) may be somewhat preserved. Stereotypic phrases (553, 559) may be the patient's only residual output (Table 4.8).

Isolation Of The Speech Area Syndrome

Isolation syndrome (Gerschwind, Quadfascl, & Segarra, 1968; Whitaker, 1976), mixed transcortical aphasia (Benson, 1979; Goldstein, 1948).

Nonfluent speech with poor comprehension but good repetition. In its severest form, the isolation syndrome is manifested in the patient's output being reduced to echolalia (i.e., compulsive repetition) in the context of apparent total loss of comprehension. The patient is likely to fail on all tasks except in repetition of single words (193-251) and, to some extent, of short sentences (254-259).

The isolation syndrome combines features of transcortical motor and transcortical sensory syndromes. Conversational speech is nonfluent with echolalia. Comprehension (23-152) is severely defective. So is naming (269-288). Since

TABLE 4.7
Conduction Aphasia

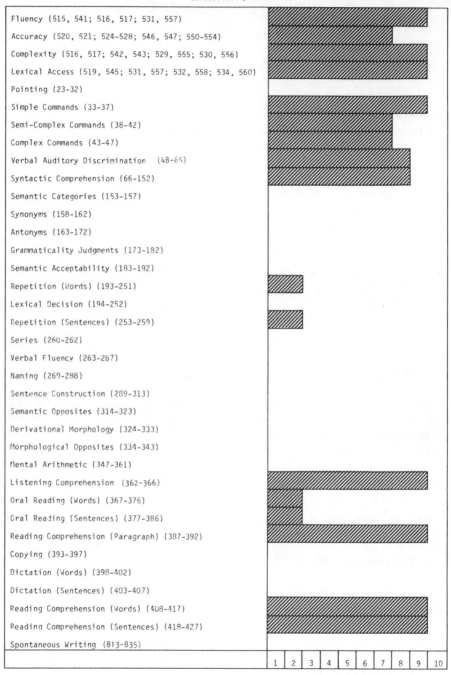

Fluency (515, 541; 516, 517; 531, 557)

Accuracy (520, 521; 524-528; 546, 547; 550-554)

Complexity (516, 517; 542, 543; 529, 555; 530, 556)

Lexical Access (519, 545; 531, 557; 532, 558; 534, 560)

Pointing (23-32)

Simple Commands (33-37)

Semi-Complex Commands (38-42)

Complex Commands (43-47)

Verbal Auditory Discrimination (48-65)

Syntactic Comprehension (66-152)

Semantic Categories (153-157)

Synonyms (158-162)

Antonyms (163-172)

Grammaticality Judgments (173-182)

Semantic Acceptability (183-192)

Repetition (Words) (193-251)

Lexical Decision (194-252)

Repetition (Sentences) (253-259)

Series (260-262)

Verbal Fluency (263-267)

Naming (269-288)

Sentence Construction (289-313)

Semantic Opposites (314-323)

Derivational Morphology (324-333)

Morphological Opposites (334-343)

Mental Arithmetic (347-361)

Listening Comprehension (362-366)

Oral Reading (Words) (367-376)

Oral Reading (Sentences) (377-386)

Reading Comprehension (Paragraph) (387-392)

Copying (393-397)

Dictation (Words) (398-402)

Dictation (Sentences) (403-407)

Reading Comprehension (Words) (408-417)

Reading Comprehension (Sentences) (418-427)

Spontaneous Writing (813-835)

1 2 3 4 5 6 7 8 9 10

NOTE: The above figures are only suggestive. Expected scores are indicated for each task as a
ratio of performance relative to other tasks. The value of absolute scores is a function of
severity. Only tasks considered to be contributing to the symptomatic picture of Conduction
aphasia are given a hypothetical relative score.

TABLE 4.8
Global Aphasia

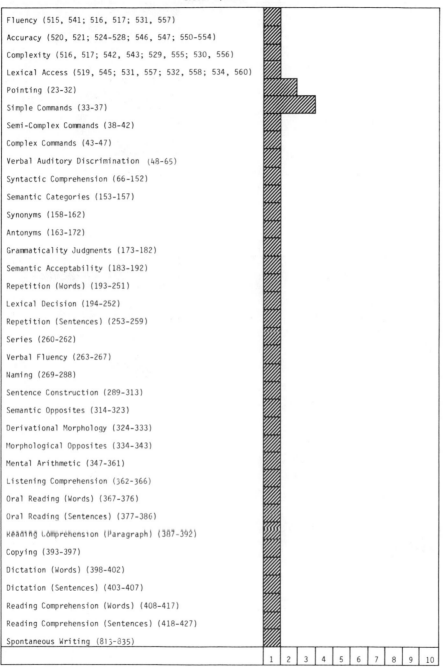

Fluency (515, 541; 516, 517; 531, 557)

Accuracy (520, 521; 524-528; 546, 547; 550-554)

Complexity (516, 517; 542, 543; 529, 555; 530, 556)

Lexical Access (519, 545; 531, 557; 532, 558; 534, 560)

Pointing (23-32)

Simple Commands (33-37)

Semi-Complex Commands (38-42)

Complex Commands (43-47)

Verbal Auditory Discrimination (48-65)

Syntactic Comprehension (66-152)

Semantic Categories (153-157)

Synonyms (158-162)

Antonyms (163-172)

Grammaticality Judgments (173-182)

Semantic Acceptability (183-192)

Repetition (Words) (193-251)

Lexical Decision (194-252)

Repetition (Sentences) (253-259)

Series (260-262)

Verbal Fluency (263-267)

Naming (269-288)

Sentence Construction (289-313)

Semantic Opposites (314-323)

Derivational Morphology (324-333)

Morphological Opposites (334-343)

Mental Arithmetic (347-361)

Listening Comprehension (362-366)

Oral Reading (Words) (367-376)

Oral Reading (Sentences) (377-386)

Reading Comprehension (Paragraph) (387-392)

Copying (393-397)

Dictation (Words) (398-402)

Dictation (Sentences) (403-407)

Reading Comprehension (Words) (408-417)

Reading Comprehension (Sentences) (418-427)

Spontaneous Writing (813-835)

1 2 3 4 5 6 7 8 9 10

NOTE: The above figures are only suggestive. Expected scores are indicated for each task as a
ratio of performance relative to other tasks. The value of absolute scores is a function of
severity. Only tasks considered to be contributing to the symptomatic picture of Global
aphasia are given a hypothetical relative score.

TABLE 4.9
Isolation Syndrome

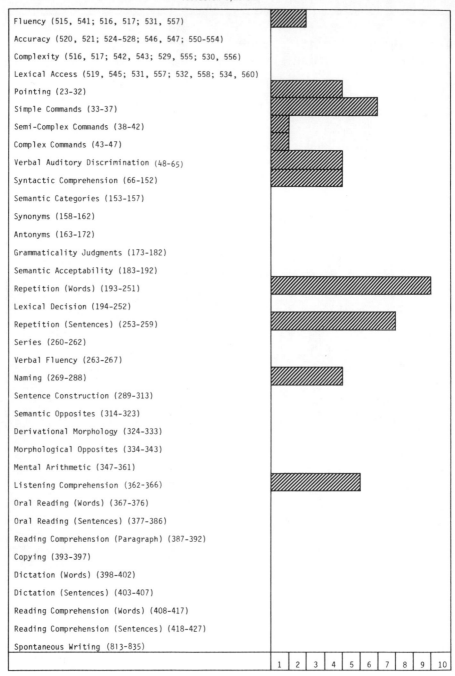

Task	1	2	3	4	5	6	7	8	9	10
Fluency (515, 541; 516, 517; 531, 557)										
Accuracy (520, 521; 524-528; 546, 547; 550-554)										
Complexity (516, 517; 542, 543; 529, 555; 530, 556)										
Lexical Access (519, 545; 531, 557; 532, 558; 534, 560)										
Pointing (23-32)										
Simple Commands (33-37)										
Semi-Complex Commands (38-42)										
Complex Commands (43-47)										
Verbal Auditory Discrimination (48-65)										
Syntactic Comprehension (66-152)										
Semantic Categories (153-157)										
Synonyms (158-162)										
Antonyms (163-172)										
Grammaticality Judgments (173-182)										
Semantic Acceptability (183-192)										
Repetition (Words) (193-251)										
Lexical Decision (194-252)										
Repetition (Sentences) (253-259)										
Series (260-262)										
Verbal Fluency (263-267)										
Naming (269-288)										
Sentence Construction (289-313)										
Semantic Opposites (314-323)										
Derivational Morphology (324-333)										
Morphological Opposites (334-343)										
Mental Arithmetic (347-361)										
Listening Comprehension (362-366)										
Oral Reading (Words) (367-376)										
Oral Reading (Sentences) (377-386)										
Reading Comprehension (Paragraph) (387-392)										
Copying (393-397)										
Dictation (Words) (398-402)										
Dictation (Sentences) (403-407)										
Reading Comprehension (Words) (408-417)										
Reading Comprehension (Sentences) (418-427)										
Spontaneous Writing (813-835)										

NOTE: The above figures are only suggestive. Expected scores are indicated for each task as a ratio of performance relative to other tasks. The value of absolute scores is a function of severity. Only tasks considered to be contributing to the symptomatic picture of Isolation syndrome are given a hypothetical relative score.

(260-262) may be completed once initiated by the test administrator. Reading aloud (367-386), reading comprehension (387-392; 408-427), and writing (398-407; 813-835) are also likely to be considerably impaired (Table 4.9).

Transcortical Motor Aphasia

Dynamic aphasia (Luria, 1966), transcortical motor aphasia (Benson, 1979; Brown, 1977; Geschwind, 1965; Goodglass & Kaplan, 1983).

Nonfluent speech with good comprehension and good repetition.   The transcortical motor aphasic typically presents a clinical picture of reduced output with relatively intact comprehension and good repetition. Hence one may expect a low mean length of utterance (516, 517; 542, 543) with relatively good scores on comprehensive tasks (362-366; 387-392). However, tasks involving pointing (48-65; 66-152; 408-427) may be affected by concomitant apraxia. Naming (269-288) is often defective. The patient may also do poorly on Semicomplex Commands (38-42) because of a difficulty in processing locative prepositions.

Reading aloud (367-386) and writing (398-407; 813-835) are usually poor. Repetition (193-251; 253-259) is relatively good but perseverations (525, 551) are generally abundant. The patient may be able to produce series (260-262) once she or he has been initiated by the examiner (Table 4.10).

Transcortical Sensory Aphasia

Sensory III (Hécaen & Dubois, 1971), transcortical sensory aphasia (Benson, 1979; Goodglass & Kaplan, 1983; Kertesz, 1979), Wernicke II (Lecours, 1974). Sometimes transcortical sensory aphasia is not distinguished from the isolation syndrome.

Fluent speech with poor comprehension but relatively good repetition.   The transcortical sensory aphasic patient generally presents with fluent, paraphasic, echolalic conversational speech in the context of severely defective comprehension of spoken language. Hence the patient is expected to obtain low scores on auditory comprehension tasks (23-152; 362-366). Reading comprehension (387-392; 408-427) is equally defective, as are reading aloud (367-386) and writing (398-407; 813-835). Naming (269-288) is also frequently impaired.

Repetition of words (193-251) and sentences (253-259) is usually relatively well preserved, as well as automatic speech, reflected in series recitation (260-262) and mental arithmetic (347-361). (Table 4.11.)

Wernicke's Aphasia

Semantic aphasia (Brown, 1977), sensory aphasia (Goldstein, 1948), Wernicke's aphasia (Benson, 1979; Geschwind, 1965; Goodglass & Kaplan, 1983; Kertesz, 1979).

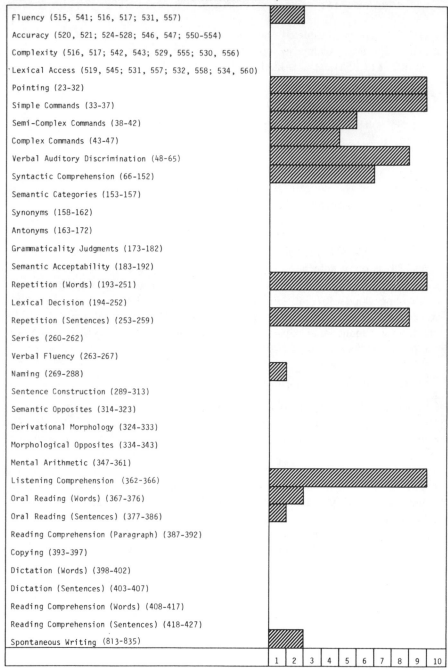

TABLE 4.10
Transcortical Motor Aphasia

Fluency (515, 541; 516, 517; 531, 557)
Accuracy (520, 521; 524-528; 546, 547; 550-554)
Complexity (516, 517; 542, 543; 529, 555; 530, 556)
Lexical Access (519, 545; 531, 557; 532, 558; 534, 560)
Pointing (23-32)
Simple Commands (33-37)
Semi-Complex Commands (38-42)
Complex Commands (43-47)
Verbal Auditory Discrimination (48-65)
Syntactic Comprehension (66-152)
Semantic Categories (153-157)
Synonyms (158-162)
Antonyms (163-172)
Grammaticality Judgments (173-182)
Semantic Acceptability (183-192)
Repetition (Words) (193-251)
Lexical Decision (194-252)
Repetition (Sentences) (253-259)
Series (260-262)
Verbal Fluency (263-267)
Naming (269-288)
Sentence Construction (289-313)
Semantic Opposites (314-323)
Derivational Morphology (324-333)
Morphological Opposites (334-343)
Mental Arithmetic (347-361)
Listening Comprehension (362-366)
Oral Reading (Words) (367-376)
Oral Reading (Sentences) (377-386)
Reading Comprehension (Paragraph) (387-392)
Copying (393-397)
Dictation (Words) (398-402)
Dictation (Sentences) (403-407)
Reading Comprehension (Words) (408-417)
Reading Comprehension (Sentences) (418-427)
Spontaneous Writing (813-835)

1 2 3 4 5 6 7 8 9 10

NOTE: The above figures are only suggestive. Expected scores are indicated for each task as a ratio of performance relative to other tasks. The value of absolute scores is a function of severity. Only tasks considered to be contributing to the symptomatic picture of Transcortical motor aphasia are given a hypothetical relative score.

TABLE 4.11
Transcortical Sensory Aphasia

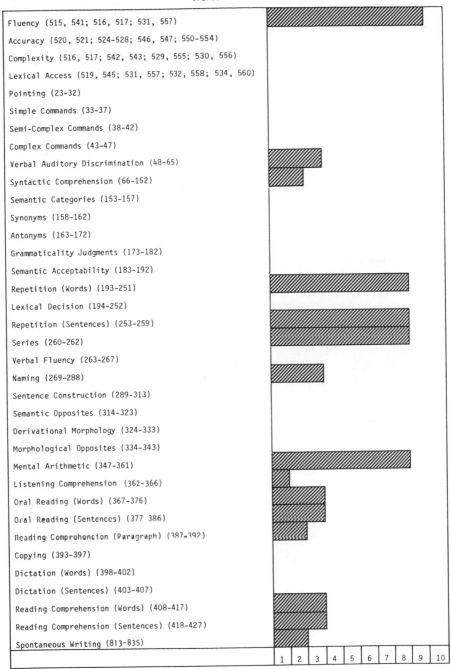

Fluency (515, 541; 516, 517; 531, 557)
Accuracy (520, 521; 524-528; 546, 547; 550-554)
Complexity (516, 517; 542, 543; 529, 555; 530, 556)
Lexical Access (519, 545; 531, 557; 532, 558; 534, 560)
Pointing (23-32)
Simple Commands (33-37)
Semi-Complex Commands (38-42)
Complex Commands (43-47)
Verbal Auditory Discrimination (48-65)
Syntactic Comprehension (66-152)
Semantic Categories (153-157)
Synonyms (158-162)
Antonyms (163-172)
Grammaticality Judgments (173-182)
Semantic Acceptability (183-192)
Repetition (Words) (193-251)
Lexical Decision (194-252)
Repetition (Sentences) (253-259)
Series (260-262)
Verbal Fluency (263-267)
Naming (269-288)
Sentence Construction (289-313)
Semantic Opposites (314-323)
Derivational Morphology (324-333)
Morphological Opposites (334-343)
Mental Arithmetic (347-361)
Listening Comprehension (362-366)
Oral Reading (Words) (367-376)
Oral Reading (Sentences) (377 386)
Reading Comprehension (Paragraph) (387-392)
Copying (393-397)
Dictation (Words) (398-402)
Dictation (Sentences) (403-407)
Reading Comprehension (Words) (408-417)
Reading Comprehension (Sentences) (418-427)
Spontaneous Writing (813-835)

1 2 3 4 5 6 7 8 9 10

NOTE: The above figures are only suggestive. Expected scores are indicated for each task as a
ratio of performance relative to other tasks. The value of absolute scores is a function of
severity. Only tasks considered to be contributing to the symptomatic picture of
Transcortical sensory aphasia are given a hypothetical relative score.

TABLE 4.12
Wernicke's Aphasia

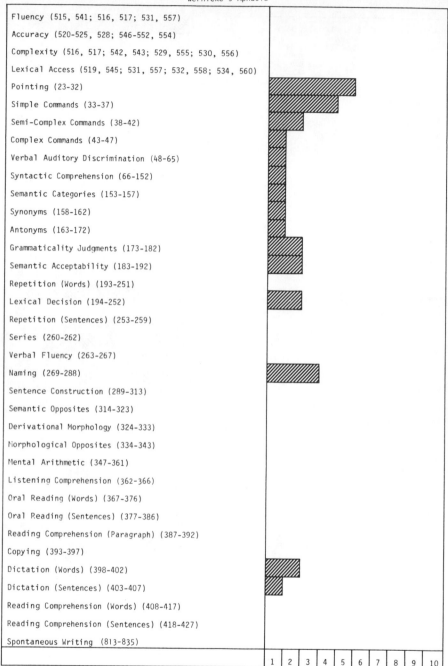

| | 1 | 2 | 3 | 4 | 5 | 6 | 7 | 8 | 9 | 10 |

Fluency (515, 541; 516, 517; 531, 557)
Accuracy (520-525, 528; 546-552, 554)
Complexity (516, 517; 542, 543; 529, 555; 530, 556)
Lexical Access (519, 545; 531, 557; 532, 558; 534, 560)
Pointing (23-32)
Simple Commands (33-37)
Semi-Complex Commands (38-42)
Complex Commands (43-47)
Verbal Auditory Discrimination (48-65)
Syntactic Comprehension (66-152)
Semantic Categories (153-157)
Synonyms (158-162)
Antonyms (163-172)
Grammaticality Judgments (173-182)
Semantic Acceptability (183-192)
Repetition (Words) (193-251)
Lexical Decision (194-252)
Repetition (Sentences) (253-259)
Series (260-262)
Verbal Fluency (263-267)
Naming (269-288)
Sentence Construction (289-313)
Semantic Opposites (314-323)
Derivational Morphology (324-333)
Morphological Opposites (334-343)
Mental Arithmetic (347-361)
Listening Comprehension (362-366)
Oral Reading (Words) (367-376)
Oral Reading (Sentences) (377-386)
Reading Comprehension (Paragraph) (387-392)
Copying (393-397)
Dictation (Words) (398-402)
Dictation (Sentences) (403-407)
Reading Comprehension (Words) (408-417)
Reading Comprehension (Sentences) (418-427)
Spontaneous Writing (813-835)

NOTE: The above figures are only suggestive. Expected scores are indicated for each task as a ratio of performance relative to other tasks. The value of absolute scores is a function of severity. Only tasks considered to be contributing to the symptomatic picture of Wernicke's aphasia are given a hypothetical relative score.

Fluent speech with poor comprehension and poor repetition.   Patients with Wernicke's aphasia are characterized by fluent, paraphasic, empty speech containing few lexical words, relatively numerous closed class words (e.g., vague pronouns) and occasional neologisms. In more severe cases, the abundance of paraphasias (521-524; 547-550), paragrammatisms (526, 552), and neologisms (520, 546) may lead to unintelligible jargonaphasia. Hence, spontaneous and descriptive speech should exhibit a high mean length of utterance (516, 517; 542, 543), a large number of sentences (514, 540), of verbs per utterance (529, 555) and of subordinate clauses (530, 556). The total number of words is also likely to be high in spontaneous (515) and descriptive (541) speech, as well as in sentence construction (289-313). Because of the repetitious vocabulary, the type/token ratio may be low. Even though the patient is fluent, she or he should be expected to score poorly on just about every subtest involving expression.

Severely impaired auditory comprehension should similarly affect every subtest to the extent that comprehension of instructions is deficient. Scores on those items that specifically test comprehension should be still worse. Hence one may expect failure in Pointing (23-32), Commands (33-47), Verbal Auditory Discrimination (48-65), Syntactic Comprehension (66-152), Listening Comprehension (362-366), Dictation (398-407). Reading Comprehension (387-392; 408-427) will also be poor. Writing (813-835) is generally also abnormal.

Since posterior aphasics have been reported to have lost a good deal of semantic organization of the lexicon (Grober, Perecman, Kellar, & Brown, 1980; Zurif, Caramazza, Myerson, & Galvin, 1974), these patients may be expected to do poorly on Semantic Categories (153-157), Synonyms (158-162), and Antonyms (163-172). (Table 4.12.)

5 Conclusion

There are many factors which contribute to the organization of the two languages in the brain of a bilingual, and it is as yet impossible to know or use these factors for prediction in a given case.
—Albert and Obler (1978, p. 247)

The present scarcity of evidence bearing on the role of biological, neurological, and environmental factors on patterns of recovery in bilingual aphasic patients is due in part to the inadequacy of testing materials and to the unavailability of sufficiently large numbers of patients in whom these parameters are known. Among the biological variables possibly influencing differential recovery one must consider age, sex, and handedness; among neurological variables, etiology, side, site, and size of lesion, number of days post-onset, type and severity of aphasia; among environmental variables, context of acquisition and use, level of education, and structural distance between languages.

Yet, the reasons why one should assess both languages of a bilingual patient are compelling. Objective assessment in each language is a prerequisite to determining which language is best available to the patient for communication. This information may in turn help one decide in which language therapy is most advisable. It is also the only way to detect symptoms that would otherwise go unnoticed in the other language, either because of the nature of specific features of the linguistic structure of one of the languages, or because of differential recovery.

Therefore, a large-scale study of bilingual aphasia will yield data of benefit to research, diagnosis, and prescription for therapy. That is, the systematic assessment of both languages of a bilingual aphasic patient will be of immediate advantage to the clinician and the language therapist. It may also eventually tell us something about the neurofunctional organization of two languages in the same brain. In addition, a methodical monitoring of the effects of various types of therapy in different circumstances will also point to the optimal conditions for prescribing which type of therapy in which language. Among other things, it will establish whether therapy is necessary in both languages or whether it is sufficient in one, and if so, in which one.

At present it is not known whether recovery significantly differs following therapy in one languagae or in both, and whether it is influenced by etiology, initial severity and type of aphasia, structural distance between the languages, patient's age, premorbid intelligence, educational level, or type of therapy. Indeed, therapy may have differential effects on the premorbidly dominant (vs. weaker) language and/or on the best (vs. the least well) recovered language. Therapeutic effects on one language may transfer to another language in proportion to the structural similarity between the languages (i.e., the positive effects on the untreated language may be proportional to the degree of similarity between the treated and the untreated language), or therapeutic effects may transfer irrespective of structural distance. Moreover, effects of therapy may transfer in the context of some aphasic syndromes, have no effect in others, and have negative effects in still others.

Therapy in one language may partially block the spontaneous recovery of other languages (Lebrun, 1976, p. 108). Recovery may be comparable for both the treated and nontreated language or may be somewhat less effective for the untreated language with one type of aphasia, but more effective for the treated language with another type of aphasia (Watamori & Sasanuma, 1978, p. 139). While Voinescu, Vish, Sirian, & Maretsis's (1977) case would lend support to such a hypothesis, Bychowski (1919) and Minkowski (1927) have reported cases in which therapy in one language had no effect on the other, even though their patients exhibited the same type of aphasia as Watamori & Sasanuma's first patient. Other authors have reported (Fredman, 1975) or assumed (Peuser, 1974) positive effects of therapy on the nontreated language, irrespective of aphasia type. But according to some, therapy in several languages will only hinder their recovery (Wald, 1961) and hence only one language should be rehabilitated (Wald, 1958). Only the systematic and detailed reporting of effects of therapy as measured by the same standard instrument in large numbers of cases can bring us closer to an answer to such complex questions.

The purpose of the BAT is not to tell us something about aphasia that we do not already know—though it will tell us something about comparative structure and the language-specific kinds of deficits subsequent to lesions in circumscribed loci. For example, we can learn how agrammatism manifests itself in languages with different structures (presence or absence of articles and copula, gender and number marking, prepositions vs. affixes, etc.). Nor is the aim to compare aphasic performance across languages. (The performance of unilinguals can tell us that—though again, of course, all factors are better controlled when the two languages are stored and processed in the same brain.) Rather, the objective of the BAT is to tell us to what extent and in what aspects of language performance one language is better recovered than another in a given patient.

Thus, the BAT provides a means of objectively evaluating the relative residual abilities in each of an aphasic patient's languages, so as to ensure that all languages are assessed uniformly and that the scores obtained on any version of the test can be meaningfully compared to scores on any other. By the same token, the BAT provides a standard method for describing bilingual aphasic patients, or groups of patients, or patterns of recovery, from one research center to another.

The BAT does not assess the patient's global communicative competence but his or her ability to communicate through each language independently. It tests how well each language (or dialect) is retained. Hence code-mixing as a communicative strategy is not tested.

Needless to say, no test can cover all aspects of language and language use exhaustively. The BAT is a comprehensive language test rather than a thorough detailed investigation of particular aspects of language. It is not intended to assess aphasic performance on individual structures. It represents only a basic assessment and is to be administered to all patients for purposes of comparison between large populations of bilingual aphasics. Shortage of personnel, the necessity of an all-around neuropsychological nonverbal assessment in addition to the administration of the BAT itself, and the fatiguability of aphasic patients prevent the BAT from being more exhaustive. It is, however, hoped that additional tests to further explore deficits in specific areas will be made available at a later stage. All the BAT can do at the moment is to provide a sufficiently detailed profile of a patient's linguistic abilities in each language to compare his or her performance in comprehension, expression, repetition, judgments, reading, and writing, or in syntax, derivational morphology, semantics, and the lexicon. The BAT will make clear whether a patient's performance is better in any or all of the psycholinguistic and linguistic areas covered.

In addition, the BAT should eventually tell us something about the way in which two languages are neurofunctionally organized in the brain and whether that organization is the same for all bilinguals (and if not, what factors influence the organization). At the very least, the BAT will enable us to testify to the existence of various patterns of recovery sketchily reported in the literature of the past century (and it will possibly enable us to identify new ones). It will also inform us about the relative occurrence of each pattern, will reveal the factor or factors correlated with each, and will discriminate between linguistic and nonlinguistic deficits. Because reasoning and conceptual knowledge are independent of language (though they interact with it), and because bilinguals do not possess two sets of cognitive functions and mental representations, any nonlinguistic deficit remains identical in both languages, irrespective of which language is being used by the patient. Nor do the patient's intelligence, education, social status, age, or the nature of his or her brain damage change when she or he changes language. Hence, any differential performance on the BAT is indicative of differential *linguistic* ability.

No task can examine one aspect of linguistic structure or of performance at the exclusion of all others. But when several sections concentrate on the same aspect it is possible to regroup the scores to obtain a clinical picture for a particular level of linguistic structure or a particular skill. Possible contaminating variables are thus somewhat controlled by varying them across tasks (i.e., some aspect of structure is tested through different skills, or some skill is tested on a variety of linguistic materials) and by testing the other concomitant aspects specifically in other sections. Such groupings can then be used to derive a patient's linguistic or syndromatic profile. The significance of such profiles is to be interpreted in the light of one's theoretical framework and classificatory scheme. Such an interpretation, in terms of the most prevalent taxonomy of classical syndromes, has been provided only as a suggestion.

Highly standardized administration procedures and objective quantitative scoring methods have been adopted for the BAT for at least two reasons: (1) The test will be given by an inexperienced administrator every time a patient speaks a language unknown to the hospital staff, and (2) the results from geographically distant centers must be comparable for research purposes. Hence, each version of the test is published in usable form and incorporates its own scoring sheet. It is practical enough to be administered in less than 2 hours, yet sufficiently comprehensive to cover most representative aspects of linguistic structure and of language use. It assesses a wide range of language skills at various levels of spontaneity and formality, from extemporaneous conversational speech to metalinguistic tasks.

Validity, in a diagnostic aphasia battery, is reflected in the degree to which aphasics can be differentiated by the test. In the case of the BAT, even though most tasks are standard aphasia battery items, validity is reflected in the degree to which a score in one language is comparable to that in another. In order to ascertain equivalence between the different versions of the BAT, in addition to the comparative structural criteria used in constructing each version, norms have been obtained in each language from 60 hospitalized non brain-damaged, non-psychotic patients in countries where the languages of the test are spoken.

The validity of the BAT as a measure of language ability also resides in its sampling a number of different language behaviors that require verbal performance on oral and written comprehension, judgment, repetition, and expression, tapping different areas of linguistic structure at the level of the word, the sentence, and the paragraph. Its content validity is further guaranteed by the inclusion of measures of the qualitative characteristics of speech which have been demonstrated to be among the most prominent features of aphasic speech. Even though formal considerations of content validity are greatly reduced because nonlinguistic effects are neutralized in a bilingual patient, the content of the BAT has been carefully selected to lie within the knowledge base of every speaker of the language.

The fact that there are many variables to consider and that consequently it might take 10 years of extensive research before results begin to form patterns is no reason to remain idle. If we do nothing, we are assured of not being any more advanced in 100 years than we are now, either in terms of our knowledge of bilingual aphasia in general, or in terms of our knowledge of the effectiveness of selective therapy in particular. If, on the other hand, we start the necessary painstaking investigation by collaborating with researchers around the world, we may hope to be closer to some answers 10 years from now.

Admittedly, the BAT is not a perfect instrument, because there cannot be a perfect instrument. But one thing is certain: As data from the over 60 pairs of languages of the *Bilingual Aphasia Test* are collected and analyzed, it will become possible to compare the linguistic abilities of bilingual aphasic patients more accurately than ever before.

References

Albert, M. L., & Obler, L. K. (1978). *The bilingual brain.* New York: Academic Press.

Altenberg, E. P., & Cairns, H. (1983). The effects of phonotactic constraints on lexical processing in bilingual and monolingual subjects. *Journal of Verbal Learning and Verbal Behavior, 22:* 174–188.

April, R., & Han, M. (1980). Crossed aphasia in a right-handed bilingual Chinese man. *Archives of Neurology, 37,* 342–345.

Arsenian, S. (1937). *Bilingualism and mental development.* New York: Columbia University Press.

Badecker, W., & Caramazza, A. (1985). On considerations of method and theory governing the use of clinical categories in neurolinguistics and cognitive neuropsychology: The case against agrammatism. *Cognition, 20,* 97–125.

Benson, D. F. (1979). *Aphasia, alexia, and agraphia.* New York: Churchill Livingstone.

Blocher, E. (1910). Zweisprachigkeit. Vorteile und Nachteile. In W. Reins (Ed.), *Encyklopädisches der Pädagogik,* vol. 10.

Boller, F., & Hécaen, H. (1979). L'évaluation des fonctions neuropsychologiques: examen standard de l'unité de recherches neuropsychologiques et neurolinguistiques (U. 111) INSERM. *Revue de psychologie appliquée, 29,* 247–266.

Boller, F., Kim, Y., & Mack, J. L. (1977). Auditory comprehension in aphasia. In H. A. Whitaker & H. Whitaker (Eds.), *Studies in Neurolinguistics* (vol. 3, pp. 1–63). New York: Academic Press.

Brain, R. (1965). *Speech disorders: Aphasia, apraxia and agnosia.* London: Butterworths.

Brown, J. W. (1972). *Aphasia, apraxia and agnosia: Clinical and theoretical aspects.* Springfield, IL: Charles C. Thomas.

Brown, J. W. (1977). *Mind, brain and consciousness.* New York: Academic Press.

Bychowski, Z. (1919). Über die Restitution der nach einem Schädelschuss verlorenen Umgangssprache bei einem Polyglotten. *Monatsschrift für Psychiatrie und Neurologie, 45,* 183–201. Translated in Paradis (1983), 130–144.

Caplan, D., Baker, C., & Dehaut, F. (1985). Syntactic determinants of sentence comprehension in aphasia. *Cognition, 21,* 117–175.

Chernigovskaya, T. V., Balonov, L., & Deglin, V. L. (1983). Bilingualism and brain functional asymmetry. *Brain and Language, 20,* 195–216.

233

Chlenov, L. G. (1948). Ob afazii u poliglotov. *Izvestiia Akademii Pedagogicheskikh NAUK, RSFSR, 15,* 783–790. Translated in Paradis (1983), 445–454.

Chomsky, N. (1965). *Aspects of the theory of syntax.* Cambridge, MA: M I T Press.

Crystal, D. (1980). *A first dictionary of linguistics and phonetics.* Boulder, CO: Westview Press.

Dalrymple-Alford, E. C. (1985). Language switching during bilingual reading. *British Journal of Psychology, 76,* 111–122.

Darley, F. L. (Ed.). (1979). *Evaluation and appraisal techniques in speech and language pathology.* Reading, MA: Addison-Wesley.

Davis, G. A. (1983). *A survey of adult aphasia.* Englewood Cliffs, NJ: Prentice-Hall.

Fredman, M. (1975). The effect of therapy given in Hebrew on the home language of the bilingual or polyglot adult aphasic in Israel. *British Journal of Disorders of Communication, 10,* 61–69.

Galloway, L. (1978). Language impairment and recovery in polyglot aphasia: A case of a heptaglot. In M. Paradis (Ed.), *Aspects of Bilingualism* (pp. 139–148). Columbia, SC: Hornbeam Press.

Galloway, L. (1980). *The cerebral organization of language in bilinguals and second language learners.* Unpublished doctoral dissertation, U.C.L.A.

Galloway, L. (1983). Etudes cliniques et expérimentales sur la répartition hémisphérique du traitement cérébral du langage chez les bilingues: modèles théoriques. *Langages, 72,* 79–113.

Geschwind, N. (1965). Disconnexion syndromes in animals and man. *Brain, 88,* 237–294; 585–644.

Geschwind, N., Quadfasel, F., & Segarra, J. (1968). Isolation of the speech area. *Neuropsychologia, 6,* 327–340.

Gloning, I., & Gloning, K. (1965). Aphasien bei Polyglotten. Beitrag zur Dynamik des Sprachabbaus sowie zu Lokalisationsfrage dieser Störungen. *Weiner Zeitschrift für Nervenheilkunde, 22,* 362–397. Translated in Paradis (1983), 681–716.

Goldstein, K. (1948). *Language and language disturbances.* New York: Grune and Stratton.

Goodglass, H., & Kaplan, E. (1983). *The assessment of aphasia and related disorders: Second edition.* Philadelphia: Lea & Febiger.

Gordon, H. W. (1980). Cerebral organization in bilinguals: I. Lateralization. *Brain and Language, 9,* 255–268.

Gordon, H. W., & Weide, R. (1983). La contribution de certaines fonctions cognitives au traitement du langage, à son acquisition et à l'apprentissage d'une langue seconde. *Langages, 72,* 45–56.

Grober, E., Perecman, E., Kellar, L., & Brown, J. (1980). Lexical knowledge in anterior and posterior aphasics. *Brain and Language, 10,* 318–330.

Grosjean, F. (1985). The bilingual as a competent but specific speaker-hearer. *Journal of Multilingual and Multicultural Development, 6,* 467–477.

Hamers, J., & Lambert, W. (1977). Visual field and cerebral hemisphere preferences in bilinguals. In S. Segalowitz & R. F. Gruber (Eds.), *Language development and neurological theory* (pp. 57–62). New York: Academic Press.

Hécaen, H., & Angelergues, R. (1964). Localization of symptoms in aphasia. In A. V. S. De Reuck & M. O'Connor (Eds.), *Disorders of language* (pp. 223–246). London: J. & A. Churchill.

Hécaen, H., & Dubois, J. (1971). La neurolinguistique. In G. E. Perren & J. L. Trim (Eds.), *Applications of linguistics* (pp. 85–99). London: Cambridge University Press.

Hemphill, R. (1971). Auditory hallucinations in polyglots. *South African Medical Journal, 18,* 1391–1394.

Hockett, C. F. (1958). *A course in modern linguistics.* New York: Macmillan.

Hughes, G. W. (1981). Neuropsychiatric aspects of bilingualism: A brief review. *British Journal of Psychiatry, 139,* 25–28.

Jackson, H. J. (1878). On affections of speech from disease of the brain. *Brain, 1,* 304–330.

Kalinowsky, L. B. (1975). Clinical observations in ECT. *American Journal of Psychiatry, 132,* 878.

Kauders, O. (1929). Über polyglotte Reaktionen bei einer sensorischen Aphasie. *Zeitschrift für die gesamte Neurologie und Psychiatrie*, *122*, 651–666. Translated in Paradis (1983), 286–300.

Kertesz, A. (1979). *Aphasia and associated disorders: Taxonomy, localization, and recovery*. New York: Grune & Stratton.

Kertesz, A. (1982). The rationale of aphasia testing with the W. A. B. Conference on Aphasia Testing, Vrije Universiteit Brussel, 22 June.

Lambert, W. E., & Fillenbaum, S. (1959). A pilot study of aphasia among bilinguals. *Canadian Journal of Psychology*, *13*, 28–34.

Laski, E., & Taleporos, E. (1977). Anticholinergic psychosis in a bilingual: A case study. *American Journal of Psychiatry*, *134*, 1038–1040.

Lebrun, Y. (1976). Recovery in polyglot aphasics. In Y. Lebrun & R. Hoops (Eds.), *Recovery in aphasics* (pp. 96–108). Amsterdam: Swets & Zeitlinger.

Lebrun, Y. (1981). Bilingualism and the brain: A brief appraisal of Penfield's views. In H. Baetens Beardsmore (Ed.), *Elements of Bilingual Theory* (Tijdschrift van de Vrije Universiteit Brussel, Nieuwe Serie 6) (pp. 66–75). Brussels: Vrije Universiteit.

Lecours, A. R. (1974). Le cerveau et le langage. *L'union médicale du Canada*, *103*, 232–263.

Lecours, A. R. (1980). Corrélations anatomo-cliniques de l'aphasie: La zone du langage. *Revue neurologique*, *146*, 591–608.

Lecours, A. R., Branchereau, L., & Joanette, Y. (1984). La zone du langage et l'aphasie: Enseignement standard et cas particuliers. *META, Journal des traducteurs*, *29*, 10–26.

Lehmann, W. P. (1983). *Language, an introduction*. New York: Random House.

Leischner, A. (1948). Über die Aphasie der Mehrsprachigen. *Archiv für Psychiatrie und Nervenkrankheiten*, *108*. 731–775. Translated in Paradis (1983), 456–502.

Lesser, R. (1978). *Linguistic investigations of aphasia*. London: Arnold.

Lewis, G. (1968). Discussion [following L. A. Jakobovits' Dimentionality of compound-coordinate bilingualism]. *Language Learning*, Special issue No. *3*, 50–55.

L'Hermitte, R., Hécaen, H., Dubois, J., Culioli, A., & Tabouret-Keller, A. (1966). Le problème de l'aphasie des polyglottes: Remarques sur quelques observations. *Neuropsychologia*, *4*, 315–329. Translated in Paradis (1983), 727–743.

Linebarger, M. C., Schwartz, M. F., & Saffran, E. M. (1983a). Sensitivity to grammatical structure in so-called agrammatic aphasics. *Cognition*, *13*, 361–392.

Linebarger, M. C., Schwartz, M. F., & Saffran, E. M. (1983b). Syntactic processing in agrammatism: A reply to Zurif and Grodzinsky. *Cognition*, *15*, 215–225.

Lipsius, L. H. (1975). Electroconvulsive therapy and language. *American Journal of Psychiatry*, *132*, 459.

Luria, A. R. (1964). Factors and forms of aphasia. In A. V. S. De Reuck & M. O'Connor (Eds.), *Disorders of language*. London: Churchill.

Luria, A. (1966). *Higher cortical functions in man*. New York: Basic Books.

Lyons, J. (1981). *Language and linguistics*. Cambridge: Cambridge University Press.

Mack, M. A. (1984). Early bilinguals: How monolingual-like are they? In M. Paradis & Y. Lebrun (Eds.), *Early bilingualism and child development* (pp. 161–173). Lisse: Swets & Zeitlinger.

Macnamara, J. (1969). How can one measure the extent of a person's bilingual proficiency? In L. G. Kelly (Ed.), *Description and measurement of bilingualism* (pp. 80–119). Toronto: University of Toronto Press.

Macnamara, J., Krauthammer, M., & Bolgar, M. (1968). Language switching in bilinguals as a function of stimulus and response uncertainty. *Journal of Experimental Psychology*, *78*, 208–215.

Meyer, J. (1979). *Meyers Enzyklopädisches Lexicon*. Mannheim: Bibliographisches Institut A. G., vol. 25.

Minkowski, M. (1927). Klinischer Beitrag zur Aphasie bei Polyglotten, speziell im Hinblick aufs Schweizerdeutsche. *Archives Suisses de Neurologie et de Psychiatrie*, *21*, 43–72. Translated in Paradis (1983), 205–232.

Minkowski, M. (1928). Sur un cas d'aphasie chez un polyglotte. *Revue Neurologique, 49*, 361–366. Translated in Paradis (1983), 274–279.

Minkowski, M. (1963). On aphasia in polyglots. In L. Halpern (Ed.), *Problems of dynamic neurology* (pp. 119–161). Jerusalem: Hebrew University.

Nair, K. K., & Virmani, V. (1973). Speech and language disturbances in hemiplegics. *Indian Journal of Medical Research, 61*, 1395–1403.

Obler, L., Zatorre, R., Galloway, L., & Vaid, J. (1982). Cerebral lateralization in bilinguals: Methodological issues. Brain and Language, 15, 40–54.

Ojemann, G. A., & Whitaker, H. A. (1978). The bilingual brain. *Archives of Neurology, 35*, 409–412.

Ombredane, A. (1951). *L'aphasie et l'élaboration de la pensée explicite*. Paris: Presses universitaires de France.

Ovcharova, P., Raichev, R., & Geleva, T. (1968). Afaziia u poligloti. Nevrologiia. *Psikhiatriia i Nevrohirurgiia, 7*, 183–190. Translated in Paradis (1983), 744–752.

Paradis, M. (1977). Bilingualism and aphasia. In H. A. Whitaker & H. Whitaker (Eds.), *Studies in neurolinguistics* (Vol. 3, 65–121). New York: Academic Press.

Paradis, M. (1980). Language and thought in bilinguals. In J. Izzo & W. McCormack (Eds.), *The Sixth LACUS Forum* (pp. 420–431). Columbia, SC: Hornbeam Press.

Paradis, M. (Ed.). (1983). *Readings on aphasia in bilinguals and polyglots*. Montreal: Didier.

Paradis, M. (1985). On the representation of two languages in one brain. *Language Sciences, 7*, 1–39.

Paradis, M. & Goldblum, M. -C. (in press). Selective crossed aphasia in a trilingual patient. *Journal of Neurolinguistics*.

Paradis, M., Goldblum, M. C., & Abidi, R. (1982). Alternate antagonism with paradoxical translation behavior in two bilingual aphasic patients. *Brain and Language, 15*, 55–69.

Peña i Casanova, J. (1986). *Programma Integrat d'Exploracio Neuropsicologica Computaritzada*. Barcelona.

Penfield, W. (1953). A consideration of the neurophysiological mechanisms of speech, and some educational consequences. *Proceedings of the American Academy of Arts and Science, 82*, 199–214.

Penfield, W. (1959). Concluding discussion. In W. Penfield L. Roberts (1959).

Penfield, W. (1965). Conditioning the uncommitted cortex for language learning. *Brain, 88*, 787–798.

Penfield, W., & Roberts, L. (1959). *Speech and brain-mechanisms*. Princeton: Princeton University Press.

Perecman, E. (1984). Spontaneous translation and language mixing in a polyglot aphasic. *Brain and Language, 23*, 43–63.

Peuser, G. (1974). Vergleichende Aphasieforschung und Aphasie bei Polyglotten. *Folia Phoniatrica, 26:* 167–168.

Peuser, G., & Fittschen, M. (1977). On the universality of language dissolution: The case of a Turkish aphasic. *Brain and Language, 4*, 196–207.

Piazza Gordon, D., & Zatorre, R. F. (1981). A right-ear advantage for dichotic listening in bilingual children. *Brain and Language, 13*, 389–396.

Pick, A. (1913). *Die agrammatischen Sprachstörungen. Studien zur psychologischen Grundlegung der Aphasielehre* (Monographien aus dem Gesamtgebiete der Neurologie und Psychiatrie, Heft 7). Berlin: Springer.

Pick, A. (1921). Zur Erklarung gewisser Ausnahmen von der sogenannten Ribotschen Regel. *Abhandlungen aus der Neurologie, Psychiatrie und ihren Grenzgebieter* (Beiheft 13 zur Monatsschrift für Psychiatrie und Neurologie), 151–167. Translated in Paradis (1983), 156–168.

Pitres, A. (1895). Etude sur l'aphasie chez les polyglottes. *Revue de Médecine, 15*, 873–899. Translated in Paradis (1983), 26–48.

Porch, B. E. (1967). *Porch index of communicative ability: Volume 1, Theory and development.* Palo Alto: Consulting Psychologists Press.

Pötzl, O. (1925). Über die parietal bedingte Aphasie und ihren Einfluss auf das Sprechen mehrerer Sprachen. *Zeitschrift für die gesamte Neurologie und Psychiatrie, 96,* 100–124. Translated in Paradis (1983), 176–198.

Rapport, R. L., Tan, C. T., & Whitaker, H. A. (1983). Language function and dysfunction among Chinese- and English-speaking polyglots: Cortical stimulation, Wada testing, and clinical studies. *Brain and Language, 18,* 342–366.

Salomon, E. (1914). Motorische Aphasie mit Agrammatismus und sensorisch-agrammatischen Störungen. *Monatsschrift für Psychiatrie, 35,* 181–208; 216–275. Translated in Paradis (1983), 118–128.

Sarno, M. T. (1969). *Functional communication profile.* New York: New York University Medical Center.

Scholes, R. J. (1984). Personal communication, letter of 4 December.

Schuell, H. M., Jenkins, J. J., & Jiménez-Pablon, E. (1964). *Aphasia in adults: Diagnosis, prognosis and therapy.* New York: Hoeber.

Schulze, H. A. F. (1968). Unterschiedliche Rückbildung einer sensorischen und einer ideokinetischen motorischen Aphasie bei einem Polyglotten. *Psychiatrie, Neurologie und Medizinische Psychologie, 20,* 441–445. Translated in Paradis (1983), 753–760.

Scoresby-Jackson, R. E. (1867). Case of aphasia with right hemiplegia. *Edinburgh Medical Journal, 12,* 696-706.

Schwartz, M. F. (1984). What the classical aphasia categories can't do for us, and why. *Brain and Language, 21,* 3–8.

Segalowitz, S. J. (1983). *Two sides of the brain.* Englewood Cliffs, NJ: Prentice-Hall.

Silverberg, R., & Gordon, H. W. (1979). Differential aphasia in two bilingual individuals. *Neurology, 29,* 51–55.

Slobin, D., & Bever, T. (1982). Children use canonical sentence schemas: A cross-linguistic study of word order and inflections. *Cognition, 12,* 229–265.

Smith, N., & Wilson, D. (1980). *Modern linguistics. The results of Chomsky's revolution.* New York: Penguin Books.

Snow, C. E., & Ferguson, C. A. (Eds.). (1977). *Talking to children. Language input and acquisition.* Cambridge: Cambridge University Press.

Soares, C., & Grosjean, F. (1981). Left hemisphere language lateralization in bilinguals and monolinguals. *Perception and Psychophysics, 29,* 599–604.

Solin, D. (forthcoming). The systematic misrepresentation of bilingual crossed-aphasia data and its consequences.

Spreen, O., & Risser, A. (1983). Assessment of aphasia. In M. T. Sarno (Ed.), *Acquired aphasia* (pp. 67–127). New York: Academic Press.

Stark, R., Genesee, F., Lambert, W., & Seitz, M. (1977). Multiple language experience and the development of cerebral dominance. In S. Segalowitz & F. Gruber (Eds.), *Language development and neurological theory* (pp. 47–55). Orlando, FL: Academic Press.

Stengel, E., & Zelmanowicz, J. (1933). Über polyglotte motorische Aphasie. *Zeitschrift für die gesamte Neurologie and Psychiatrie, 149,* 292–311. Translated in Paradis (1983), 356–375.

Swischer, L. (1979). Evaluation of M. T. Sarno's Functional communication profile. In F. L. Darley (Ed.), *Evaluation of appraisal techniques in speech and language pathology* (pp. 205–207). Reading, MA: Addison-Wesley.

Thiery, C. (1978). True bilingualism and second language learning. In D. Gerver & H. W. Sinaiko (Eds.), *Language, interpretation and communication* (pp. 145–153). New York: Plenum.

T'sou, B. K. (1978). Some preliminary observations on aphasia in a Chinese bilingual. *Acta Psychologica Taiwanica, 20,* 57–64.

Vaid, J., & Genesee, F. (1980). Neuropsychological approaches to bilingualism. *Canadian Journal of Psychology, 34,* 417–445.

Veyrac, G. J. (1931). *Etude de l'aphasie chez les sujets polyglottes.* Thèse pour le doctorat en médecine, Paris. Translated in Paradis (1983), 320–338.

Vildomec, V. (1963). *Multilingualism.* Leyden: Sythoff.

Voinescu, I., Vish, E., Sirian, S., & Maretsis, M. (1977). Aphasia in a polyglot. *Brain and Language, 4,* 165–176.

Wald, I. (1961). Problema Afazii Poliglotov. *Voprosy Kliniki i Patofiziologii Afazii* (pp. 140–176). Moskva. Translated in Paradis (1983), 641–669.

Walters, J., & Zatorre, R. (1978). Laterality differences for word identification in bilinguals. *Brain and Language, 2,* 158–167.

Watamori, T. S., & Sasanuma, S. (1978). The recovery process of two English-Japanese bilingual aphasics. *Brain and Language, 6,* 127–140.

Weinreich, U. (1963). *Languages in contact.* The Hague: Mouton.

Weisenburg, T. H., & McBride, K. E. (1935). *Aphasia, a clinical and psychological study.* New York: Commonwealth Fund.

Whitaker, H. (1976). A case of the isolation of the language function. In H. Whitaker & H. A. Whitaker (Eds.), *Studies in neurolinguistics* (Vol. 2, pp. 1–58). New York: Academic Press.

Whitaker, H. A. (1978). Bilingualism: A neurolinguistics perspective. In W. C. Ritchie (Ed.), *Second language acquisition research. Issues and implications* (pp. 21–32). New York: Academic Press.

Zatorre, R. (1983). La représentation des langues multiples dans le cerveau: vieux problèmes et nouvelles orientations. *Langages, 72,* 15–31.

Zurif, E. B., Caramazza, A., Myerson, R. & Galvin, J. (1974). Semantic representations for normal and aphasic language. *Brain and Language, 1,* 167–187.

Author Index